THE POLITICS OF RESTORATIVE JUSTICE

THE POLITICS OF RESTORATIVE JUSTICE

A CRITICAL INTRODUCTION
SECOND EDITION

**ANDREW WOOLFORD
& AMANDA NELUND**

FERNWOOD PUBLISHING
HALIFAX & WINNIPEG

Copyright © 2019 Andrew Woolford and Amanda Nelund

All rights reserved. No part of this book may be reproduced or transmitted in any form by any means without permission in writing from the publisher, except by a reviewer, who may quote brief passages in a review.

Editing: Jessica Antony
Cover design: John van der Woude
Printed and bound in Canada

Published by Fernwood Publishing
32 Oceanvista Lane, Black Point, Nova Scotia, B0J 1B0
and 748 Broadway Avenue, Winnipeg, Manitoba, R3G 0X3
www.fernwoodpublishing.ca

Fernwood Publishing Company Limited gratefully acknowledges the financial support of the Government of Canada, the Canada Council for the Arts, the Manitoba Department of Culture, Heritage and Tourism under the Manitoba Publishers Marketing Assistance Program and the Province of Manitoba, through the Book Publishing Tax Credit, for our publishing program. We are pleased to work in partnership with the Province of Nova Scotia to develop and promote our creative industries for the benefit of all Nova Scotians.

Library and Archives Canada Cataloguing in Publication

Title: Politics of restorative justice : a critical introduction / Andrew Woolford & Amanda Nelund.
Names: Woolford, Andrew John, 1971- author. | Nelund, Amanda, 1985- author.
Description: Second edition. | Includes bibliographical references and index.
Identifiers: Canadiana 20190137223 | ISBN 9781773631417 (softcover)
Subjects: LCSH: Restorative justice—Political aspects. | LCSH: Restorative justice.
Classification: LCC 2019 | LCC HV8688 .W65 2019 | DDC 364.6/8—dc23

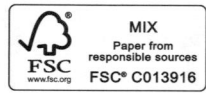

CONTENTS

Preface and Acknowledgments I

1. **What Are the Politics of Restorative Justice?** 5
   Restorative Justice 6
   The Politics of Restorative Justice 15
   Politics and Justice 23
   Questions for Discussion 24

2. **What Events Trigger a Restorative Response?** 25
   Trigger Events 27
   Questions for Discussion 47

3. **Delineating the Restorative Justice Ethos** 49
   Traditions of Dispute Resolution 50
   Theories of Restorative Justice 55
   The Restorative Justice Ethos 68
   The Truth and Reconciliation Commission of Canada 70
   Questions for Discussion 72

4. **Restorative Justice Styles** 73
   Mediation and Community Mediation 74
   Victim Offender Reconciliation
   and Victim Offender Mediation Programs 76
   Family Group Conferencing 79
   Circles 81

  Truth and Reconciliation Commissions..88
  Restorative Justice and Reparations for Crimes of Mass Violence....95
  Grey Areas of Restorative Justice..99
  Does Restorative Justice Work?...101
  Micro-Politics of Restorative Practices...110
  The Embodied Politics of Restorative Justice..................................115
  Questions for Discussion..119

5. Constructing Restorative Justice Identities.................................**120**
  Victims..122
  Offenders...132
  Communities...143
  Facilitators...147
  Opening Restorative Identities..150
  Questions for Discussion..151

6. Restorative Justice Contexts...**152**
  Level of Analysis..152
  Restorative Justice and Gender...155
  Restorative Justice and Race..158
  Restorative Justice and LGBTQ Communities................................159
  Restorative Justice and Class...160
  Restorative Justice and Age...162
  Intersecting Structures of Domination..165
  Restoration and Neoliberal Politics..166
  Culture, Meaning, and the Politics of Restorative Justice.................173
  Restorative Justice and Other-than-Human Actors.........................175
  Questions for Discussion..180

7. Restorative Justice Criticisms..**181**
  Technical Criticisms..182
  Substantive Criticisms...188
  Criticism and the Politics of Restorative Justice..............................193
  Questions for Discussion..194

8. Transformation and the Politics of Restorative Justice 195
    Transformative Justice.. *199*
    Recognition, Redistribution, and Representation.............................. *200*
    The Politics of Transformation *209*
    Final Thoughts.. *220*
    Questions for Discussion 220

References 221

Index 240

PREFACE AND ACKNOWLEDGMENTS

This book has been significantly reworked for its second edition. Transformative justice is an always unfinished project. It must engage with the world, but also retract into the arena of criticism to sharpen ideas and open up blind spots. What better way to challenge and expand thinking on a topic than to bring on board another author? The first edition was based on Andrew Woolford's initial researching, teaching about, and volunteering in the world of restorative justice. However, his views grew and developed through reading the work of and engaging in conversation with Amanda Nelund. She now joins as the second author, providing new insight and experience to the text. While the previous edition was friendly to an intersectional approach to understanding the politics of restorative justice, this approach was too much in the background. Amanda Nelund brings to this edition her work in feminist criminology, helping to better accentuate the intersectional politics of restorative justice.

Both of us share a degree of ambivalence about restorative justice. On the one hand, we are trained as critical scholars and deploy insights drawn from critical social theory to interrogate topics in criminology and socio-legal studies. On the other hand, we are committed to improving the experiences of those who, out of necessity, must engage with the criminal justice system. Restorative justice can make a difference for such individuals, however they are involved in the criminal justice system. Our ambivalence is reflected in the makeup of this book. We challenge restorative justice, which emphasizes the involvement of those affected in resolving the harms associated with crime, for all its potential faults, but also leaves room for its improvement and advancement — for it to become something more than what it already is.

This book is also the product of our work teaching criminology courses focused on restorative justice at the University of Manitoba and MacEwan

University for the past sixteen years. There remains an absence of introductory-level texts that offer a critical sociological investigation of restorative justice concepts. Works by scholars such as George Pavlich provide critical social theoretical insights into the conceptualization and practice of restorative justice, but are written for more advanced students. In contrast, this book aims to bring critical sociological awareness of restorative justice to students in their second or third year of university or college classes, as well as to practitioners and those in the general public interested in matters of restorative justice. This does not mean that this text is always an easy read. We push students at all levels of learning to expand their vocabularies and to contend with abstract and complicated ideas. While we try to clearly communicate theoretical concepts, we do not boil them down to the point where they become oversimplified and deprived of their full critical force.

We also are motivated to offer a second edition of this book because insufficient thought is still given toward "the politics of restorative justice." This is not to say that politics have not factored into many previous studies of restorative justice. However, many authors tend to work with a narrower conception of politics, locating restorative justice within a political world, but not questioning the ways in which restorative justice is itself complicit in certain forms of politics. In addition, there is a noted communicative divide between the theory and practice of restorative justice whereby the insights of restorative justice theory find less traction within actually existing restorative justice programs (Gavrielides 2007). In our view, the bridge to cross this divide can be forged through a theoretical investigation of the political context and political meanings of restorative justice, which can then contribute to a strategic conceptualization of the way forward for restorative justice.

We offer these thoughts as a preface out of the belief that all projects should begin from a point of reflexivity. As authors presenting a description of what restorative justice is and a vision of what restorative justice could be, it is important to reflect upon our grounding assumptions since these factors certainly inform and influence the interpretations presented in this book. So, let us reveal upfront that, intuitively speaking, the values of restorative justice feel right in many respects, in the sense that we have seen the immediate human benefits that can be obtained from a restorative justice approach that is sensitive to the particular needs of individuals and communities. However, we also understand that this desire for collaborative and meaningful conflict resolution is positioned within a socio-political framework that blocks its fullest actualization. This is the first guiding framework for this book. The second is a preference for viewing the world as dynamic rather than static. Whereas some may be drawn to the parsimony and analytical clarity of an airtight typology, our goal is always to leave room in our conceptual models for process and change. Although the world is consistently structured and sufficiently regular in a manner that allows us to navigate our day-to-day lives, it is also constantly in movement, requiring us to adapt and change our actions and thoughts to particular circumstances. We seek to demonstrate that the boundaries of this so-called justice alternative are not firmly set, and to leave room for the debates and discussions that create and re-create the universe of restorative justice.

This manuscript owes much to Wayne Antony, who proposed the initial project. As well, we would like to acknowledge the excellent work of the Fernwood production team, especially Jessica Antony (copyediting), Beverley Rach (design and layout), Debbie Mathers (pre-production), and John van der Woude (cover design). Funding for the research that informs this book has come from the Social Sciences and Humanities Research Council (SSHRC) of Canada and the University of Manitoba. The book has benefited from conversations with Diane Crocker, Bob Ratner, Bryan Hogeveen, George Pavlich, Frank Cormier, Jens Meierhenrich, Rob Vallis, Noelle Dietrich, Dragan Milanovic, Elizabeth Comack, Steve Brickey, Peter Karari, Adam Muller, Struan Sinclair, and many others. In addition, the constructive suggestions made by Kearney Healey and the two anonymous readers helped us refine and expand our initial manuscript. A great debt is also owed to Rene Durocher for generously allowing us to begin the manuscript with his amazing story.

Andrew thanks Jessica and Ella Woolford, who have supported him and who always keep things lively. Amanda thanks the many students who have and continue to think carefully about injustice and the potential and limits of restorative justice along with her. She also thanks Fraser and Abi for support and encouragement.

— *Andrew Woolford and Amanda Nelund*

1

WHAT ARE THE POLITICS OF RESTORATIVE JUSTICE?

Rene Durocher spent twenty-three years of his life as an inmate in seventeen different penitentiaries. He entered his first correctional institution at the age of seventeen for an act of armed robbery. At the time, the Crown decided to try Mr. Durocher as an adult to teach him a lesson — one for which he was not yet ready. Raised in a large family by an abusive father, Mr. Durocher had learned to use his fearlessness and daring to get what he wanted. And although he never wanted to physically hurt anyone, he did not expend much thought on the emotional and financial harm he was exacting upon his victims.

Rene Durocher was released in 1963, but found himself back in prison within the year. He had walked into a store while firing a newly purchased shotgun into the air. Once again, he was arrested, and this time, he was sentenced to fourteen years. While in prison, he took lessons from the more experienced inmates and eagerly awaited parole to test his new criminal knowledge. However, when at last he was released on parole, this knowledge soon failed him, and he was re-arrested only four months later. In this instance, he and some associates had purchased machine guns and were using them to conduct bank robberies. One robbery went wrong, and a shoot-out transpired. Mr. Durocher exchanged fire with the police with little thought of the risk to himself and others. He was the only one of the bank robbers who was not shot that day.

In prison again, this time for twenty-two years (and only 25 years old), Mr. Durocher had earned the respect of his fellow inmates. He was the "crazy Frenchman" who had shot at the police. However, Mr. Durocher ignored his notoriety and sought to improve his formal education. While in prison, he also fell in love with a woman he would later marry. Upon his third release from prison, he tried to lead a law-abiding life, but after several bad jobs and a failed business venture, Mr. Durocher found himself in debt to organized crime, with a wife and two children to support. To correct the situation, he returned to what he knew best — crime — and participated in what was, at that time, the biggest robbery in Canadian history. On July 8, 1985, Mr. Durocher and his partners robbed a Brinks truck. He used the money from the robbery to buy a house and pet store. He was arrested for a final time six months later.

It was only at this point in his life that Mr. Durocher began to try to change himself. He worked with the prison psychologist at Stony Mountain Penitentiary in Manitoba learning to take responsibility for his crimes and to recognize the harm he had done to others. Upon his final release from prison, he committed himself to helping others and later worked with agencies — such as Lifeline, the John Howard Society of Manitoba, and the St. Leonard's Society — to assist inmates in turning their lives around.

The retributive mode of punishment, which seeks to be tough on offenders in order to deter future criminal activity, clearly did not help reform Mr. Durocher. For Rene Durocher, prison often felt like home, and it was not until he was prepared to change himself that he was able to shake his criminal career. This raises the questions: might another approach to justice have helped lead Mr. Durocher to this realization sooner? If so, are we as a society ready to think differently about justice and to provide people meaningful opportunities to reform themselves? And are we ready and willing to reform society in the process?

RESTORATIVE JUSTICE

To answer these questions, we must first look at our justice impulses because when we hear about crimes like those committed by Mr. Durocher, our first instinct is, typically, to call for punishment, no matter how counter-productive this punishment may be. Indeed, the punitive conceptualization of justice is deeply ingrained. From early in our lives, we are inculcated with notions of right and wrong, and of just and unjust punishment. This conditioning is further reinforced by a cultural mythology of criminal justice. A common motif of our culture is the good (eventually) receive rewards and the bad are punished. We learn this when young, watching superheroes save the day and villains pay the price of punishment. The notion that people get what they deserve is invoked explicitly when commenting on those who receive prison sentences and implicitly when remarking on the hard work of successful public figures. Thus, justice is culturally constructed as an either/or dichotomy and is assumed to have winners and losers. Imagine the difficulty, then, of trying to encourage a different notion of justice, one designed to care for the different needs of those who commit harms and those who are harmed. Such a project would require more than just platitudes and good ideas; it would require a politics — a strategic plan for countering the current arrangements of social power — to challenge entrenched and dominant notions of justice. Restorative justice is an idea that needs to achieve traction and resonance within a distinctly political environment. Moreover, restorative justice must develop an enabling politics so it may more effectively spread its messages throughout society and contribute to social transformation. However, first we must contend with the question of what restorative justice is.

Restorative justice is a term deployed with great frequency within contemporary criminal justice systems. More and more, criminal justice programs aimed at diverse goals — such as reintegrating offenders, healing victims, and dealing with crime in communities — describe their principles and their mission statements in the language of restorative justice. As well, restorative justice is receiving greater recognition in formal law. The 1999 Youth Justice and Criminal Evidence Act in England and Wales and the 2003 Canadian Youth Criminal Justice Act both make room for restorative practices within their respective youth justice systems (Crawford and Newburn 2002; Charbonneau 2004). In 2002, the United Nations released its guidelines for applying restorative justice to criminal matters, touting restorative justice as a legitimate and beneficial means for dealing with criminal harms (United Nations Economic and Social Council 2000; see also United Nations 2007). In 2015 the European Union included restorative justice in its Victims' Rights Directive and Canada included the right to be informed of restorative justice in its new Victims Bill of Rights. Thus, restorative justice has achieved a great deal of political recognition over recent years and has come to be viewed in many quarters as a viable alternative within the criminal justice system. This trend is evident in the numerous restorative justice programs sprouting up worldwide.

Increasing acceptance of restorative justice occurs not only within the criminal justice system. School-based restorative justice is used to address a broad array of issues, from reintegrating criminalized youth back into the school system to addressing everyday instances of bullying (Morrison 2006). Such expanded usage presents further challenges for delimiting a distinct theory and practice of restorative justice. The frame of reference for identifying what is the core of restorative justice must move beyond the criminal justice system and embrace diverse actors and harms.

Despite its growing popularity, or perhaps because of it, restorative justice does not lend itself to easy definition. For example, it is often described as a participatory practice that involves the victim, offender, and community in resolving the harm caused by a specific crime. More directly, according to Tony Marshall (1999: 5), "[it] is a process whereby all the parties with a stake in a particular offence come together to resolve collectively how to deal with the aftermath of the offence and its implications for the future."

An image that immediately may spring to mind is of a (rural) community hall where neighbours gather to discuss a criminal event, such as a break and enter. The offenders are present with heads bowed to demonstrate the deep shame they feel as they stand before their community. The victims are there as well and are surrounded by their supporters. And what unfolds is a conversation that results in a novel solution: the offenders, sincerely apologetic, offer to help the victims clean the mess and recover their losses; the community unites around victims and offenders, offering their collective support; the victims forgive and move forward with neither hatred nor fear nesting in their hearts. This romantic narrative is a potential reality, but it does not reflect the typical practice or outcomes of restorative justice (Daly 2003). In many cases, offenders are slow to repent, victims refuse to participate, and communities are largely indifferent to or unaware of the entire business. In response to these and other challenges, restorative justice programs will often adapt their practices while, at the same time, seek to remain located within a more general restorative justice conceptual framework. For example, they may choose to work with an offender who appears ready to take responsibility and change their behaviour, even without direct victim and community involvement. The absence of these key stakeholders may perhaps be addressed through the involvement of proxy victims (that is, victims of similar crimes who communicate to the offender the experience of being a victim of this sort of incident) or through a written statement made by the victim. The program workers may themselves stand in for the community, articulating the fear and distrust crime breeds. However, with these adaptations, the restorative justice program strays from Marshall's definition of restorative justice: that is, it is a stretch to say the offence is being collectively resolved when such changes are put into effect.

Perhaps, then, a more flexible and accurate definition of restorative justice would be along the following lines: "Restorative justice attempts to address the harm(s) caused by crime in a manner that meets the specific needs of the involved parties while using the resources available." This definition

WHAT ARE THE POLITICS OF RESTORATIVE JUSTICE? 9

communicates the adaptability of restorative justice. However, it is unsatisfactory in that it lacks precision. What is there in this definition to differentiate restorative justice from other criminal justice practices? Do not criminal courts, at times, also fit this description? Imagine, for example, two individuals awaiting a court hearing. One, the accused, sits nervously with their lawyer, wondering about their fate. The other, the victim, is ready to serve as a witness and has prepared a victim impact statement to express the harm they suffered at the hands of the accused. The act of writing this statement has afforded them some relief, allowing them to name the confusing emotions they felt in the aftermath of the event. Then, immediately before the trial, the crown attorney approaches the victim to inform them the crown is considering a plea bargain. The attorney reports that the accused has taken responsibility for their actions, has begun alcohol and anger management treatment, and is not perceived to pose a threat to the community. The victim, relieved to see the accused is making positive efforts to change their life, as well as happy to avoid the stress of the courtroom, gives their blessing to the plea bargain (although the crown could move forward with the plea bargain without this blessing) and subsequently leaves the courthouse feeling the matter is resolved. Is this restorative justice? If so, how is it that a restorative moment arises within the alleged adversarial environment of the criminal justice system?

It is perhaps worth taking a moment here to reflect on what we do when we define a concept. For many students reading this text, you may be scanning these pages looking for a clear definition to underline so that you can relay it flawlessly on an upcoming test. But we ask your patience. Hold off on memorizing any of the definitions covered thus far. We provide them only to illustrate that such definitions attempt to encapsulate complex phenomena and reduce them to their most basic qualities, and in so doing sacrifice some of the fluidity and flexibility of actual practice. Moreover, such definitions can involve choices that impose limitations on our understanding. Definitions can, in and of themselves, be political, as they advance a particular vision of how the world is or should be. For example, where one is situated in the criminal justice system may result in certain emphases in how restorative justice is defined. An advocate for victim's rights may be more prone to highlight victim safety and involvement in their definition than someone whose work focuses on offender reintegration into the community. And someone using restorative justice outside of the criminal justice system, such as within a school, may reject the tendency thus far to define restorative justice in relation to crime.

Let's try to move from memorizing a definition to gaining a feel for a concept. We can understand this movement through an analogy to the rule and the game. To say that ice hockey is a game played on skates where one team of five players and a goalie tries to score more goals than another does not communicate a great feel for the game. Moreover, neither would knowledge of any particular rule such as hooking, interference, or unsportsmanlike conduct, especially when interpretation of the latter seems to vary by referee and the stage of the season (as these things seem less enforced during the playoffs). To have a feel for the game is to be able to adapt to its shifts and energy, to build off momentum, and to draw from training and practice to respond to the immediacy of the play. Concepts, too, are something for which we must gain a feel. Restorative justice is better understood not by memorizing its definition, but by obtaining a sense of its ideals, its vision of the world, and its shifting dimensions as it responds to the action in the social world.

One may assume that, if restorative justice amounts to anything at all, there must be something at its core that would allow us to differentiate it analytically from adversarial approaches to justice. It is not enough to say it is informal, healing, and participatory, since all of these aspects were present in the plea bargain example offered above. In this example, the lawyers for each party informally negotiated the plea bargain, the offender was set on a path of healing, and the victim was offered a modicum of participation. For the sake of conceptual clarity, there are several ideal traits of restorative justice:

1. *Open and actively participatory*: Restorative justice is open to the participation of all interested parties, although it does not mandate their participation. Moreover, this participation is *active* in the sense that it allows participants more than just a consultative role; indeed, they have an actual say in the process and outcomes. In the plea bargain example used above, the victim was set to act as a witness, and was later consulted on the plea bargain, but their role could hardly be described as active participation in the sense that they would be able to offer suggestions or information that would sway or alter the course of the justice process.

2. *Empowering*: This active role for participants is intended to offer participants in restorative justice a significant degree of ownership over the process. They play a part in determining how the process will unfold and in the decision making that is the crux of restorative

justice practice. This offers them an investment in the resolution, which ideally results in them becoming the principal agents of its implementation. Returning to the plea bargain example, the victim left the courtroom more with a feeling of relief than empowerment. They held no personal investment in the resolution, but rather merely experienced some peace of mind that their assailant was now set upon a more positive path and unlikely to re-offend in the near future. However, they received nothing from this experience that will allow them to better manage future conflicts.

3. *Satisfying and offers a relational healing process*: Restorative justice derives its legitimacy not from state support or by achieving state-designed outcomes; instead, its primary objectives are to satisfy participants with respect to their collectively negotiated resolution and to start them on a process toward healing the harms associated with the wrongful event (Llewllyn and Howse 1998). In short, it seeks to give participants an opportunity to fashion something positive out of a negative event. Certainly, the plea bargain described above brought the parties a degree of satisfaction, but much of this occurred through the independent actions of the parties (for example, the accused took it upon themself to seek help with anger and alcohol issues), rather than through a relational process, which refers to an interactive process that both engages existing relationships and creates new ones.

These ideal traits provide a basic framework with which we might assess the restorativeness of any given program, but we still must be prepared to find anomalies. In any specific application of restorative justice, moments may arise when these ideals are unreachable or temporarily suspended. Take the case of Don and Mary Struefert, who in 1991 lost their 18-year-old daughter, Carin, at the hands of Guy Sullivan and Jim Swanson in Minnesota. Guy Sullivan and Jim Swanson forced Carin at gunpoint into their van before taking her to a wooded area where they raped and murdered her. The arrest and prosecution of the two culprits left the Strueferts feeling unfulfilled, thus leading Don to consider restorative justice as a post-sentencing reconciliation option. This means the restorative justice meetings would have no bearing on Sullivan's and Swanson's sentences, which had already been determined by a judge. Rather, the restorative justice program, in this case, was intended largely to allow the victims to ask questions of the offenders as a step on their personal journey of

has been used not to resolve the outcomes of the case, but to involve victims and their family and provide satisfaction recovery. Sullivan agreed to meet with the Strueferts, resulting in some very emotional and oftentimes frustrating sessions (see Konowal 1997).

Returning to the ideal traits listed above, while Don maintained a largely positive attitude toward the restorative justice process throughout its course, Mary experienced moments when she felt neither empowered nor satisfied. For example, when Sullivan told the Strueferts that Carin's last words amounted to a plea for him to help her, Mary was overwhelmed at the thought that Sullivan just stood there and did nothing, and she felt intense anger toward him. Yet, a decade after first meeting with Guy Sullivan, Mary told a crowd in Winnipeg she had forgiven Sullivan. She had only realized this when she learned Sullivan had overcome his illiteracy, and she discovered that she was, at that moment, very proud of him.

When examining *actually existing restorative justice*, one is confronted with the limits of such lists of ideal traits. The Strueferts' experience of restorative justice can be described as open, participatory, empowering, satisfying, and healing, but not consistently throughout its application. There were moments of deep hurt before healing eventually occurred. There were times when empowerment was frustrated by conversations characterized by problematic communication, and satisfaction was not an immediate or guaranteed outcome of the Strueferts' interactions with Sullivan. Of course, analytical categories, like the ideal traits listed above, are only intended as a guide to our thinking and should not be taken to be perfect realizations of the actual world. Thus, to complement this list of ideal traits, and to add an important reminder of its limits while also capturing inconsistencies within actual restorative justice practice, let us try to establish some of the basic *morphological properties* of restorative justice. Morphological properties are those that alert us to the malleable or shape-shifting qualities of restorative justice.

1. *Restorative justice is contextually specific*: Restorative justice must adapt its practice to specific harm contexts rather than applying a "one size fits all" approach. Crime is a term with varying meanings that is used to describe a diversity of events, ranging from minor offences against property and person to massive-scale destruction, such as genocide. It would be naïve to expect we could develop a concept of restorative justice that would definitively prescribe the processes used and outcomes to be achieved in response to such a broad range of events. This is even more true, for those restorative programs that want to deal

with harms beyond those that are designated as crime (such as regulatory offences like those related to the spread of pollutants). Thus, whatever restorative justice *is,* it will change as it is applied in multiple and complex circumstances. Restorative justice will also adapt to specific cultural contexts with respect to both its practice and outcomes. For example, whereas certain cultural communities employing restorative justice may reject all forms of punishment (such as prison) as inappropriate, others may find punishment (such as banishment from the community) as a reasonable outcome for a restorative meeting.

2. *Restorative justice is a process*: it does not follow a pre-set linear course. Instead, it is a process through which the parties are offered an opportunity to create new positive meanings out of a situation that they, in most cases, experienced as negative. Given this processual character, it is impossible to impose specific desired outcomes on restorative justice. Restorative justice facilitators may enter restorative meetings with an ideal script in mind of how they would like the meeting to transpire (for example, that the parties will move from describing and emoting about the events toward problem solving). They still must be prepared to allow this process to unfold in an uneven manner, with fits and starts, progress and fallbacks. [handwritten: will not look the same everytime]

3. *Restorative justice is negotiated and can be the subject of heated debate and disagreement*: it is not guaranteed that participants will simply embrace one another in a desire to resolve their conflict. Restorative outcomes are difficult to reach and often require contentious negotiations to arrive at a point of resolution. This point can also help us better accept the debates and disagreements that exist over the definition of restorative justice. Restorative justice, as a social movement, is in a constant process of negotiating its meaning, or identity, and therefore, it is perfectly understandable that there exists no one master definition. [handwritten: will not fit a single definition]

4. *Restorative justice is a living model*: it is not any unitary thing but, rather, a continuously evolving body of ideas intended to articulate a method of justice built upon the active participation of stakeholders. What we understand restorative justice to be today will not be the same as what it is in the future. We will see a restorative justice that has developed, reformed, and/or revised itself to meet future chal-

lenges. We could also see a restorative justice that has been neutered or diluted by political forces seeking to deploy it toward their own ends.

The threat of dilution brings a final ideal to mind, but one we cannot claim to be true for all forms of restorative justice: restorative justice should be transformative (Morris 1994; Sullivan and Tifft 2001). By transformative, we mean restorative justice creates conditions for pursuing forms of personal and, perhaps more importantly, social change that address multiple forms of domination. Indeed, restorative justice should be concerned with more than just the crime or conflict that triggers an initial restorative justice meeting. It must be about fostering opportunities for individuals and groups to evaluate their lives and their worlds, and to initiate attempts to bring change into these arenas: to address injustice and to improve the lives of the many. We saw in the example of the Strueferts and Guy Sullivan that the participants were able to take a very negative event and to fashion something positive out of it. This is not to say the positive can ever outweigh something as negative as the loss of a loved one; however, we can take a negative experience and learn from it in hopes of individual and societal improvement. Restorative justice should be mobilized for purposes of transformation. That can be in the form of everyday transformations, such as a commitment to greater personal literacy. It can also be societal transformation, such as what is hoped will follow when restorative justice is employed in the aftermath of mass violence, or when people use a restorative justice meeting to discuss more broadly the social problems that affect their lives and to devise strategies for addressing these challenges. As will become increasingly evident, our preference is toward a transformative restorative justice that strives to address the very conditions that make injustice possible.

Another example further illustrates the transformative potential of restorative justice, but also the role of politics in transformation. The South African Truth and Reconciliation Commission (SATRC) was intended to create public awareness about the harms committed under the racial system of apartheid and to initiate a society-wide conversation toward collective healing. For years, the apartheid government had used violence and torture to suppress Black South African demands for equal rights and freedom. When victims sought justice for acts of state violence, their claims were denied. Authorities told people who lost family members, or who had themselves been seriously scarred by apartheid violence, that their complaints were unfounded. In the aftermath of such circumstances, it was believed revelation of the truth of apartheid would have a transformative effect, and the SATRC was to be the primary vehicle for this transformation. It should also be noted that the SATRC was, in part, a product of a political compromise. When the apartheid government fell, and Nelson Mandela's African National Congress was elected to power in 1994, this new government faced a tricky challenge: how could they deliver justice for past misdeeds when the people who committed these misdeeds still held a great deal of power in South African society? The civil service, the judiciary, and the military, for example, still rested in the hands of the whites, and there was a risk civil war would erupt if the new government sought to drag too many of these people before a tribunal. Thus, the SATRC owed its existence to favourable political circumstances that made its brand of justice appear more palatable (Adam 2001). Moreover, in offering a mechanism to redress the apartheid past, the compromise-focused nature of the SATRC also placed limits on what victims could demand in terms of justice. In particular, gross human rights violations were to be the subject of the SATRC's hearings. The systemic economic and social inequalities that had made white South Africans the beneficiaries in terms of status, property, wealth, and opportunity were not.

In this case, the transformative potential of restorative process was narrowed by prevailing political conditions. For restorative justice to live up to its transformative potential, there needs to be a deeper understanding of the political contexts in which restorative justice is situated and through which it operates so restorative justice may be more effectively strategized as a form of transformative politics.

THE POLITICS OF RESTORATIVE JUSTICE

Restorative justice is a *political* process. It is political in at least four senses:

1. Restorative justice exists in a political context that is, at different times, favourable, unfavourable, or indifferent to its practice, and which influences its conceptual development. Dominant political discourses and ideologies (that is, the way the criminal justice system "thinks"), as well as institutional arrangements (that is, the way the criminal justice system "works"), have an impact on how alternative policies, such as restorative justice, are received and implemented (if at all).

2. This political context is also a structured context. This means that there are persistent social patterns or tendencies that shape our dominant ways of both thinking and acting. These include intersecting structures of patriarchal, racialized, heteronormative, settler-colonial, class-based and other forms of social domination. This is important to keep in mind because restorative justice is not magically free of these forces on the basis of its good intentions. Restorative justice can be theorized, legislated, implemented, and practiced in a manner that is gendered, racialized, heteronormative, and settler oriented. However, there may also be potential for restorative justice to subvert and disrupt these patterns of domination.

3. Restorative justice is itself a form of governance in that it aspires to change behaviour, heal individuals, and revitalize communities (Pavlich 2005). These efforts complement governmental goals, such as ensuring social peace and minimizing costly forms of conflict. Following from this, because restorative justice can assist in social control, it faces the constant danger that it may be co-opted and set to the task of reproducing dominant social relations. This is the case when restorative justice is used as a mild punishment for perpetrators of minor crimes who might otherwise be ignored by the criminal justice system. The goal in such instances is often to better govern a seemingly unregulated group, rather than to contribute to forming more positive social relations.

4. Restorative justice needs to mobilize a politics in order to realize its broader social justice and transformative goals. Restorative justice advocates, sometimes referred to as "restorativists" (Walgrave 2004), need to be capable of navigating the political world. One danger of failing to mobilize a politics of restorative justice is that other political actors will appropriate restorative justice and employ it toward their own instrumental ends. This has been the fate of other ethically charged notions, such as human rights, which, although promoted as being somehow apolitical in a pure conceptual sense, are still used by political powers to launch wars for strategic gain, such as the belated human rights justifications used to legitimize the 2003 U.S. invasion of Iraq or the 2011 NATO-led military intervention in Libya.

To fully understand restorative justice, we need to move beyond outlining the justice ideals that inform the principles and practices of restorative justice and to initiate consideration of the challenges faced in implementing a transformative restorative justice under difficult political conditions. However, in this context the political must be understood broadly, not just the narrow world of party politics and government, but also the politicized forces of economy, society, and culture that shape contemporary governance, as well as everyday life. The notion of the political, then, refers to the ever-present forces of power and domination. These forces work to maintain and entrench the current state of affairs in which economic and cultural control are predominantly in the hands of powerful actors, such as the political, economic, and state/military elites. Moreover, restorative justice is not merely an object of politics, in the sense that it is debated by political actors looking to tackle crime or gain popular support; rather, restorative justice is a political project — as a social movement working toward important forms of social and political change.

To refer to restorative justice as a social movement (Daly and Immarigeon 1998; Sullivan and Tifft 2001; Johnstone and Van Ness 2007) is not to say that restorative justice programs comprise a fully unified group of individuals or that restorative justice philosophies form an undifferentiated body of ideas. This is clearly not the case for restorative justice, but this is also not true for most, if any, social movements. Social movements are networks in which actors with varying interpretations of what the movement is about, and different levels of commitment to the movement, negotiate the meaning of a linked set of big ideas as well as their ideal application in everyday life. According to Mario Diani (1992: 1), social movements are "networks of informal interactions between a plurality of individuals, groups and/or organizations, engaged in political or cultural conflicts, on the basis of shared collective identities." Thus, a social movement is not a single group or organization but rather a host of individual and collective agents engaged in a process of movement definition, issue or grievance articulation, activism, and program implementation. For example, within the environmental social movement, we see a number of agencies and individuals engaged in articulating the dangers posed by environmental neglect and damage and proposing recommendations as to how we might rectify these problems. However, among this movement's supporters, we are likely to find a wide range of perspectives. The groups under the environmental movement umbrella range from those that are quite radical and use disruptive measures to sabotage logging operations, such as Earth First, to those that often seek to work in partnership with government, such as the David Suzuki Foundation.

Efforts may be initiated to create conversations across these diverse groups, but the conversations are always ongoing and never fully resolved, other than, perhaps, in the form of occasional policy or protest statements framed around a single pressing issue (such as the harmful effects of clear-cut logging).

Such diversity is also true of the restorative justice movement. There, heated debates occur among practitioners, theorists, and agencies with respect to questions like: can restorative justice work in cooperation with the formal criminal justice system, or does it require a completely separate institutional framework? How important is the involvement of offenders, victims, and community members in restorative justice processes? Should restorative justice be defined based on outcomes or processes? Is restorative justice a set of values or practices? What sorts of practices can be considered "true" forms of restorative justice? (See Gavrielides 2007: 36–43 and Daly 2006: 135 for a list of restorative justice "faultlines.") Rather than any particular answer to one of these questions being definitive of the restorative justice movement, it is the case that the process of negotiating possible answers to such questions is what constitutes the movement. In this book, therefore, we do not seek to resolve these questions, but rather to critically trace, and in some cases add to, the variety of considerations that are navigated by participants in restorative justice.

As a social movement, the meaning of restorative justice is negotiated by a group of actors that includes:

1. *Governing authorities:* Even though they would not necessarily be considered part of the restorative justice social movement, state agencies and other governing bodies have an obvious influence on the restorative justice movement since they provide the resources (such as money and referrals) that make the practices of restorative justice possible. Much economic and administrative support for restorative justice programs comes from federal, provincial (or state), and/or municipal governments, each motivated by a specific set of goals, but also potentially wary of the bad optics that might arise from this support (for example, if an offender who is processed through a restorative justice program recidivates by committing a high-profile offence). Therefore, restorative justice agencies cannot rely on unconditional governmental support and often need to turn to non-governmental funding agencies, such as the United Way or private investors, to ensure their continued and unfettered operation. In such cases, non-

governmental funding agencies play a role as governing authorities for restorative justice.

2. *Restorative justice agencies:* These are the groups (both state-based and not-for-profit) that deliver actually existing restorative justice programs. Through their implementation of restorative justice, they play a significant role in defining what restorative justice is. They also face the difficult task of negotiating demands placed upon them by the governing authorities while still trying to remain faithful to the principles of restorative justice, as laid out by various restorative justice proponents.

3. *Restorative justice proponents:* This is the group of often charismatic practitioners, academic theorists, and other restorative justice advocates who contribute to the discussion about the collective definition of the restorative justice movement (for example, what are its essential values and practices? What outcomes are truly restorative?). These are the people who are seen attending restorative justice conferences and writing books on the topic, trying to convince a broader public of the benefits of the restorative approach.

4. *Third-party interests*: Restorative justice is not an isolated field of justice activity. The application of restorative justice has a significant bearing on the work performed by activists and practitioners in connected areas of concern, such as victim rights, prisoner rights, family violence, and prison abolitionism, to name but a few. Therefore, it is no surprise that critical and/or supportive contributions from these individuals are part of the restorative justice social movement. For example, Susan Herman (2004) of the National Centre for Victims of Crime has offered support to the idea of restorative justice but also expresses reservations that it still appears to be a very offender-centred process, much like the criminal justice system. Such criticisms have contributed to debates within restorative justice about the lack of attention to victim's needs and the overemphasis in some programs on offender reintegration, leading to attempts to define a more victim-centred model of restorative justice.

5. *Participants:* Too often, the voices of victims, offenders, students, and community members who are the primary subjects of the restorative justice movement are ignored within the larger movement, even though they are the ones who participate in restorative justice pro-

grams. This should not be the case. Any appreciation for or dissatisfaction with restorative justice issuing from these participants should become part of the broader discussions about what restorative justice is and should be.

It must be noted that an individual could move between categories or find that they fit within multiple categories. However, despite this potential for fluidity and overlap, there are tensions existing between the categories that make it unlikely there will ever be complete agreement across the entire field of restorative justice. For example, whereas the governing authorities often seek to have restorative justice implemented in a manner that meets state goals of lowering recidivism and reducing the cost of justice, the proponents tend to view the values and desired outcomes of restorative justice in a more holistic light, emphasizing goals such as individual and community healing. As mentioned above, restorative justice agencies must therefore navigate these perspectives, while also taking input from third parties and participants.

To become a transformative social movement, restorative justice must resist conservative tendencies within this broader dynamic. Typically, for example, governing authorities are not seeking to foment social change through their (often limited) support of restorative justice; they are invested in the status quo and see restorative justice as a means to preserve it or to modestly improve it. Thus, it is with respect to the goal of transformation that a politics of restorative justice becomes most crucial. Returning to the four senses of the political, a transformative politics of restorative justice would mean:

1. *Assessing the political context in which restorative justice operates*. What are the policy rationales that guide current government and donor thinking? We emphasize neoliberal politics and the influence it has had on criminal justice thinking in contemporary societies. Like restorative justice, neoliberalism is a flexible and context-specific ideology, but it does attempt to shape local contexts to favour the profit and mobility demands of transnational corporations and investors. Neoliberals often support competing justice strategies rather than putting all of their eggs in the basket of one justice form. For minor crimes, they turn to informal, more cost-effective measures (such as restorative justice) as a way of making offenders more responsible for their actions and therefore less prone to re-offending. However, for repeat or major offenders, neoliberals often seek to bring the full

might of the state to bear on the offender, using instruments such as minimum sentences, zero-tolerance measures, and other forms of "tough on crime" punishment. Under such conditions, restorative justice advocates must be sensitive to the perpetual threat of co-optation. In other words, there is concern restorative justice will be adopted and supported by state actors so they can direct it toward acting as an accompaniment to the punitive criminal justice system, dealing with only the small fish (Hogeveen and Woolford 2006).

[margin note: attempts to avoid the adoption of political perspectives]

2. *Refusing to reproduce structures of domination.* Racialized, gendered, classed, heteronormative, and settler-colonial biases are easily imported into restorative justice processes. Given the general persistence of these patterns of domination, this should be expected. The restorative justice movement cannot simply assume that it is outside these patterns of domination, they must be addressed directly in restorative justice practice. For example, a restorative justice program working with Indigenous victims and offenders may feel that it is paying homage to Indigenous traditions by using in restorative justice strategies that share similarities with Indigenous justice practices. However, such borrowings can also serve as a means of cultural appropriation, taking Indigenous knowledges and re-packaging them for white service providers to deliver to Indigenous "clients." When this occurs, settler-colonial systems of Indigenous dispossession are maintained rather than subverted. The same thing can occur with respect to patriarchal domination if restorative justice practices fail to critically address gendered expectations of how women and men are to conduct themselves in public. Restorative justice could be a very retrograde force, for instance, if it were to allow a community to bully an abused spouse to "stand by her man" in a case of family violence. Moreover, these structures overlap with and reinforce one another, adding further complexity. Were a restorative program to operate in a context of a settler heteropatriarchy, a combination of settler colonialism, gender domination, and heteronormativity would define the experiences of the participants (Arvin, Tuck, and Morrill 2013).

3. *Restorative justice constitutes a form of governance.* As an approach to criminal justice, restorative justice offers a means for dealing with actors who violate state-defined norms. Thus, restorative justice is inevitably immersed in the task of governing such unruly individuals.

For this reason, it needs to find ways to think and apply its governance in a manner that goes beyond the dictates of the state, or, once again, it faces the threat of co-optation. Resistance to co-optation involves a reflexive assessment of restorative justice theories and practices to try to establish for restorative justice a foundation that does not depend solely on governmental definitions of wrongdoing or import government assumptions about crime and criminals into its practice.

4. *Social movements articulate grievances in the hopes of seeing them register with the general public, as well as to foster or prevent social change.* To shift society from retributive and toward restorative justice standards requires strategic political engagement in order to spread the message of restorative justice and to have it resonate with the broader public. The Italian Marxist, Antonio Gramsci (1971), famously spoke of the need to launch both a "war of movement" and a "war of position." Whereas the war of movement consisted of the deployment of troops to achieve military control, the war of position aspires to win the battle for the people's hearts and minds. In Gramsci's view, society is entrenched by the *hegemony* of the ruling class, a dominant worldview that shades the way we all see and act within the world. Through fostering their hegemony, the ruling class is able to transform its interests into a general common sense, and thereby make ruling class goals and objectives seem natural and inevitable. According to this perspective, social change requires more than just the overthrow of the ruling powers — it necessitates an effort to transform the ways that people think about the world around them. Simply put, a restorative justice war of position entails overcoming assumptions that punishment is the natural response to wrongdoing. However, this assumption intersects with many other assumptions about the place of women in society, racial hierarchies, and the legitimacy of settler colonial dispossession. For example, Elizabeth Comack and Gillian Balfour (2004) have shown how discourses of race, gender, class, and social space influence the decisions made by crown attorneys on whether or not to pursue criminal charges. Structures of domination in this manner inform the likelihood of whether or not one is accused and punished for an alleged wrong. A transformative war of position necessitates examining these linkages and pushing restorative justice beyond a narrow focus on changing our practices of punishment.

POLITICS AND JUSTICE

Much of the writing about restorative justice focuses upon what it means to be restorative. While that is important, a more pressing concern is that of justice. On what grounds does restorative justice claim to be justice? What does it mean to be just? Without in-depth discussions of such questions, restorative justice risks operating based upon unacknowledged or disguised presuppositions, and therefore, it is more likely to solidify rather than transform existing relations of governance. That is to say, it fails to be honest (with others, but also with itself) about the basis for its principles and practice. This failure can result in notions of restorative justice that are grounded upon naïve and overly idealistic foundations.

The question of justice will receive more attention later. For now, a basic definition of justice is that it is a means to solving a problem by offering "a way out of a morass of conflicting claims" (Fisk 1993: 1). Justice can address such conflicts in two basic ways. First, substantive theories of justice provide us a moral framework for deciding upon justice. In other words, the theory of justice guides us in deciding what the substance or content of justice should be. It provides an answer to the question, "what is right?" In contrast, procedural theories of justice offer no prescription for the substance of justice. Instead, they define a procedure through which fair and agreed-upon decisions might be made. They help us address the question, "how can we come to a fair decision about what is right?" Although restorative justice is often described as a process or procedure (see Marshall's definition on page XX), there are substantive qualities embedded within its practice (Pavlich 2007).

Whether the approach to justice is substantive or procedural, there still might be an expectation that just decisions will somehow be beyond politics. For example, in the tradition of justice inspired by the philosopher Immanual Kant, the just individual is expected to separate themself from the everyday world and to assume a reflective position that allows them to make a moral decision. In such a process, the mundane world of politics would simply be noise distracting the individual decision maker and therefore must be blocked out. However, such an ideal of justice is often far moved from reality. As Jürgen Habermas (1990) has argued, philosophers and judges can no longer assume themselves above or outside of the social world and therefore in a position to cast judgment on the requirements of justice. We are always already immersed in the social world and cannot simply bracket away its influences. Instead, we are left with the world of communicative engagement, where justice must be negotiated among individuals whose lives are deeply political.

Thus, justice is inseparable from the political, and, moreover, its pursuit requires a politics. Justice is inseparable from the political in that it involves processes of negotiating the competing claims of politically situated actors, who each bring their own socially constructed worldviews to the negotiation table. Justice requires a politics because, in order to advance an alternative vision of justice or to institute new justice procedures, we must engage in political debates and discussions. Thus, justice is both a critical and a communicative project in that it involves assessing current political conditions and strategizing ways to advance a different vision of the world.

QUESTIONS FOR DISCUSSION

1. What is the difference between gaining a feel for a practice and memorizing a definition? Why do we want you to focus more on the former than the latter?
2. What are some of the advantages and disadvantages of not having a firm definition of restorative justice?
3. Identify some specific local examples of each social movement group of actors. What are some concrete ways in which their interest in restorative justice may differ?

2

WHAT EVENTS TRIGGER A RESTORATIVE RESPONSE?

How does a restorative justice process begin? In a typical example, a criminal offence is committed, a suspect is apprehended, and something about the suspect makes them seem suited to restorative justice. Perhaps the accused takes immediate responsibility for their actions, or maybe they come from a close family and has good community supports to draw upon (although such criteria could result in a whole host of biases, since "good families" are often assumed to look a particular way: two parented, middle class, white). For such reasons, this person is considered a promising candidate for an alternative justice option. They are typically referred to a restorative justice program by a police officer, judge, lawyer, counsellor, or other criminal justice gatekeeper — that is, someone who has sufficient authority or decision-making power to facilitate another person's progress through the criminal justice system.

Victims, however, can also initiate restorative justice processes, as was the case for Don and Mary Struefert (see Chapter 1). In that case, Don felt unsatisfied with the criminal justice system response and turned instead to a restorative justice program, arranging for a post-sentencing meeting with Guy Sullivan. There are a number of persons who are able to initiate a restorative justice intervention.

There are also a variety of times when an accused person may be referred to a restorative justice program. It is important to note, though, that once they enter restorative justice, they in most cases accept responsibility and thereby forego their status as "accused." There are several stages at which restorative justice may be introduced:

1. *Pre-charge:* Police officers and other gatekeepers are on occasions empowered to divert perpetrators of minor crimes to restorative justice

programs. In cases such as shoplifting, this may be done to correct a young person's behavior without burdening them with the record of a criminal charge.

2. *Post-charge*: Restorative justice encounters may be held post-charge, but prior to the initiation of a formal sentencing process. This may serve to clarify the matters of the dispute or so the meeting-derived recommendations can be passed along to the deciding judge. Or, an alternative measures or extrajudicial sanction may be assigned through the process. The majority of restorative justice applications in Canada take place at the pre-charge or post-charge stage (Federal-Provincial-Territorial Working Group on Restorative Justice 2016).

3. *Sentencing:* Restorative justice encounters may take place for purposes of sentencing. Here, the participants decide upon an appropriate sanction and strategy for the offender to earn redemption. In many instances, participants will receive guidance from various justice professionals as to what sort of programs are available within the community to help the offender (such as addiction or anger management programs). It is also quite often the case that a judge may need to approve the recommended outcomes to ensure the agreed upon sanction meets formal legal standards, including terms of the *Canadian Charter of Rights and Freedoms*.

4. *Post-sentencing:* Victim and offender may meet in a mediated session after a judge has delivered the sentence. The offender may be held within a correctional institution or living within the community. In this process, the restorative justice meeting has no bearing upon their sentence (other than potentially demonstrating the offender's commitment to taking responsibility and making positive changes, which could potentially be admissible to the proceedings of a parole hearing). Most importantly, such meetings are intended to address unanswered questions (for example, "why did you do it?") for the concerned parties.

5. *Reintegration:* Some programs use restorative justice principles when assisting offenders with community reintegration. This includes several John Howard and Elizabeth Fry Societies, who assist a variety of former offenders as they transition from incarceration back into their regular lives. It also includes Circles of Support and Accountability (or COSA), which works specifically with sex offenders, using the

circle as a means to create supportive social networks that will help prevent recidivism.

The Nova Scotia Restorative Justice Program (NSRJP) is an example of a program designed to allow referrals at all of the stages we outline above. The NSRJP is one of the most comprehensive, institutionalized restorative justice programs in the country. It is fully funded and mandated by the province of Nova Scotia under the Public Safety and Security Division in the Department of Justice and offers restorative justice options for both youth and adults. In Nova Scotia police can refer before a charge is laid (pre-charge), crown attorneys can refer a case to restorative justice after a charge is laid, judges can refer after a conviction and before a sentence is imposed (post-conviction/pre-sentence), and finally staff of either Correctional Services or Victim Services can refer after a sentence has been imposed (post-sentence). Each referral point allows for different types of cases to be referred, with lower level offences being the only available for pre-charge. The different stages at which restorative justice might take place are a further testament to its flexibility, as programs must adapt their practices according to the stage at which they enter the conflict. A pre-sentencing session designed to inform the judge and counsel about various issues related to the case is much different than a post-sentencing meeting intended to answer victim questions and to move the parties toward reconciliation.

TRIGGER EVENTS

These stages of possible introduction only touch upon the individual initiators or gatekeepers for restorative justice. This is how restorative justice processes begin under most contemporary criminal justice systems. However, taking a step back addresses a more fundamental question: What sort of events *should* trigger a restorative response? This is a question of what sort of crimes, conflicts, harms, normative violations, wrongdoings, or injustices are the basis for launching a restorative justice response. It is problematic to assume restorative justice is restricted only to the harms prohibited under various national criminal justice codes. To base restorative justice on such a limitation would burden it with existing presuppositions about what justice is (that is, it would suggest justice is only what the law says it is) without asking exactly what is meant by the "justice" of restorative justice. Simply put, restorative justice needs to identify its object or target independent of the criminal justice system. As critical criminologists have long alerted us, the criminal law is not reflective of an overarching collective consciousness or consensus, but rather the product of specific political circumstances. We cannot take crime to be a naturally occurring object, rather we must remember it is socially constructed. For example, while some events are defined as crimes under our criminal code (for example, amphetamines used outside of medical prescription), other comparably harmful behaviours are not (for example, excessive alcohol consumption). A restorative justice program that focuses its energies on the 25mg of speed in the pocket of a student accused of harassing a classmate would most likely be ignoring the primary source of harm. As well, not all crimes are necessarily well-suited to a restorative response. A person growing a couple of marijuana plants in Manitoba may violate the law, but it is not necessary to hold a restorative justice conference to discuss this crime and its effects on the community, unless we know for certain that someone else feels harmed by this behaviour. To avoid the ethical confusion that comes with an over-reliance on a politically charged criminal code, restorative justice needs to strike out on its own and to define its own terms. [cannot simply adapt to the terms of the CJS]

In addition, aspiring toward a transformative approach to restorative justice leads to considering harmful events that are not recognized under criminal codes. The structural harms of gendered inequality, racist misrecognition, or unfair economic distribution, for example, are often at root in the everyday social conflicts that are the fodder of restorative justice. Therefore, any concept of restorative justice that does not open restorative meetings to discuss these and other such issues is unlikely to inspire much in the way of social transformation. [↑ needs to be done differently]

[margin: targets other issues that lead to social conflicts and injustices]

Crime

The event that triggers restorative justice, in most cases, is a crime. By crime, we typically refer to an act that has been designated criminal by the state and that is codified within domestic or international criminal law. However, this is an odd starting point for a justice paradigm that claims to be alternative (Zehr 1990, 1995) or even oppositional (Sullivan and Tifft 2001) to the formal criminal justice system (CJS) (see Pavlich 2005). By accepting the laws of formal criminal justice as its starting point, restorative justice does much to reproduce criminal justice ways of thinking (adapted from Pavlich 2005: 11–15):

1. *Harms hierarchy:* CJS restorative justice can privilege some harms (such as property crime) over others (such as the spread of pollutants). As mentioned above, criminal codes are rarely neutral and apolitical. The process of establishing something as a crime often involves an intensive political lobbying effort to place a certain form of wrong within the criminal code, as well as the political self-interest of the state. A stunning example of this is the way the crime of genocide is defined within the Canadian criminal code: as the intent to destroy an identifiable group by either "killing members of the group" or "deliberately inflicting on the group conditions of life calculated with the intent to destroy any identifiable group." Canadian law mirrors international conventions on genocide closely in these aspects of the definition. Yet, it is notable that Canada did not include the *United Nations Convention on the Prevention and Punishment of the Crime of Genocide* (1948) clause that describes "forcibly transferring children of the group to another group" as genocide. Can you think of reasons why Canada would not introduce this clause into its domestic laws? It is also worth noting that Canada was part of a group of nations who fought actively against inclusion of a broader section on techniques of cultural genocide, which included the offense of prohibiting language use among members of the targeted group, in the UN Genocide Convention (Woolford 2019).

2. *Victim and offender identities:* CJS restorative justice often constructs the reductive identities of victim and offender, even though there may be multiple and overlapping levels of victimization and offence. In other words, the labels of victim and offender are sometimes too simplistic to describe the dynamics of conflict situations (see Nelund 2017). For example, crimes are at times (if not most often) committed by individuals who have themselves experienced a great deal of victimization. The story of Yvonne Johnson demonstrates the breadth of suffering that lies behind a single criminal act (see Wiebe and Johnson 1999). Yvonne Johnson was sentenced to twenty-five years for first-degree murder for the September 14, 1989 killing of a man she believed to be a child molester, but antecedent to this incident were years of poverty, addiction, and abuse, including sexual assaults at the hands of her grandfather, father, brother, and a stranger. Restorative justice, if true to its principles, requires a language that allows it to be

sensitive to cases such as this, where there exists many levels and layers of victimization and wrongdoing.

3. *Increasing the power and status of governing criminal justice institutions and actors*: Because police personnel, judges, and lawyers are the primary gatekeepers who determine which individuals will be referred to restorative justice, they amass new powers through the introduction of restorative programs. While many will seek to use this gatekeeping power in a helpful and caring manner, there is always the possibility that restorative justice will be deployed in a manner that is self-serving or addresses CJS rather than societal objectives. Youth justice, for example, could be administered in a manner that uses restorative justice to expedite less serious cases so that more resources could be directed toward tougher treatment of certain young offenders (such as repeat offenders). Even more problematically, this latter group may feature primarily racialized or poor youth who do not receive the same opportunities and who are more likely to be targeted, accused, charged, and sentenced for their wrongful acts.

4. *Fostering non-disruptive behaviour that allows for the maintenance of the status quo*: Although we often place high value on peaceful and conciliatory behaviour, in its extreme form, such behaviour can be viewed as passive and subservient, and therefore in danger of lessening motivation for social change. There are times in any society's existence where individuals need to stand up to disrupt the social order, whether this is with respect to racialized inequalities or the wanton destruction of the environment. Conflict resolution should not be a tool for promoting a docile and less engaged populace.

For restorative justice programs that seek social transformation in the form of equal social participation in justice decisions and expanded community input into determining social norms, the affirmation of existing criminal justice laws through restorative justice processes presents acute problems. How can restorative justice transform a CJS when it takes the presuppositions of this system for granted? The problem is one of placing limits on the potential of restorative justice by restricting it from the outset to a narrow criminal justice focus. When crime is the primary trigger event for restorative justice, it becomes harnessed to the CJS in a way that discourages a broader rethinking of what we consider to be right and what we consider to be wrong. For instance, should restorative justice not concern itself with inter-ethnic tensions in a neighbourhood when they have not yet spiraled into criminal actions? It would seem most practical and preventative for restorative justice to involve itself at an early stage in such matters, rather than waiting for a crime to occur.

[handwritten: ↑ address the issues before they lead to crime]

Harm

Some have proposed that the ideal trigger event for restorative justice is harm, not crime (Mika and Zehr 2003). Following in the footsteps of peacemaking criminology (Pepinsky and Quinney 1990), which turned criminological attention toward the broader issue of suffering instead of crime, some restorative justice advocates have suggested their true concern is for all forms of harm, criminal or non-criminal, experienced by human beings. However, whereas crime is too narrow a trigger event for restorative justice, harm is too broad. There are many things that cause harm that may not be well-suited to a restorative approach. When a natural disaster strikes, such as an earthquake that destroys an apartment complex, an individual may have cause for a facilitated restorative justice meeting with their landlord to discuss the unstable construction of the building that contributed to its demise. This individual will not, however, be able to hold a mediated session with the earthquake. To suggest that restorative justice might nonetheless play a role in healing this individual from the trauma caused by the earthquake is to conflate restorative justice with victim counselling and other individual-based approaches to healing. Restorative justice is a *relational* approach to justice that depends on real or potential relationships between people. In other words, restorative justice responds specifically to interpersonal harms — that is, it addresses harms caused through interaction between two or more individuals. Interaction may include consideration of harm to an other-than-human entity, such as a river or stream subject to pollutants, but the needs of that other-than-human entity must still be represented by human actors who have a relationship with it (see Chapter 6 for more discussion of the possibility of restorative justice for other-than-human actors).

Conflict

Others have argued that crime is a form of conflict and therefore place restorative justice under the broader rubric of conflict resolution. This approach begins with the work of Nils Christie (1977), who suggested that conflict is a form of property that is "stolen" from communities. When communities are deprived of this resource, they lose the ability to creatively address their problems and to build something new and hopeful out of a troubling event (see Chapter 3). Other theorists have continued within this tradition of thought, offering arguments that most criminal harms are simply forms of conflict that are officially prohibited. Under this logic, a property offence, such as shoplifting a pair of basketball shoes from a store, is really just a conflict between the store's owner, who wants to charge high prices and earn a profit from the shoes, and the young offender, who desires the shoes and cannot afford the high prices. Similarly, a drug offence is a conflict between the drug user, who wishes to feel the effects of a prohibited substance, and the state, which has forbidden its use.

These examples imply that this understanding of conflict as a restorative justice trigger event bears a resemblance with Austin Turk's (1969) non-partisan conflict theory of crime. Turk suggested that crime is a mode of conflict between authorities who define, interpret, and enforce the law, and subjects who obey or resist the same laws. However, in the case of crime as conflict, the notion of conflict is extended well beyond Turk's understanding of the term to encompass a very broad array of behaviours. It becomes difficult to discern which conflicts deserve restorative attention and which do not. This approach can make it seem as though conflict is necessarily a problem that needs to be resolved. As is often noted within the broader conflict resolution literature (see Kriesberg 2008), some conflicts need to be played out and should not be forced toward an early resolution, since new or intensified hostilities would potentially arise, or entrenched injustices may persist. This speaks to the issue of the ripeness of the conflict and the timing of conflict resolution, since conflicts are ripe for peacemaking interventions when certain political, historical, cultural, and social conditions are present (Aggestam 1995; McEvoy and Newburn 2003). For example, a victimized group may be too disempowered to achieve a fair settlement with a wrongdoer, making conflict resolution premature. Along these lines, many of the still surviving "comfort women," who hail from Korea, China, and other nations, and were forced into sexual slavery by the Japanese military in the 1930s and 1940s, have refused privately funded reparations and an unofficial apology from Japan. Their insistence is that a dialogue be initiated within Japanese society about the injustices imposed upon them, bringing an end to the nationalist denial that has branded these women as willing "prostitutes." In this case, the conflict has not yet reached the point where a viable and acceptable resolution can be achieved, and the remaining "comfort women" and their supporters have little choice but to continue their struggle for a more meaningful outcome. A compromise settlement in such circumstances may be premature, since the Japanese government is unwilling to accept the basic premise of the conflict — that the Japanese state was directly responsible for perpetrating this wrong and needs to negotiate directly with survivors on the issue of compensation.

Conflict resolution specialists also draw a distinction between "constructive" and "destructive" conflicts (Deutsch 1973; Kriesberg 2008), with the former leading toward maximal benefits and minimal harm between adversaries and the latter producing suffering on all sides. It is possible that conflicts sometimes have a purpose. When the Black inhabitants of South African "homelands" took to the streets to protest the indignities of apartheid, many suggested this conflict was indeed justified and that it would have been irresponsible to try to impose upon it an early resolution. Instead, the governors of the apartheid system had to feel the sting of local and international protests for many years before they were ready to come to the table and negotiate a peaceful resolution to their conflict.

Norm Violation

Given the interpersonal dimension of restorative justice, one could suggest that restorative justice is truly concerned with *norm violations*. Norms are group-established behavioural codes that guide the activities of individuals belonging to the group. These norms, and the sanctions that arise in response to their violation, can be formal or informal. They may be recorded in a legal code, such as the criminal law, or simply known through socialization into the group in question, such as standards of politeness. For example, if a young person riding a bus vandalizes the seat in front of them by tagging it using a black felt marker, they have violated a formal norm, one that is contained within the criminal code and could possibly result in a formal sanction. If they do not rise to offer their seat to an elderly person or pregnant woman who boards the bus, they have broken an informal norm. Such a violation will not result in a formal punishment, but could lead to informal sanctions, such as the disapproving stares of fellow passengers (for distinctions between norm and law, see Weber 1946; Simmel 1908; Durkheim 1984 c. 1933).

Using norm violation as a trigger event, restorative justice might respond to any number of breaches of the normative order. Property crime or interpersonal violence would certainly constitute formal normative breaches, but so might the careless spread of pollutants or even the hurt caused by name-calling. In the latter case, using Instagram or Snapchat to insult one's classmate may not constitute a formal normative violation if it does not meet the criteria of existing criminal code offences (including criminal harassment, intimidation, extortion), but it certainly could cause a great deal of hurt to the person targeted. Indeed, rather than speculate we can look at the real-life example of what has become known as the Dalhousie Dentistry Scandal. In 2014, it came to the attention of the female members of the fourth-year dentistry cohort that their male colleagues had a private Facebook group called "Class of DDS 2015 Gentlemen." This group frequently posted content that was misogynistic and harassing. The incident that the female students first heard of was a poll created in the group asking members who they would "hate fuck" and listing several of their female classmates. The harm to those women and the feelings of betrayal and disgust were such that they filed complaints under the University's Sexual Harassment Policy. In response, the University offered a restorative justice process as a resolution and this option was taken up by twelve of the thirteen male students in the group, along with three other male dental students, and six of the nine women directly targeted on Facebook, along with eight other female dental students. For many, this process was necessary and useful for sanctioning the sexist norms that they felt pervaded the Dentistry culture at Dalhousie (see part of the participants' statement in Box 2.1). Others, however, felt that this was a disproportionate reaction to behaviour that was unseemly perhaps but certainly not worthy of such strong condemnation. The Task Force on Misogyny, Sexism and Homophobia in Dalhousie University Faculty of Dentistry Final Report notes there were letters to the editor of Halifax's main newspaper decrying the restorative justice process as a witch hunt (see the Report's comments in Box 2.1 about these varying interpretations).

For many conventional practitioners of restorative justice, this norm-violation definition would be sufficient. For them, the goal is to maintain social order and to return affairs to the status quo. However, for those adhering to a transformative notion of restorative justice, this definition is problematic. In fact, one criticism of the notion of norm violation as a trigger event for restorative justice is much the same as that offered with respect to the notion of conflict. In particular, basing restorative justice upon normative violations assumes the value of the normative social order, ignoring that breaches of this order might be fully justified or even necessary. The example of Rosa Parks illustrates this

Box 2.1 Restorative Justice at Dalhousie University Dentistry Program

Report Excerpt: Participants' Statement

As participants in the restorative justice process from the Dalhousie Dentistry Class of 2015, we write to you again as our time in the process comes to a close. To rephrase that, our time in the restorative justice process is officially coming to a close but we can all attest that we will carry the lessons it has brought us long after we graduate. As we reflect upon our five-month journey, we recognize how far we have come not only individually but collectively. We have challenged and supported one another as we confronted what happened with Facebook and the climate and culture within our school. These uncomfortable, difficult and complicated conversations have required us to delve deeper into societal and cultural issues of sexism, homophobia, and discrimination and how they erode the foundations of supportive and healthy communities. We did not create these issues, but we have come to understand our parts in perpetuating and tolerating them within our relationships and community. We have experienced acutely how harmful and destructive people can be to one another, and how people bring each other down. We have consciously learned to support one another and we have begun the process of building each other and our community back up. Having endured such a public fracturing of our class community and many of our personal relationships, our focus throughout the process has not been to return to normal but to create a new "normal" for the future.

Source: Report from the Restorative Justice Process at the Dalhousie University Faculty of Dentistry May 2015. Prepared on behalf of the participants by Jennifer J. Llewellyn, Jacob MacIsaac, and Melissa MacKay.

Report Excerpt: Perspectives on the Meaning of What Happened

Early on in our work, we were struck by wide-ranging, often conflicting understanding of the events. Understanding was far more varied than the frequently polar division of opinion over sexual misconduct against women — one view considers the response inadequate to the gravity of the conduct and its impact on the victims, and the other view considers the response excessive in light of the presumed intent of the perpetrators. The Facebook posts inspired vigorous debate over whether the remedy lay

> in individualized punishments or systemic change. Those who took the position that an effective response needed both elements did not agree on which should come first. Perspectives differed over interpretations of the content of the Facebook posts and what they revealed about Dentistry, as well as over the broader implications of social media and rape culture. We also heard diverse views about the University's response and what it said about the University's capacity to deal with such matters.
>
> Source: Report of the Task Force on Misogyny, Sexism and Homophobia in Dalhousie University Faculty of Dentistry.

point. On December 1, 1955, Rosa Parks, an African-American seamstress from Tuskegee, Alabama, refused to relinquish her seat on the bus to a white passenger. At this time, racial segregation was the norm in this part of the US, as was deference by those of African ancestry to those of European heritage. By violating these norms, Rosa Parks sparked the Montgomery Bus Boycott, which was one of the influential events that inspired Martin Luther King Jr. and the US Civil Rights Movement. Therefore, if a norm violation is assumed to be something that must be corrected (and the status quo thereby restored), restorative justice would fail to acknowledge that Rosa Parks' actions were a legitimate response to an unjust situation. In this sense, norm violation as the trigger event for restorative justice potentially possesses a conservative bias.

Norms are socially and politically constituted codes and therefore must be left open to criticism. Although in some cases norms may reflect the considered agreement of a community or other social grouping, it is just as likely they reflect the current confluence of power relations. For this reason, restorative justice cannot simply accept existing norms, conflict, or crime as its object, since this would serve only to reproduce dominant societal codes, for good and for ill. Instead, restorative justice requires guidelines that will allow it to actively and critically assess the norms and harms it takes under consideration.

Injustice

It seems we have reached something of an impasse. On one hand, crime is too narrow a trigger event, potentially limiting restorative justice to matters officially defined as criminal. Conflict, harm, and norm violation are too broad to serve as triggers, potentially lending themselves to what we will later refer to as "net widening" (the extension of the net of social control to previously non-criminalized behaviours).

As such, injustice offers a preferable frame for identifying restorative justice trigger events (see also Sharpe 2004). In Chapter 1, we offered a very basic definition of justice, but such a notion requires more in-depth investigation. In particular, the idea of justice presupposes a specific form of wrong — an injustice — that calls forth the need for justice. But what is an injustice and what should a restorative justice response to injustice be?

Under liberal principles of justice, such as those espoused by John Stuart Mill, Immanuel Kant, or John Rawls, injustice is often viewed as a violation of the public good or of universally afforded rights. For example, according to John Stuart Mill's (1993 [1861]) theory of utilitarianism, that which is of the most utility to society is considered morally good. Injustices are those events that violate the social order, thus, representing a disutility. To commit a crime like a bank robbery or a mugging is to act selfishly and in a manner that harms the public good. Thus, there would be a utilitarian interest in punishing these crimes to deter such acts.

The efforts of Kant and Rawls are directed less toward prescribing the content (or substance — see Chapter 1) of justice (and thereby defining injustice) and more toward outlining the ideal procedures for arriving at just decisions. With Kant, this involves the "categorical imperative," which is a principle that strikes invalid any norm that cannot be assented to by all who might be affected by it (Kant 1873; see also Habermas 1990). This does not require that some/all individuals actually meet and discuss the norms that govern their society, but rather that decision makers reflect on these various interests and consider the potential for collective assent to their decisions. Such an approach, however, assumes a shared (or universal) understanding of injustice and what sort of justice is needed to remedy it. But do we all share similar notions of injustice? Think for a moment about what causes you offence. Compare that to what might offend someone from another generation or culture. Are these sensibilities always universally shared? For some, marrying outside of one's religious or cultural group could cause great offence, while for others, intermarriage is an accepted practice of modern, pluralistic societies. For this reason, it is highly questionable that one person could alone reflect upon all the hurts and harms that might possibly constitute an injustice and separate themselves sufficiently from their private beliefs in order to ably reach a broadly agreeable resolution.

Rawls (1993) recognizes that belief systems differ among various cultures and subcultures, and thus claims his "political" model of justice is only appropriate to modern constitutional democracies. This is because the rights-based nature of a constitutional democracy presupposes that individuals are to be provided political equality and liberty. Indeed, for Rawls (1993: 52), these principles are ingrained within our understanding of "society as a system of fair cooperation between free and equal persons." Thus, Rawls limits his focus to a particular form of injustice — violations of the rights of equality and liberty. He does not discount that individuals and groups of individuals possess divergent and sometimes intractable visions of the good; however, the conditions of a constitutional democracy direct us toward a "reflective equilibrium," whereby any strictly political conception of justice must be in accordance with our convictions about the inherent importance of equality and liberty within a democratic society (Rawls 1971). When conflicts arise, those engaged in the conflict must step away from their privately held or culturally specific conceptions of the good and think in terms of the underlying political values of their society. Individuals are directed to resolve conflict by referring to the "original position," that is, by seeking a position outside of their own particular lives from which they can decide what is fair, based on the requirements of the political system. An integral feature of the "original position" is the "veil of ignorance," which Rawls refers to a self-imposed ignorance that allows individuals to step away from the immediate conditions of the social world so they can avoid being influenced by the power imbalances that are inevitably part of the institutional context of the conflict and that threaten the so-called fairness of any instance of conflict resolution.

In more concrete terms, we could understand Rawls's theory of justice as offering an ideal model for a judge in a democratic society. For example, Justice Beverley McLachlin (2004) of the Supreme Court of Canada describes the judge's role:

> The judge's role is the human role of resolving the legal disputes our society throws up as impartially as is humanly possible. This function is basic, not only to justice but to democracy.... In a democracy, citizens are entitled to bring their disputes and claims before an impartial arbiter with full confidence; the judge will decide the issue impartially, without fear or favour.

Here, the judge is not presented as a robotic dispenser of a justice that is fully prescribed by the legal code. Instead, the legal code is indeterminate, and the judge must do their best to make fair decisions that are free from undue bias or error. By seeking to take a neutral stance, the judge helps ensure citizens of fair and impartial conflict resolution, and of the protection of their rights.

This appears, on the surface, a fair way to determine the nature of injustice and justice in our liberal democratic societies. Since we are all assumed to have consented to live in such societies, one would think we could unite around these common values. However, this position rests too heavily upon the capacity of a lone individual to step back from their social situation and to reflect fairly upon what is in the best interests of all persons. Yet, we know from the world of law that adjudication is a "human process" (see Hogarth 1971), subject to the cultural and social assumptions of those in positions of power. Asking such individuals to remove themselves from what are deeply socialized, embodied, and intuitive beliefs about the social world is bound to lead to bias. For example, it took feminist activists many years to convince judges and lawmakers their masculine and patriarchal biases influenced the justice they sought to define and deliver, and still these activists work to point out masculine assumptions in the world of law. For instance, in the case of *Murdoch v. Murdoch*, which reached the Supreme Court in 1973, Irene Murdoch petitioned the court for rights to a portion of the property she had helped her former husband to acquire and sustain. But, in denying her claim and awarding her former husband sole ownership of the property, the Supreme Court agreed with a lower Alberta court, which had ruled the work Irene Murdoch had done in "sewing, cooking, cleaning, mowing, driving trucks, haying, dehorning, branding, and quieting horses" was "only a normal contribution as wife, to the matrimonial regime" (Supreme Court of Canada 1975).

It is also worth noting that Rawls' model of justice and injustice is a poor guide for restorative justice, since it emulates the traditional justice system by asking decision makers to take on a role very similar to that occupied by a judge when reflecting on matters of justice. Restorative justice, as a communicative process, requires a theoretical framework that can support its emphasis on dialogue. Moreover, it is through dialogue and communication that we are more likely to challenge our existing worldviews and open our minds to transformative change.

The challenge that arises with liberal philosophies of justice is that they offer what is primarily a political definition of injustice. Although scholars such as Rawls admit as much up front, we increasingly face the perplexing challenge of dealing with injustices within competing polities and intercultural settings, where such shared agreement about norms and what constitutes their violation does not yet exist. How do we claim such broad agreement in nations such as Canada, where the unity of the nation itself is called into question by competing self-determination claims from Indigenous peoples and Québécois? For this reason, we turn instead to theories that suggest an open notion of justice (and injustice) that must be subject to ongoing negotiation.

Jürgen Habermas (1984, 1990) offers a strong statement of the negotiated nature of norms and justice. For Habermas, reason and argumentation are necessary components of our world. When communicating, even if we intend to argue that human faculties of reason are inherently flawed or problematic, we are required to use these very same faculties to convince others of our position. Therefore, when one tries to deny the power of reason, one is immediately caught in a "performative contradiction" — the expression of reasonable arguments against the power of reason exposes the very power of reason. Thus, Habermas views reasoned argumentation as a universal practice upon which a system of ethical communication can be built.

Habermas contends it is the active participation of people taking part in a reasonable discussion about what is right and wrong (or what is just and unjust) that is the ideal basis for reaching agreement about justice. In this manner, Habermas differentiates his theory of communicative ethics from the theories of justice offered by Kant and Rawls when he identifies his approach as dialogical (that is, based on dialogue) rather than monological (that is, based on an individual monologue or thought process, as was the case for Kant and Rawls). For a communicative dialogue to act as a vehicle for fostering normative agreement, certain conditions must be in place:

1. Every subject with the competence to speak and act is allowed to take part in discourse.
2. a) Everyone is allowed to question any assertion whatever, b) everyone is allowed to introduce any assertion whatever into the discourse, c) everyone is allowed to express his attitudes, desires and needs.
3. No speaker may be prevented by internal or external coercion from expressing his rights as laid down in (1) and (2). (Habermas 1990: 89)

When these procedural conditions are met, the discourse that follows allows for the development of a normative consensus — or agreement about right and wrong. Following from this, Habermas (1990: 65) states a norm is valid when "all affected can accept the consequences and side effects its general observance can be anticipated to have for the satisfaction of everyone's interests (and the consequences are preferred to those of known alternative possibilities for recognition)." Discourse or communicative ethics, then, rests upon the process through which norms are validated, whereby "only those norms can claim to be valid that meet (or could meet) with the approval of all affected in their capacity as participants in a practical discourse" (Habermas 1990: 66). Unlike the models put forward by Kant and Rawls, an actual public discourse is necessary to define what is just and what is unjust. It is important to note that Habermas is speaking here of a "practical discourse," and acknowledges it is unlikely all interested parties will be involved in the actual discussion. What is necessary is they, or their representatives, receive opportunity to participate in the actual discussion.

Injustice, under this framework, can be understood as a matter to be negotiated rather than something that is pre-set. In this manner, although a particular event — a mugging, a violent assault, or parental emotional violence — may spark a restorative justice meeting, the meaning and boundaries of such an event should remain open to discussion within the actual meeting. In other words, restorative processes would ideally facilitate dialogue on what injustices occurred, as well as on other related injustices, so the group can reach a deeper sense of the forms of suffering that exist within their social world and reflect on a specific problem from this light. As well, restorative justice encounters are an opportunity for public discussion of community normative standards rather than for the unquestioning defence of these standards. Based on such a principle, a restorative justice meeting would not work to try to convince Rosa Parks to obey Alabama's racial laws but would make possible a broader collective questioning of these unjust standards.

Habermas's theory of discourse ethics does appear to offer a vision of justice and injustice that is suitable to flexible restorative justice processes. The theory, however, presents some difficulties for the restorative approach. For example, in Habermas's theorizing, individuals are expected to hold back their particular life views when they enter into communicative situations. The primary goal of establishing consensus is impossible if we are too immersed in the specific struggles of our day-to-day lives and not thinking of the general good. Such a perspective is imperfect for a restorative philosophy that prides itself on opening processes to the specific needs of participants, since our particular needs are shaped by our everyday lives, not solely by an abstract notion of the general good. Other theorists have revised Habermas's theory of discourse ethics so the "particular other" — that is, an individual with all their specific experiences and identifications — can engage in normative discussion (Benhabib 1992). Under this refinement of Habermas's approach, less emphasis is placed on achieving consensus, and more on using the discussion as a means for expanding our justice horizons and learning about the specific needs of others.

Benhabib's correction to communicative ethics points to the notion of an "ethic of care." Historically speaking, the ethic of care has been opposed to a masculine ethic of justice. Psychologist Stanley Kohlberg's work on moral development was criticized by Carol Gilligan (1982) for exhibiting a male bias by privileging a masculine approach to justice — the supposed objectivity and neutrality of the judge — as the apex of moral development. In contrast, Gilligan argued that women held to an ethic of care as their primary ethical focus is on learning the specific needs of those with whom they are in a direct caring relationship. A mother may not strive for objectivity when faced with the delinquency of their child but may instead want to understand the motivations and feelings that drove the child to crime. Gilligan's conceptualization of the ethic of care was subsequently criticized for making assumptions about the essentially feminine nature of the ethic of care and for how such an ethic can be used to impose expectations of specific practices of femininity and motherhood upon women in their everyday lives (Bartky 1990). But this does not mean that the baby of seeking to understand the particular needs of the other has to be thrown out with bathwater of essentialism (that is, the assumption that women are feminine and beholden to a particular ethic because of their nature). Indeed, intersectional feminism has provided a means for understanding particular needs through its conceptualization of interlocking structures of domination and its promotion of narrative and standpoint-based methodologies. The most basic insight to be drawn from intersectional feminism is that identity is not singular. Instead, individuals are placed within the multiple patterns of domination that transverse our social world. Legal scholar Kimberlé Crenshaw (1991) argues that when feminists talk about women they are often talking about *white* women and at the same time when critical race scholars talk about African Americans they are often talking about African-American *men*. Neither perspective captures the unique ways that African-American women are positioned. One may be privileged in one realm, while disadvantaged in another. As well, some may simultaneously experience multiple forms of injustices, and the intersection of these injustices results in distinct biographies of suffering (Burgess-Proctor 2006; Comack and Balfour 2004). Awareness of these multiple and interlocking patterns of domination can therefore help guide us when discerning the specific needs of a particular justice context. One would not, under this line of thinking, necessarily approach restorative justice for an Indigenous woman sexually harassed by her employer in the same way for a white woman. In the former case, the woman's indigeneity modifies in significant ways this unfortunately common experience of patriarchal domination.

The need to connect restorative justice processes to discussion of the very nature of the injustices that are at stake can also be connected to the work of Jacques Derrida (1992). Derrida points to deconstruction and the role it might play in exposing law's "mystical" foundations, as well as the force that brings law into existence. Often, within its ideological framework, law hides the fact it is a reflection of the economic and political interests of dominant forces in society. These interests have been codified as law in society through a moment of force. To say law arises from a moment of force does not necessarily mean powerful people employed physical violence in order to subject others to their law and rules, although this is possible. Force also arises through everyday acts of interpretation (or interpretive violence) through which one particular interpretation of justice is disseminated amongst a larger public. For example, consider how we commonly employ terms such as offender or property crime in our everyday language. We too often take these things as givens, as matters of common sense, and ignore that certain acts or individuals are being interpreted through a specific cultural lens. In this regard, when Will Goodon shot a ringneck duck near Turtle Mountain in October 2004, the state charged him with hunting out of season. Goodon disagreed with the state's interpretation of his action. He argued his Métis Harvester Card was sufficient to demonstrate he had an Indigenous right to hunt in this area. In his case before the Supreme Court of Canada, Goodon questioned the state's power to define such laws, and, more generally, he challenged the state's power to define what it means to illegally hunt or fish (see CBC News 2009). Should a history of Indigenous rights be ignored because of the imposition of colonial law and the existence of often-violated treaties? What about the rights of Indigenous peoples to continue their traditional activities?

Deconstruction exposes the mythical foundations of law not merely out of some spirit of academic sport, but in hopes of bringing about change; that is, to intervene in the construction of law or norms in a responsible manner. However, it does not claim for itself a standpoint from which it can say the force that constructs these mythical foundations is unjust, since this would imply deconstruction itself possessed some direct knowledge of justice, which Derrida sees as being impossible. For Derrida, law, authority, and most other supposed absolute concepts are deconstructable — we can examine how they are founded or constructed through historically and socially contingent interpretations. None of our concepts has a natural origin; they have all arisen through human actions and carry with them the taken-for-granted assumptions that are characteristic of specific times and places. For Derrida, what is important about justice is it cannot be deconstructed. Justice is an "experience of the impossible," by which he means justice, in its idealized sense, represents something that is always "to come" rather than realizable in any immediate form.

In a more concrete sense, for Derrida, justice represents a concern with the singularity of the Other. This means addressing oneself to the Other in the language of the Other. Although it is impossible for one to fully understand what another person means (you can never see entirely into the head or be in the shoes of another person), we must nonetheless try to place ourselves in their position and seek to comprehend the very specific qualities of their life experiences. We too often fail to truly hear what others are saying and instead translate their words from the perspective of our own specific experiences of the world. In Woolford's research on treaty negotiations in British Columbia, for example, he frequently witnessed this failure to communicate. On occasions when Indigenous groups spoke about their territory and its centrality to what it means to be an Indigenous person, and thereby told of the deep injustice of colonial land appropriation, the government negotiators often heard these statements as demands for resources and territory. They were understood to want control over property rather than stewardship over land, which was part of their Indigenous identity, and the capitalist notion of property ownership framed much of the subsequent discussion (Woolford 2005).

Derrida's conceptualization of justice clearly opposes Habermas's notion that there exists a universal reason that allows for the possibility of unproblematic speech under certain conditions. In contrast, Derrida suggests communication is always and inevitably problematic. For this reason, he argues deconstruction *is* justice. It is a form of responsibility to the Other in the sense that it seeks to uncover points in any conversation where certain worldviews or culturally based understandings are imposed. Furthermore, Derrida's perspective requires us to always accept any consent or common understanding that we reach as tenuous and uncertain. Perhaps put too simply, deconstruction is justice because it never allows us to settle upon taken-for-granted assumptions; we are always required to question, to probe, to interrogate commonsense meanings so we become aware of their arbitrary foundations. In this way, deconstruction is always ready to denounce injustice because it vigilantly watches out for the forceful imposition of meaning on any situation.

Derrida concludes it is beyond our ability to completely reflect justice in our laws, to calculate its requirements. However, we cannot simply use this as an excuse for staying out of conflict or for allowing conflicts to rage on. Justice requires that we attempt to calculate the just, but that we do so in a way that we are always reflecting on these calculations (laws) and renegotiating their boundaries. Although Derrida places great emphasis on the work of deconstruction in taking apart our commonsense views, this does not mean we can simply stand back and criticize without taking any forward-looking action. Injustice is immediate, it is there in our presence, and demands our response, but we must be willing to critique, re-examine, and potentially alter any specific remedy or response. For example, legal practices relating to rape and other forms of sexual violence in Canada have shifted over time, in part through the critical engagement of feminist legal scholars and activists. Until the 1980s, it was very difficult to convict a male rapist for his crime on the sole basis of testimony from a woman or child. Both women and children were viewed as too unreliable to provide convincing evidence and their testimony had to be supported by another, preferably male, witness or expert. The Badgley Commission reviewed these practices and challenged the assumption that women and children were unable to provide reliable evidence with respect to their experiences. These changes were later subject to further refinement, such as through "rape shield" provisions, established in 1992, that prevent complainants in rape cases from having their sexual histories used by the accused to discredit their evidence. Justice remains a continuing project in such cases rather than ever reaching a final, perfect end state.

The insights of Habermas, Benhabib, intersectional feminists, and Derrida are, to a great degree, incompatible, since Derrida problematizes both the prospects for uncoerced conversation and of knowing the Other in a full manner to truly meet their needs. However, Derrida's deconstruction does offer guidance that can help restorative justice practitioners to foster transformative communication in a more open, reflexive, and critical fashion. On the one hand, these other scholars offer a means for establishing a communicative framework for reaching restorative agreements, even to the point of allowing us to decide what is and what is not unjust in any particular situation. On the other hand, Derrida's model of deconstruction demands that, once reached, we probe these agreements even further, to look for the traces of power — the unspoken presuppositions that are at work in such agreements — and be willing to turn a critical eye toward these conversations. Thus, by combining Derrida's insight with these dialogue-based models, we arrive at a means for understanding restorative justice as an agonistic or contention-based space in which we continuously strive to meet the demands of justice.

What does this all mean in the concrete world of restorative justice practice? It means that if we take injustice to be the trigger event that sparks a restorative justice, we do so with some reservations. The injustice that sparks the restorative encounter is not the full extent of the injustices that might be discussed; it is just an immediate need to which we must respond and may also be a symptom of or signal to larger harms. Therefore, a break-and-enter may be the trigger event that leads us to restorative justice, but the restorative meeting has the potential to raise issues of ageism (if, say, an elderly person was victimized), neighbourhood poverty or economic disparities, youth disempowerment, or any number of issues. Unfortunately, not all restorative justice programs meet the standard that C. Wright Mills proposed for sociology. That is, they do not draw the link between private troubles of crime commission and victimization and public issues of structural disadvantage and inequality (Mills 1959). But there are some that try.

To illustrate this point with an example, in the case of a 17-year-old male, who admitted responsibility for a serious act of arson in Renfrew, Ontario, the restorative justice conference was directed primarily toward exposing the young person to the harmful consequences of his actions. He had been careless while smoking and drinking behind a local school, which had resulted in a wooden trash container catching fire. The fire subsequently spread, causing $14,000 damage to the building. The principal, vice-principal, teaching aid worker, as well as the youth's parents all impressed upon this young man their deep upset and the many challenges the school faced as a result of his actions. However, the report from this conference offers no details of discussion concerning the situation faced by youth in this community — such as their sense of boredom, disconnection, alienation, and other factors that might have attracted him to this behaviour (see Hunt 2000). A restorative justice program based on open communication, where the intersectionality of the youth's experiences as a young, disenfranchised member of an economically disadvantaged community had been brought to the table for discussion, may have offered a more well-rounded response. While the message of harm would still need to be communicated to the youth, it would be possible to deconstruct the power structures at the school that left this young person feeling disconnected and bored, as well as to open the meeting to solutions beyond simply shaming the young person for his wrongdoing.

The crucial issue here is that restorative justice can aspire to a form of communicative ethics around an injustice, but if the restorative justice program is to have any transformative potential, the discourse must be open to other possibilities — to new potential problems or understandings of a specific problem. It must be more than the collective imposition of shame for what is presumed to be an isolated act. This is something many restorative justice practitioners intuitively know: a crime or other single injustice that triggers restorative justice is only an initial pathway of what may be, in fact, a complex network of injustices.

This self-corrective capacity of a restorative justice guided by communicative ethics is not enough, however. The practices of restorative justice cannot simply be taken as a foundational means for uncovering injustice and finding its remedy. Instead, restorative justice must continually reflect upon its practice to see where new injustices might arise: does restorative justice tend to get assigned to individuals in a particular age, ethnic, or class bracket? Is restorative conflict resolution being used, in a particular case, to placate and dampen a necessary and righteous dispute? The insights of intersectional feminism and the practice of deconstruction remind us we must not allow restorative justice practices to become sedimented — to become unquestioned and frozen, and therefore no longer open to critical questioning. In addition to fostering open dialogue amongst various parties who have experienced a common harmful event, restorative justice must continue to foster dialogue about its own practices and grounding assumptions, never allowing itself to become an unchanging orthodoxy.

QUESTIONS FOR DISCUSSION

1. We outline many of the potential dangers in limiting restorative justice to crime. Are there any benefits of retaining this category as the trigger event for restorative justice?

2. What would a restorative justice process have looked like for the Dalhousie Dentistry case if it had begun from each of the justice theories — liberal, communicative, intersectional, deconstructive — discussed in this chapter? What would the focus have been? What harms would be identified? What would the goal of the process be?
3. Reflect on the arson case outlined above. What may be some other, connected injustices that restorative justice may be able to address in that case?

3

DELINEATING THE RESTORATIVE JUSTICE ETHOS

Restorative justice theorizing has gone through some major developments in recent years. Some thinkers and practitioners have tried to create a consolidated or universal restorative justice theory — that is, a theory of restorative justice that would apply in all times and places, and to all restorative justice programs. It is more useful, however, to identify a restorative justice *ethos* — the dispositions or guiding beliefs of the restorative justice movement. The restorative ethos is built upon a common set of assumptions that links together even the most conservative and radical restorative justice programs. The notion of a restorative justice ethos allows one to include the debate and contention that characterizes the restorative justice movement (see Chapter 1) without forcing closure onto this debate by declaring a full and final theorization of the principles of restorative justice. As well, the act of delineating a restorative justice ethos allows for a more fundamental critique of the tendencies within the restorative justice movement that inhibit rather than foster transformative change.

Some contend that restorative justice was first a practice, and it has only subsequently been theorized. Attempts to theoretically grapple with restorative justice can seem somewhat after-the-fact in that they try to add conceptual flesh to what has been an intuitively rational and culturally salient approach to communal conflict. A brief history of restorative justice addresses this claim, as well as explores the roots of the restorative justice ethos.

TRADITIONS OF DISPUTE RESOLUTION

A claim sometimes put forward by restorative justice proponents is that restorative justice is a natural historical approach to justice. This, however, ignores that the histories we carve out to support this claim, or any claim for that matter, are themselves politicized in the sense that the truth they purport to uncover has implications for how things are perceived in the present. Skepticism about the motivation behind historical truth claims should not, however, be taken to mean there is no real history. Certainly, there are uncontested historical events, such as the fact that there were multiple fronts of battle during an era we refer to as World War II, and during this period the Nazi regime worked to eliminate European Jews and other targeted groups through a variety of killing methods. Denial of such events is, without doubt, revisionist. There is nonetheless a large degree of contestation over the interpretation of such events. There is even, at times, contestation over the historical details that comprise these events. For example, although only the revisionist fringe disputes the occurrence of the Holocaust, there is much argument over what we consider the Holocaust to be. Historians have long debated the question of when precisely the Holocaust began. Did Hitler plan the extermination of European Jews prior to his rise to power, but wait until international war provided him a cover for carrying out his deadly ambitions? Or did the Holocaust emerge gradually as the Nazi regime radicalized and other plans for dealing with Jews, such as a proposal to ship them to Madagascar, failed (see, for example, Browning 2004)? Debates such as this are seldom simply contestations of fact; they also reflect specific political leanings. With the former, the Holocaust is the product of a calculated and long-held hatred that suits a liberal viewpoint prioritizing the thinking agent as the source for historical change. With the latter, the Holocaust is still an intended horror, but it arises haphazardly out of a very specific social and political context. This view appeals to those who see social structures to be, at least partially, responsible for the way events unfold. In each case, history cannot escape politicization because it has implications for how we understand the crime of genocide in the present — is it necessarily the product of consciously premeditated and deadly hatred? Or can it also or instead result from immediate and extreme radical response to perceived problems? Therefore, because historical claims are often subject to competing socio-political interpretations, we must approach any claim to true historical representation with a critical eye and great caution so we can assess the assumptions that are built into whatever act of historical representation we are witnessing.

Most attempts to represent the history of dispute resolution use and abuse history in order to serve a contemporary agenda. For example, an author approaching this history from the perspective of the state is likely to present a narrative of civilizational progress. Accordingly, prior to the twelfth century, the world (usually meaning Europe) was a dark and violent place. With little systematic dispute regulation in place, there was always the potential that any wrong committed would spark a bloody cycle of vengeance. In the worst-case scenario, they would take the form of a blood feud between kinship groups. Into this chaos entered the state, which declared certain forms of wrong to be public harms, thereby making itself solely responsible for the adjudication of justice. An example in the progress narrative is the system of *composition*. Defined by the Laws of Ethelbert of Kent (approximately 600 A.D.), this "law" enforced a practice whereby wrongdoers would pay *bot* for injuries that did not cause death and *wite* to the state to offset the costs of administering justice for the case (Weitekamp 2003). This system of dispute resolution is often viewed as an early stage in the gradual rationalization of justice. However, this story of state progress and the humanization of law tends to ignore or minimize the injustices that accompanied newer, more "rational" approaches. The system of compensation often led to further injustices, since the rich could easily pay their debts, while the poor, at times, had little choice but to sell themselves into slavery to cover their debts. As power became more concentrated in the hands of leaders such as paramount chiefs, feudal lords, and kings, it became more brutal, as these leaders sought to display their might through the administration of punitive violence (Kueneman 2008). In its early incarnation, the criminal justice state was still unfair and brutal in its dispensation of justice, offering cruel punishments. Proponents of a progress narrative argue that the state became gradually more humane and enlightened in response to wrongdoing, thus producing due process rights and other procedural protections to prevent abuses of state power (for further discussion, see Johnstone 2002).

Michel Foucault (1977), in *Discipline and Punish*, exposes the mythic nature of this progressive rendition of criminal justice history. Foucault begins with the story of Damiens, who attempted to kill King Louis XV of France. Damiens, according to the ritualistic regulations of eighteenth-century punishment, was to be tortured, drawn, and quartered. The performance of his death was compromised when the horses failed to pull him apart, and the executioner had to intervene to try to expedite the process by hacking at Damiens's limbs. In a spectacle such as this, which is designed to illustrate the unchallengeable power of the king, performance disruptions can be highly problematic. For instance, the crowd's animosity toward the offender may turn into sympathy, and then there is the potential for a public protest or riot to erupt. The spectacle fails when the crowd begins to identify with the punished rather than fear and respect the might of the punisher. According to Foucault, this is part of the reason that punishment began to change course during the eighteenth century. Following the lead of various disciplinary institutions, such as the monastery, the military, and the school, governments sought to retrain criminals rather than brand upon them the power of the sovereign. Foucault, however, portrays this shift as an uneven and elliptical development, and not as the product of a linear and increasingly enlightened progress.

In contrast to Foucault's complex history of punishment, restorative justice advocates have too often offered their own simplified historical narratives to compete with the progressive triumph of an enlightened criminal justice. In what Johnstone (2002) describes as a story in which informal justice responses are lost, we see prior to the twelfth century not a period of widespread violence, but, rather, a world where restitution and negotiation are the primary features of dispute resolution. Small-scale societies were viewed to seek mediated settlement of conflicts, sometimes through the intervention of a respected community member, so as to maintain the social peace. It is only when the state "steals" crime from communities that things begin to unravel (Christie 1977). In closely interconnected and interdependent small-scale societies that existed for much of human history, there was a definite interest in resolving conflict amicably so as to preserve the harmony of the community. Once the state declared certain wrongs to be public wrongs, then victims and communities were shut out of dispute resolution processes, depriving these groups of an important opportunity to participate in public deliberation and creative problem solving (Braithwaite 1999). The story of the rise of the state and the concentration of political power is one in which our primordial restorative tendencies are displaced in favour of retributive, state-centred justice.

Although ours is a simplified story, the restorative justice historical narrative we present is that justice becomes more distinctly political after the twelfth century. It is in this period that justice is appropriated to serve state purposes and is more strategically crafted as a technology for regulating broad and diverse populations. But this "story of loss" cannot be taken uncritically. The increased politicization of justice does not necessarily mean we have linearly descended from a paradise of informal justice into our present retributive criminal justice reality. Formal and informal justices have always overlapped and operated in combination with one another during this period, as the example of plea bargaining from Chapter 1 attests. There is not a single story of progress or loss, but rather of different combinations of formality and informality, in different times and different places. Patterns of domination and politics have had a role in how these combinations manifest.

It is not just European restorative justice history that has been oversimplified. One can, for example, be equally critical of the ways in which some restorativists employ the traditions and histories of Indigenous peoples when advancing their claims. To begin, it is an error of presentism — of interpreting the events of the past through the ideas of the present — to suggest that past Indigenous justice practices were restorative justice. Yet, many restorativists do so when they review the past and claim Indigenous justice as part of their lineage. This is not to suggest these practices do not exhibit elements of what we might today view as restorative justice; however, it is important to recognize they were developed in distinct cultural contexts. Take, for example, the traditional justice practices of the Indigenous peoples who reside on Turtle Island, what is now Canada. One of the primary forms of dispute resolution employed by some of these Indigenous groups, especially those in the Prairie regions, was the use of circles, or community meetings, to determine a resolution to the harm caused. Contemporary restorative justice practitioners have since adopted circles as a means to bring a variety of stakeholder voices to bear on a particular case of wrongdoing, but there is not a straightforward and unbroken line between traditional Indigenous circles and those used today. Nor is there a single, unitary practice of circling that was used across the diversity of Indigenous groups that populated Canada prior to colonization (Laroque 1997).

For these reasons, we must trace the lineage of restorative justice carefully. Beginning with the traditional justice practices of Indigenous peoples on Turtle Island, it would be disingenuous to suggest all such groups used a justice that was predominantly restorative (Laroque 1997). Much depends upon factors such as cultural region, historical period, and the conflict to be addressed. In some cases, such as when a male combatant was caught by a competing war party, punishment could involve a sentence as retributive as death or slavery. Typically, however, given that Indigenous societies were more tightly knit with strong interdependencies and shared cultural norms, there was a clear interest in conciliatory forms of dispute resolution. Given the reliance of one group member upon the other, Indigenous groups often could not allow conflict to continue in a never-ending spiral, since such conflict could seriously disrupt group life. Therefore, compromise and mediated settlement were widely practised to ensure group harmony. However, the compromises viewed as culturally appropriate in these communities, at times, diverge radically from contemporary restorative sanctions. In some west coast Indigenous communities, wrongdoing by a member could result in a community recommendation of banishment: the wrongdoer would be asked to leave the community, perhaps to live alone on an uninhabited island for a period of time.

Still at the core of such practices was a desire to restore community harmony. The link to today's restorative justice can be found in this common goal, but this ignores the historical processes of colonialism, which extracts wealth from a region to enrich a colonial power, and settler colonialism, which operates to replace Indigenous peoples with a settler population, dispossessing the former of their lands. After a period of relative cooperation between Indigenous peoples and the traders and explorers who ventured to what is now Canada (approximately sixteenth to early seventeenth century, mainly through the fur trade), colonial settlement (beginning in earnest in the mid-seventeenth century) brought deep disruptions to Indigenous nations. Suffering first from the European diseases that came with the explorers, Indigenous peoples subsequently felt the force of European law as it stretched across the continent. Legal documents were signed to remove Indigenous territories, acts of parliament such as the Indian Act (1876) defined all Indigenous peoples legally as Indians, with a determinate set of rights and obligations. Eventually, the Canadian police and judicial systems included even the most remote Indigenous community within their regulatory domain. The world of Indigenous dispute resolution was not simply forgotten or lost; instead, it was colonized. It was forcibly replaced through the imperial march of Canadian law. Therefore, to simply claim to be renewing Indigenous justice traditions, without serious consideration of the colonial acts that disrupted the social conditions that made these traditions possible, is to risk performing new acts of colonial appropriation and erasure. The authenticity of such an "imagined noble savage justice" is drawn upon to lend credence to modern practices, but without any real historical continuity existing between the two justices. Even worse, as restorative justice is reintroduced into Indigenous communities, but now at the discretion of a Canadian criminal justice system, there is a fear that Indigenous justice is being appropriated in an act of neo-colonialism. Indeed, whereas Indigenous traditional justice practices once achieved their saliency from being culturally embedded in self-determining Indigenous cultures, contemporary circle sentencing achieves legitimacy through state sanction (for discussion of Australian Indigenous peoples see Cunneen 1997, 2002, and 2007). Renewals of Indigenous justice traditions could strengthen the colonial state as much as they do Indigenous communities. Must recognize the practice

This is not to suggest that we cannot learn anything from the past. Nor is the caution an underlying radical historical relativism that suggests the past and present are so incommensurate that knowledge cannot travel through the ages. In contrast, Indigenous knowledge is itself a resource belonging to specific communities that have experienced the onslaught of colonialism. Restorativists must be very careful not to simply appropriate or wrongfully borrow that knowledge without proper recognition of its source and a commitment to decolonizing the social conditions that contributed to the removal and repression of Indigenous justice traditions.

Based upon these challenges, theoretical engagement with restorative justice cannot be avoided. There is no natural or inevitable tendency toward restorative justice. We must explore theoretical questions about why restorativists believe what they believe, as well as questions about the assumptions that are built into restorative justice practice.

THEORIES OF RESTORATIVE JUSTICE

The use of the term "theory" to describe the conceptualization of restorative justice may seem overly ambitious. Restorative justice writings are not typically systematic theorizations of the epistemological (how restorative justice proponents know what they claim to know) and ontological (the assumed nature of the social and political world that restorative justice inhabits) foundations of restorative justice (see Hay 2006). More often, we find instead clusters of ideas that represent a rethinking of contemporary criminal justice and conflict resolution practices. Much restorative justice theorization represents an attempt to construct a theory of the practice of restorative justice. It offers an explanation as to why restorative justice is effective in what it seeks to accomplish, and of how it might be even more effective in the future. The emphasis on the social theory of restorative justice focuses less upon the everyday practice of restorative justice and more upon its grounding assumptions: how does restorative justice know what it claims to know? What assumptions does restorative justice make about the nature of the social world? What is the restorative vision for society? The answers offered to these sorts of questions provide insight into the underlying restorative justice ethos that shapes restorative thought and practice.

The modern variant of restorative justice emerged in the 1970s, as a confluence of forces made possible a re-evaluation of our responses to crime. These forces included:

1. An earlier effort to reform criminal justice as rehabilitation was dismissed by advocates of the notion that "nothing works" (Martinson 1974; see also Duguid 2000), saying society is unable to change the behaviour of offenders and has little option but to incarcerate and warehouse them. The hopelessness of the "nothing works" mantra led more idealistic criminologists, justice workers, and prisoner advocates to search for a new alternative.
2. Radicalism of the 1960s spearheaded an era of identity mobilization in which individuals began to organize around gender, race, ethnicity, and sexual orientation rather than their class positions. These efforts contributed to demands for greater community autonomy and control over local matters, as identity-based communities sought greater participation in the decisions affecting their day-to-day lives.
3. A move toward deinstitutionalization (removing power and control over social life from the hands of bureaucratic organizations) and deprofessionalization (removing power and control over social life from the hands of professionals) accompanied the era of identity mobilization, leading to demands to scale back the power of institutions, such as the prison, the asylum, or even the hospital, and to re-empower communities to deal with local concerns (see, for example, Illich 1977 and Illich et al. 1977).
4. Spiritual groups and reformist criminal justice agencies began to experiment with alternatives to incarceration, using conciliatory and negotiative approaches to encourage social harmony through reconciliation.
5. Underlying these developments was an economic shift from welfarism toward the neoliberal policies of Margaret Thatcher, Ronald Reagan, and Brian Mulroney. Under welfarism, the state established a social safety net to ensure the well-being of all citizens and to protect

citizens against social harms, such as unemployment and poverty. However, the maintenance of the social safety net was perceived by some economic and political elites to be too costly and difficult for government. This perception produced a call to roll back the welfare state and to impose policies designed to make individuals responsible for their own well-being, rather than tasking the state with this objective. Under these political conditions, one can anticipate the appeal of alternative justice strategies like restorative justice, which promise to ease the burden on our criminal justice system by asking communities and offenders to become more responsible and accountable for repairing criminal harms.

Amid these and other conditions, reformist scholars emerged to capture and theorize a new vision of criminal justice (see, for example, Barnett 1977; Zehr 1990; Wright 1991; Van Ness 1993; Galaway and Hudson 1996; Kurki 2000). Although the contributions were many, there are a few key moments in the development of the restorative justice ethos. There is no better person to start with than Nils Christie.

A Norwegian criminologist and anti-prison activist, Nils Christie (1977) published "Conflicts as Property." Christie argued that crime, as a form of conflict, is a valuable resource or "property." Possession of this property allows communities to participate in key forms of decision making and creative problem solving, as well as to contribute to local processes of norm development and clarification. When the state, through the work of state professionals, "steal" these conflicts and make them cases for the criminal justice system, a great community loss is suffered. Criminal issues become removed from the everyday life of communities, and community members are not required to confront these problems with creative solutions. In addition, the distance of the courts from the community contributes to the dehumanization of offenders, who are no longer perceived as community members, but rather as excluded parties removed from the realm of community life. For Christie, this system required replacement by community-based and victim-oriented courts that would provide citizens greater input into justice outcomes.

In the early 1990s, restorative justice would receive fuller formulation by Howard Zehr, a Mennonite scholar who had become familiar with the idea through his involvement in a victim–offender reconciliation program. Zehr called for a "paradigm shift" away from a criminal justice system that had failed

Table 3.1 Paradigms of Justice: Old/Retributive and New/Restorative

Retributive	Restorative
Crime defined as violation of the state	Crime defined as violation of one person by another
Focus on establishing blame, on guilt, on past (did he/she do it?)	Focus on problem solving, on liabilities, and obligations, on future (what should be done?)
Adversarial relationship and process normative	Dialogue and negotiation normative
Imposition of pain to punish and deter/prevent	Restitution as a means of restoring both parties; goal of reconciliation/restoration
Justice defined by intent and process: right rules	Justice defined as right relationship; judged by outcome
Interpersonal, conflictual nature of crime obscured, repressed; conflict seen as individual versus the state	Crime recognized as interpersonal conflict; value of conflict is recognized
One social injury replaced by another	Focus on repair of social injury
Community on sideline, represented abstractly by state	Community as facilitator in restorative process
Encouragement of competitive, individualistic values	Encouragement of mutuality
Action directed from state to offender • victim ignored • offender passive	Victim and offender's roles recognized in problem/solution • victim rights/needs recognized • offender encouraged to take responsibility
Offender accountability defined as taking punishment	Offender accountability defined as understanding impact of action and helping decide how to make things right
Offense defined in purely legal terms, devoid of moral, social, social, economic, or political dimensions	Offense understood in whole context — moral, economic and political
"Debt" owed to state and society in the abstract	Debt/liability to victim recognized
Response focused on offender's past behavior	Response focused on harmful consequences of offender's behavior
Stigma of crime unremoveable	Stigma of crime removable through restorative action
No encouragement for repentance and forgiveness	Possibilities for repentance and forgiveness
Dependence upon proxy professionals	Direct involvement by participants

Source: Zehr 1985.

victims by not meeting their needs or empowering them, and that had failed offenders by not holding them to a standard of real accountability whereby they would need to face those who they had harmed (Zehr 1995). By a "paradigm shift," Zehr means a new way of seeing the world — a new lens that will allow us to surpass all of our notions of criminal justice that are entrenched within a punitive worldview. Zehr argues this punitive worldview is the dominant interpretive lens in contemporary societies, leading us to automatically expect retribution to be the response to any harm, even if retribution proves to be a counterproductive means that neither deters potential offenders nor rehabilitates those who are apprehended. Zehr begins the project of encouraging such a shift from this punitive worldview by drawing a series of oppositions between restorative and retributive justice.

Zehr has since been criticized for creating too stark an opposition between restorative and retributive justice, that the two justice forms overlap more than Zehr admitted. It is also the case that such an exercise defines restorative justice predominantly in terms of what it is not. Such an act of definition by negation has a way of anchoring restorative justice to criminal justice by making the two ideas conceptually dependent on one another. Pavlich (2005) points out that binding these two ideas makes it very difficult to establish a truly alternative justice, since restorative justice ends up using retributive justice as its eternal reference point, and thus allows formal criminal justice to set the terms of debate and development. Due to this dependency, restorative justice often ends up reacting to criminal justice policy and practice rather than creating an approach to justice that is truly new.

In the late 1980s, John Braithwaite explored a similar set of ideas that would eventually merge with the notion of restorative justice. Braithwaite's thinking helps insert restorative justice more firmly within existing criminological theory. Specifically, Braithwaite addresses the related conundrums of labelling and stigmatization. When an individual commits an initial act of deviance, they may, as of yet, be uncommitted to a criminal identity. Indeed, it is common for young people to drift in and out of criminal behaviour (Matza 1990). However, the way in which we process people through the criminal justice system may have the effect of committing them to a criminal lifestyle. Courts, for example, represent "degradation ceremonies" (Garfinkel 1956) that serve to publicly lower the status of the offender, marking them as a devalued person. This change in status is most clearly illustrated by the criminal record, as is evident in the troubles experienced by the young man in Box 3.1, even after he has

Box 3.1 Canadians Who Are First Time Offenders and Looking for Jobs

"I just wanna see how many people out there in Canada have a criminal record and are looking for jobs and having a hard time. This is strictly for first time offenders and I'll explain why later. It seems like every company and business are starting to do criminal record check and most likely if you have a record your not gonna get the job.

I have talked to so many people where I live who have a criminal record, their first one and they all say that its hard to get a job and the only other option they have to do is illegal stuff to make money. I have also talked to people who had a first offense and then ended up getting themselves charged again because they went the wrong way to start to make money.

Now we all know that you can pay a x-amount of dollars to get your record erased or sealed after so many years and that's only if you have been keeping out of trouble. First how are you to get a job if you have a criminal record, secondly how are you to pay that fee if you can't get a job, and thirdly to not be able to find a job and have no money ends you up getting into trouble because your gonna do what it takes to make money even if its to break the law.

Now alot of you reading this are probably saying well you shouldn't have gotten yourself into trouble in the first place. Well first there's reason why people do certain things that got them into trouble in the first place, secondly just in the wrong place at the wrong time.

As a first time offender myself, I have had a hard time finding a job where I live now, I did my dues, I paid for my crime and it seems that having a criminal record, your punished for life. I have been crime free for years now it opened my eyes up, but it was a mistake when I did the crime and I apologized for it. I was going through tough times at the time of the crime that I committed.

But as I walk down the streets everyday, I see a new sign saying they are hiring, and businesses/companies are starting to feel the pain as they can't find people to fill positions and I'm sure there are tons of people out there who are qualified to do the job but can't because of their criminal record. As years go by I believe its only gonna get worst, more and more

[margin note: our current system stigmatizes crime and labels people]

> companies/businesses are gonna require a criminal record check.. I like to hear some other stories out there who have a criminal record.
>
> So the reason why I wanted only first time offenders is because I like to see the law changed and that is if its your first offense and depending on the charge its erased or sealed as they call it, and that's only if you have done your dues and have been crime free for 5 years, your still on record but when a criminal record is done it doesn't show and its as if you haven't done anything wrong."
>
> Source: Comment by Rocky1982 Posted to <http://forum.kijiji.ca/about6774494.html> on November 6, 2008 1:47 pm

paid his debt to society. Here, Rocky1982 uses an online forum to express his frustration at the difficulty he is having finding a job with his criminal record for a first-time offence.

In addition to the practical consequences of public stigmatization — such as the difficulty an offender may experience finding a job or suitable housing — degradation ceremonies contribute to the further alienating offenders from law-abiding society. Through processes of labelling and stigmatization, the offender may feel they have little choice but to embrace a criminal identity, since they sense the rejection of the mainstream world. Thus, a criminal subculture or gang may become a more appealing form of group identification, and/or the person may accept offender or criminal as their "master status" — the primary identity that defines who they are.

In contrast to this self-defeating and self-perpetuating criminal stigmatization process, Braithwaite (1989; see also Braithwaite and Mugford 1994) recommends we fashion instead "reintegration ceremonies" for offenders. The underlying principle of such ceremonies would be that they shame the act and not the actor. This modification of the Christian tenet of "hating the sin and not the sinner" reflects Braithwaite's concern that we not simply do away with shame. For him, correcting the problems of criminal justice is not as simple as reversing the labelling process so there is no more shame. Instead, there is good shame and bad shame. Bad shame stigmatizes individuals and leads to their disconnection from their networks of support, but good shame would aim to reintegrate them. Indeed, in his study of societies that effectively prevent offenders from committing new crimes (such as Japan), Braithwaite (1989) identified the productive use of shame as the most important factor.

[margin note: good shame vs bad shame]

[bottom note: Not to say crimes are not committed but we must remove the individual from the crime and allow them to make a change]

Therefore, rather than treating the act as fully representative of the character of the offender, we must be tough in admonishing wrongful actions, we must also seek to re-affirm the admirable qualities of those who have done wrong. A young offender should not be subjected to endless tirades about their misbehaviour in a restorative justice session. Time must also be given to discussing what is good in that person — their more noble traits — to accentuate a positive identity and to make room for their re-immersion in community life (Braithwaite 1989).

Braithwaite has also contributed to the development of a more systematic theorization of restorative justice (in this case, theory with a capital T). Indeed, Braithwaite's work with Phillip Petit (Braithwaite and Petit 1990) on a "republican theory of criminal justice" does more than most theories of restorative justice in the sense that it seeks to formulate a more general vision of ethical and political life (see also Braithwaite 2002; Braithwaite and Daly 1994; Walgrave 2002). This perspective centres on the notion of dominion, which refers to the rights and freedoms assured to citizens of democratic societies. Domination, in contrast, refers to incursions upon these rights and represents the primary form of social harm that is to be minimized within justice contexts. It is the state's role to create opportunities for dominion and to minimize the likelihood of domination. This entails the state acting to maintain space for community-based restorative justice programs to freely arrive at their own justice sanctions, while simultaneously ensuring general principles of human rights are maintained. For example, restorative justice might provide citizens the chance to interact and address harms within their community, but this is done within legal limits enforced by the state, which ensures the rights of each party to the restorative justice encounter are respected, and intervention occurs when they are not.

Braithwaite and Petit's republican theory of criminal justice intersects with a more recent area of restorative justice theorizing that borrows heavily from deliberative democracy (see Chapters 6 and 7 for further discussion). Like the ideas of Habermas discussed in Chapter 2, deliberative democracy emphasizes open public participation in decision-making processes (Habermas 1999; Benhabib 1996; Fishkin 1991; Dryzek 2000). The deliberative democratic vision of society is one in which ordinary citizens have a voice in their governance. As Dzur and Olson (2004: 99) note, there are "close resemblances between restorative justice ideals and deliberative democratic ideals of public participation and reasoned value-oriented debate in political forums." Dzur and Olson contend that restorative justice could follow deliberative democracy in the establishment of basic guidelines or norms, which direct participants in deliberative settings toward rational, respectful, and consistent discussion (similar to Habermas's communicative presuppositions). Moreover, they argue such guidelines provide a means for assessing the communicative potential of restorative justice by identifying the places where it fails to live up to the ideals of deliberative democracy. In this regard, they point to coercive and unequal moments within restorative justice encounters, where offenders are intimidated into participation through the threat of formal judicial action, or victim's voices and accounts are privileged over those of offenders. If an offender is strongly encouraged (or, some would say, coerced) by court or police authorities, or even by restorative justice practitioners, to take responsibility and proceed through a restorative process rather than face a potentially punitive judge, their participation in restorative justice can no longer be described as free and uncoerced. Likewise, if the victim's version of the events is automatically accepted as truth, and the offender's counterclaims disregarded as exculpatory rationalizations, then the communication can hardly be described as open and democratic. For Dzur and Olson, it is necessary that progressive restorative justice advocates seek to improve the communicative potential of restorative justice by measuring restorative justice encounters up against the ideals of deliberative democracy so they can better ensure open and fair participation.

Most of the theorists discussed thus far are white and male (as is one of the authors of this book). We mention this fact not to diminish or dismiss their contributions, but rather to bring attention the existence a politics of representation in the work of knowledge production that can result in certain perspectives being treated as more canonical than others. Certainly, these scholars were prominent in the creation of the field of restorative justice, but what voices contributed to building the movement from the margins? Earlier we recommended caution in claiming a direct lineage between Indigenous justice practices and contemporary restorative justice out of concern for the cultural appropriation of Indigenous knowledge to prop up a colonial justice system. However, in so doing, the role of Indigenous thinkers and practitioners in creating the restorative justice ethos should not be minimized. For example, Māori scholar Juan Tauri (2009) has challenged the move toward restorative justice standardization in New Zealand and Canada. This standardization begins from an initial Indigenization as states seek to respond to Indigenous over-incarceration by integrating community-based justice practices long promoted by advocates. However, these practices are soon incorporated into top-down state managerial strategies rather than from the ground up in a manner that responds to community distinctiveness and self-determination. This is a key facet of resurgent approaches to Indigenous justice that are influencing the restorative justice movement.

Such approaches do not aspire to a universal theory of justice, but rather local practices of justice that are holistically rooted in Indigenous languages, territory, and relations (Youngblood Henderson and McCaslin 2005). John Borrows (2016) has drawn upon Anishinaabe narratives to illustrate Indigenous law, drawing on key figures such as heroes, tricksters, monsters, and caretakers to demonstrate aspects of Anishinaabe responses to harm and conflict within their communities. Borrows (2016: 832) writes of the trickster figure, Nanaboozhoo:

> Nanaboozhoo's narratives expose Anishinaabe law's hidden cultural assumptions and disorders. In so doing, Anishinaabe people gain access to the world of dissenting opinions, minority reports, and oppositional viewpoints within their legal tradition. Discord, dissention, and disagreement are not outside Anishinaabe law. Conflict and differentiation are firmly rooted within it, thus providing access to creative and innovative ways of recalibrating regulatory and adjudicatory decisions.

The need for deliberation and contention is thus built into Anishinaabe law. Recognizing that Canada exists not under a single legal regime, but rather in a condition of legal pluralism, helps us understand how diverse approaches to justice, such as this one, come to influence continuous formation of the restorative justice ethos.

Likewise, intersectional feminist and critical race perspectives are also important contributors to the restorative justice movement. Barbara Hudson (2006) sees potential in restorative justice to realize some of the justice ideals of these scholarly traditions. She sees complementarity between intersectional feminism, critical race theory and the restorative principles of discursiveness, relationalism, and reflectiveness. These principles offer the promise of a justice that is not just the "white man's justice" in the sense that any claimant must first prove herself or himself to be the same as the white man in order to merit justice. Discursiveness, for Hudson, means that those traditionally marginalized from justice discussions must be brought inside the circle. In restorative justice terms, each person, no matter what their identity or position in relation to the harm (such as victim or perpetrator), is allowed to speak to the harmful event in their own terms, and to define this harm in a manner beyond the

Box 3.2 Anishinaabe Seven Grandfather Teachings

Among our many original instructions as Anishinaabeg, as well as among countless teachings and principles, are the Seven Grandfather Teachings. They were given to the Anishinaabeg to live in a good way, to live without conflict or contradiction, and to live in peace with all of our relations.

They are:

Debwewin:
"To Speak Only to the Extent We have Lived or Experienced."
Deb: To a certain extent.
We: Sound through speech.
Win: Nominalizer. A way it is done.
It is commonly referred to as "Truth."

Dabasendiziwin:
"To Think Lower of Oneself (in Relation to All That Sustains Us)."
Dabas: Low, lower.
End: Pertaining to thought.
Izi: State or condition.
Win: Nominalizer. A way it is done.
It is commonly referred to as "Humility."

Manaaji'idiwin:
"To Go Easy on One Another," meaning all of Creation.
Manaaji: To go easy on someone.
Idi: In a reciprocal way.
Win: Nominalizer. A way it is done.
It is often referred to as "Respect."

Zaagi'idiwin:
"Unconditional Love Between One Another," meaning all of Creation — including humans and non-humans, seen and unseen, of yesterday, today, and tomorrow.
Zaag: To emerge, to come out, to flow out.
Idi: In a reciprocal way.
Win: Nominalizer. A way it is done.
It is commonly referred to as "Love."

> *Gwayakwaadiziwin:*
> "To Live Correctly and with Virtue."
> *Gwayak:* Correctly, straightly, and rightly.
> *Aadizi:* He/She lives.
> *Win:* Nominalizer. A way it is done.
> It is commonly referred to as "Honesty."
>
> *Zoongide'ewin:*
> "To Live with a Solid, Strong Heart."
> *Zoongi:* Solid, strong.
> *De'e:* A form of "heart."
> *Win:* Nominalizer. A way it is done.
> It is commonly referred to as "Bravery" or "Courage."
>
> *Nibwaakaawin:*
> "To Live with Vision"
> *Waa:* Pertaining to sight.
> *Kaa:* An abundance
> *Win:* Nominalizer. A way it is done.
> It is commonly referred to as "Wisdom."
>
> Through our teachings and original instructions, including the Seven Grandfather Teachings, the Anishinaabeg seek Mino Bimaadiziwin. Mino Bimaadiziwin, the Good Life, describes a way of living in a good way, in a respectful relationship to all our relatives, and establishes a framework for Anishinaabe to live by which our ancestors envisioned as we make our way through this life.
>
> Source: Presented by the Seven Generations Education Institute

dictates of formal law. Relationalism "recognizes individuals as embodied in a network of relationships, which include relationships with community and with the state" (Hudson 2006: 37). Through such relations we negotiate our identity, our sense of right and wrong, and our rights and responsibilities as citizens, neighbours, and so forth. Thus, restorative justice should be a space where such relationships can be fostered and explored. Finally, reflectiveness speaks to the distinctive elements of a crime or act of wrongdoing. Too often our justice processes seek to shoehorn cases into a particular legal box rather than deal with their particularity on their own terms. One's experience of loss

Box 3.3 Kimberlé Crenshaw on Intersectionality, More than Two Decades Later

In 1989 Kimberlé Crenshaw coined the term "intersectionality" to explain the oppression of African-American women. This concept is central to discussions of racial justice and identity politics.

Q: You originally coined the term intersectionality to describe bias and violence against black women, but it's become more widely used — for LGBTQ issues, among others. Is that a misunderstanding of intersectionality?

Intersectionality is a lens through which you can see where power comes and collides, where it interlocks and intersects. It's not simply that there's a race problem here, a gender problem here, and a class or LGBTQ problem there. Many times that framework erases what happens to people who are subject to all of these things.

Some people look to intersectionality as a grand theory of everything, but that's not my intention. If someone is trying to think about how to explain to the courts why they should not dismiss a case made by black women, just because the employer did hire blacks who were men and women who were white, well, that's what the tool was designed to do. If it works, great. If it doesn't work, it's not like you have to use this concept.

The other issue is that intersectionality can get used as a blanket term to mean, "Well, it's complicated." Sometimes, "It's complicated" is an excuse not to do anything.... We want to move beyond that idea.

We try to take ideas and make them into hands-on tools that advocates and communities can use. Part of it is public education. We use art and other projects to show how people are experiencing intersectional harms, such as mothers of women killed by the police, or young girls expelled from school. We work directly with advocates and communities to develop ways they can better see these problems and better intervene in advocacy.

Source: Columbia Law School 2017.

is defined in terms of criminal law, such as sexual assault, though this term may only scratch the surface of what was suffered through sexual violence. For the philosopher Claudia Card (2010), sexual violence carries the potential to cause "social death," which is an experience of utter powerlessness that disconnects one from social relations. The principle of reflectiveness would require the restorative justice practitioner to think more holistically of what the person subject to a sexual assault has experienced and to address not just the legal definition of harm, but the broader impact of this violence on the life of the individual and their community.

Hudson posits that together these principles allow for the possibility of a restorative justice more responsive and less marginalizing to the intersecting experiences of domination and privilege participants bring with them into restorative justice encounters.

THE RESTORATIVE JUSTICE ETHOS

Through this brief conceptual overview, we can begin to piece together the elements of a restorative justice ethos. At base, the following assumptions appear operative in the restorative justice ethos:

1. *Conflicts are knowable*. The idea that conflicts are intractable, or that they present an impossibly complex array of disputes is anathema to restorative justice thinking. For restorativists, there always exists the possibility of understanding the parameters and antipathies of a given dispute, and therefore making a deliberate intervention toward resolving the conflict.
2. *We can get to know conflicts through the act of communication.* The means to understanding a conflict is through effective communication. When people gather together to discuss openly and freely their understandings of a given situation, a clearer sense of the conflict is developed.
3. *Conditions can be established in which communication is unproblematic.* With the right processes or conditions in place, people are able to communicate with one another in a non-coercive manner. According to this way of thinking, people may enter the restorative justice meeting with various advantages and disadvantages, but it is possible to level these inequalities through careful preparations and interventions conducted by the facilitator.

4. *Human behaviour can be changed*. Our behaviour is not set in stone or predetermined. Various social forces have assembled to influence and shape our current behavioural patterns, and it is possible to replace these influences with a new set of influences, such as reintegrative shaming and positive social networks, that will place us on a more caring course.
5. *Humans possess the capacity for communication and for creative problem solving*. Due to our capacities for communication and behavioural change, we are also able to arrive at creative solutions for changing the conditions that led to conflict and for re-fashioning the world around us.
6. *A society built upon effective communication will be more peaceable and progressive*. For all these reasons, effective communication provides the foundation for a society where people are able to live peacefully with one another, as well as to make changes and adapt to the social world when new problems arise.

Within this ethos, we see the primary components of a restorative justice epistemology and restorative justice ontology. With respect to epistemology (how we know), we glean a sense that the social world — in particular, the world of conflict — is knowable through our efforts to speak to one another. Derrida's concern (see Chapter 2) that we are never fully able to hear the voice of the Other, and that we are always engaging in an act of translation when we communicate, would be ignored or dismissed by many restorativists. With respect to ontology (assumptions about the nature of the social world), we see a social world where, despite multiple potential obstacles to communication, we are nonetheless able to speak with one another (assuming the right conditions are in place) and to change ourselves and the world around us. We live in a malleable world. This leads us to what we might refer to as the restorative justice *teleology* — the end state to which restorative justice hopes to lead us — which is a vision of a world where communication is liberated so humans can collectively recreate society for the betterment of each and every one of us.

These underlying presuppositions appear common to most restorativists and are therefore presented here as constitutive of the restorative justice ethos. However, these presuppositions are not unproblematic when examined in light of actual conflicts such as the Truth and Reconciliation Commission of Canada.

THE TRUTH AND RECONCILIATION COMMISSION OF CANADA

In the 1880s, the Indian Residential School (IRS) system began to take shape. Though there existed prior efforts to use schooling to forcibly assimilate Indigenous children, it was at this point that the Canadian government enlisted various Christian denominations (Catholic, Anglican, Presbyterian, and Methodist) in a concerted project to eliminate Indigenous cultures by transferring their children to carceral schools designed to erase Indigenous languages, traditions, and connections to territory (see Woolford 2015; Woolford and Gacek 2016). Indigenous parents were pressured, and in many cases forced, to send their children to residential schools for most of the year, only to see them for brief holidays and for a period of the summer. It was believed that separation from parents and community would shift Indigenous children away from their attachment to Indigenous ways. By 1920, these schools were made mandatory for all Indigenous children. At many of the schools, conditions were so inadequate that large numbers of children died from ill health, exposure to the elements, and poor nutrition (Milloy 1999). They also suffered physical and sexual abuse, as well as a constant verbal assault upon their cultures, traditions, communities, and families. Upon completing their education, many no longer felt at home or welcome in their communities, leaving them isolated, detached, and without a supportive social network. Deprived of the experience of being parented, they later found it a great struggle to raise their own children (Haig-Brown 1988; Monture-Angus 1999). Continuing cycles of emotional, physical, and sexual abuse, as well as addiction, suicide, and other markers of intergenerational trauma within Indigenous communities, are often cited as residual effects of the IRS experience.

In developing a truth and reconciliation commission, which involves creating opportunities for victims to tell their stories so as to foster greater social understanding of their plight, restorativists would operate on the assumption that the world of residential schooling and the trauma it has caused is, to a certain degree, knowable and communicable. This means the residential schooling experience can be distilled into a narrative that communicates this complex experience to a general public that did not live through its reality. Through this understanding, the general public should achieve a better sense of the plight of IRS Survivors and a window into the sorts of trauma they faced in the aftermath of these so-called schools. Non-Indigenous people are not likely to fully understand the IRS experience in the way those who lived through this era (and its aftermath) understand it. Instead, non-Indigenous people will simply receive a picture of what it may have been like, and on the basis of this, might become more empathetic to the current challenges facing Indigenous peoples in Canada, and even commit to transforming our settler colonial society to ameliorate its many injustices. The restorative justice ethos presumes that through such an understanding, a public discussion could then take place toward broadly improving Indigenous and non-Indigenous relations in Canada.

The restorative justice epistemology and ontology are geared toward providing us a way forward, whether from a troubled period or a distinct traumatic event. This is the basis for an ethos that it is resolutely optimistic that most, if not all, human problems can be fixed. However, this ethos requires a critical political sensibility to avoid charges of naïve hopefulness. In the everyday world of conflict resolution, barriers to communication arise and threaten to disrupt even the best-intentioned efforts at repairing harm. Restorative projects, such as truth and reconciliation commissions, are devised and implemented by political actors who possess clear interests and pre-formed assumptions about the social world.

Remaining with the Truth and Reconciliation Commission of Canada, there are the fears of government liability for civil suits stemming from the abuses of residential schools that helped motivate government participation. Such lawsuits present the risk of high costs to the government. In contrast, the symbolism of a truth commission, accompanied by a public apology and lump sum payments, offers a calculable pathway to resolving what has been a seemingly intractable and potentially expensive social problem. For this to be the case, great care must be taken to manage these reparation processes to ensure compensation is not too widely distributed and the symbolic acts of atonement do not compromise government legitimacy and authority by admitting too much (for example, the government is unlikely to admit their contribution to widespread genocidal destruction through colonial policies such as residential schooling). In a situation such as this one, where many aging IRS Survivors live in conditions of dire poverty and are in grave need of whatever financial compensation they can achieve, a degree of power is in the government's hands to shape the restorative process in its favour. Therefore, it will mobilize this power to place limits upon the degree of justice offered to Survivors. For example, rules are created to exclude some groups of Survivors, such as those who attended assimilative day schools, or those who cannot be found in poorly kept IRS records. Through such mechanisms, the communicative project of

[margin note: the RJ ethos is overly optimistic]

[bottom note: the current process of repairing harms done limits access and reparation.]

truth and reconciliation can transform into a technical and actuarial model for assessing truthfulness and circumscribing costs. The Truth and Reconciliation Commission, as a body independent from government, sought to counter these tendencies by creating victim-centred processes. Nonetheless, the government's role as controller of the funds and records could not help but influence the sort of communication that occurred. For this reason, those committed to the project of reconciliation cannot simply engage in the pursuit of truth and efforts at symbolic redress — they need to also seek political avenues to advance these goals.

This example illustrates the hopefulness of the restorative justice ethos often comes up against the crass political realities of conflict. This ethos needs to be strengthened by a political sensibility that allows it to better navigate the troubled waters of conflict resolution. As well, one must approach the restorative ethos, as it is described above, with a degree of caution. The ethics of communication and understanding that is contained within its principles needs to be examined within the power dynamics of both the actual practices of restorative justice (Chapter 4), as well as in the broader collective and social-structural circumstances in which restorative justice is implemented (Chapters 5 and 6).

QUESTIONS FOR DISCUSSION

1. Why is it of political concern if Indigenous justice is claimed to be a form of restorative justice?
2. What is a restorative justice ethos? How does it influence they ways that people think about and practice restorative justice?
3. Reflect on what you have learned about the Truth and Reconciliation Commission of Canada. In what ways might this process be considered restorative?

4

RESTORATIVE JUSTICE STYLES

[Handwritten annotation: pg 73-88, pg 110-119]

There are several primary forms of restorative justice, most of which are still in use today. We need to know what these practices are. More importantly, we need to delve deeply and critically into restorative justice practices so we may explore their embodied and affective politics. Actions do not simply reflect a straightforward display of our ideas and beliefs: they also derive from habituated dispositions that guide our day-to-day behaviour (Bourdieu 1990) as well as cultural contexts through which our emotions take shape (Ahmed 2004). Put in simpler terms, our everyday actions often reflect deeply ingrained sensibilities of which we are often unaware. Think, for instance, of practising a sport, such as hockey. The drills you run in practice are designed to habituate you to certain actions, so when the moment arises in a game, you can react in an almost automatic, but also somewhat creative fashion. For example, if you have practised breakaway after breakaway, a game-time opportunity to break free from the defence and approach the goalie unchallenged may play out almost instinctively. Instead of overthinking your moves, you may instead rely on your training to guide you, as you move to the backhand, knowing (although not necessarily consciously thinking) from experience the goalie will not be able to move backward to stop the shot you lift into the top of the net. Now think of a fan, let's say a parent, watching this hockey game. This person may feel an incredible surge of emotion when witnessing your deke. This may include excitement of certain victory for your team, as well as pride that your hard work is paying off. But beyond these immediate emotional triggers is a cultural context that valorizes hockey skill as a particularly noteworthy attribute associated not only with hard work but also Canadian identity. This concrete moment thus has behind it a complex set of social and cultural relations.

When put into practice, restorative justice seeks to guide us in the

[Handwritten annotation: We are shaped by social & cultural relations]

development of new conflict resolution dispositions and forms of affect based upon the restorative justice ethos that lead us toward improved communication and creativity, as well as feelings of relief, healing, safety, and community. There are a number of types of retraining programs restorative justice has to offer.

MEDIATION AND COMMUNITY MEDIATION

[margin note: we are deeply rooted in social + cultural relations and RJ aims to reshape some of those]

Paul McCold (2006) notes the shared origins of mediation and restorative justice. Although most scholars are careful to differentiate between the two practices, as they do have significant overlaps, it is worthwhile to take some time to discuss this antecedent to restorative justice (see Woolford and Ratner 2008a for further discussion).

As mentioned in the previous chapter, the 1970s was a time when many people experienced disenchantment with the formal law. The courts were viewed to be inaccessible, as much of the business of law was carried out in esoteric and jargon-laden legal discourses, and legal decisions were most favourable to those who could afford the services of lawyers. The courts were also viewed to be unnecessarily adversarial. Courtrooms were perceived as spaces of combat, where there could be only winners and losers and nothing in between. For these and other reasons, many began to wonder if it might be possible to return to an earlier form of justice in which communities and local actors were empowered to creatively resolve the problems in their midst (Burger 1979).

This turn toward the community led to the development of community justice centres, community credit unions, neighbourhood-based health and food cooperatives, and other local experiments that were established under this new influence (Coy and Hedeen 2005). Most relevant to the rise of restorative justice are the community justice centres, where lay mediators volunteered to facilitate the resolution of neighbourhood-based disputes. These lay mediators were expected to use their status in the community to help persuade disputants to resolve their differences, all the while not seeking to advantage their own personal power. At the onset of these justice experiments, it was assumed these mediators would facilitate both civil and minor criminal conflicts; however, over time, community justice centres came to concentrate their efforts on civil disputes (Olson and Dzur 2004).

The San Francisco Community Boards (SFCB) is one of the most studied examples of community justice (see, for example, Fitzpatrick 1995; Pavlich

[neighbourhood mediation]

1996a). Established in 1976, the aim of the SFCB is to build community harmony by addressing conflicts before they grow into more disruptive struggles, reduce fear of crime within the community, and provide residents with conflict resolution skills so they can apply them in their daily lives (Shonholtz 1984). In their neighbourhood mediation program, the dispute might be based on a landlord/tenant disagreement, conflict between roommates or neighbours, a noise complaint, or some other matter that threatens social harmony in the community. During SFCB meetings, disputants present their conflict to members of a volunteer-based panel that attempts to facilitate an agreed-upon resolution. The members of the panel are selected on characteristics shared with the disputants rather than based solely upon social status. Presumably, these shared characteristics allow the disputants to better identify with and feel understood by the panel. They also help give the impression of equality amongst all participants in the SFCB process, so the disputants would trust their own authority within the process rather than look toward panel members for decisive interventions.

[idea that we can remove stigma + other social harms]

Community justice boards like this one offer many the hope that a deprofessionalized and deinstitutionalized local justice is, indeed, possible. However, community justice has also come under criticism for failing to live up to its promise. Instead of a local and autonomous justice, critics argue the justice process sometimes serves as a means for extending and entrenching state power at the local level, where social workers and community volunteers take the place of state officials in ensuring community conflicts do not become socially disruptive (Abel 1982; Hofrichter 1982; Matthews 1988). Community justice boards have also been accused of providing the formal justice system with a means to preserve its legitimacy by allowing it to overcome the many crises the latter faces, such as overloaded court dockets and citizen alienation from the justice process (see, for example, Abel 1982; Selva and Böhm 1987). Other critics argue community justice serves to pacify the workforce, resolving conflicts that might otherwise threaten capitalist means of production (Hofrichter 1987). For example, conflicts such as marital disputes or neighbourhood conflicts over property lines do not only disrupt the everyday lives of workers, they also threaten to spill over into their working lives, as they distract working people and affect their potential productivity. In addition, when these squabbles are brought to the courts, they risk draining legal resources that are viewed to be the privilege of the middle and upper classes (Hofrichter 1987). For these reasons, scholars such as Hofrichter argue the capitalist system has had a direct interest in supporting gentle means of social control, such as those promoted through community mediation.

VICTIM OFFENDER RECONCILIATION AND VICTIM OFFENDER MEDIATION PROGRAMS

The community justice ideal has found expression in criminal justice. In 1974, an early victim offender reconciliation program was developed in Elmira, Ontario, not far from Kitchener-Waterloo (Peachey 2003). At this time, Mark Yantzi, a probation officer, was assigned the task of working with two teenagers who had gone on a vandalism spree in the small town. Yantzi felt it would be in the interests of all parties concerned if an effort was made to reconcile the teenagers with their fellow community members. He approached the judge for the case and proposed that, as part of their sentence, the young offenders be required to approach their victims and offer to make restitution for the damages done. The judge agreed, and Yantzi, together with David Worth, who worked for the Mennonite Central Committee, soon found himself escorting the teenagers as they visited the houses of those whom they had harmed. The teenagers met with their victims and agreed to make reparations to them, but also gained a clearer sense of the harm they had done. The success of this endeavour led the two men to create a post-sentencing reconciliation program (Peachey 2003).

Victim offender reconciliation (VOR) and victim offender mediation (VOM) are used almost interchangeably to refer to programs that follow this model. According to Mark Umbreit et al. (2006), the core elements of VOR and VOM are:

- establishing a safe environment;
- preparation;
- voluntary participation;
- a face-to-face encounter; and
- follow up.

Based on these criteria, it is important to note the encounter between the victim and offender is but one small, albeit crucial, part of the VOR and VOM processes. The activities that precede this encounter are central to the encounter's success, since this is how stakeholders are readied to meet one another. To begin, all parties must feel safe, develop a sense of trust in the mediator, and be reassured

Box 4.1 Victim Offender Mediation for Family Victims of Homicide

"Ann" was one of a number of children whose father, a police officer, was murdered in the line of duty by two men whom he had pulled over on the highway. Ann and her siblings had adored their father and were devastated by his loss.... As in far too many cases, while the people responsible were arrested and sent to prison, the needs not only went on, but magnified, over time....

Many years had passed when "Charles," one of the men responsible for her father's death, contacted Fraser Region Community Justice Initiatives through his Institutional Parole Officer. Charles had heard from another inmate who had met with family survivors ... it had been an astonishing experience, one he would recommend to others. That began a time when we visited with Charles from time to time to try to discern together whether or not to attempt to reach the victims/survivors in his case. Charles was torn between wanting to share with them the depth of his sorrow for having taken their father's life, and wanting to avoid the possibility of retraumatizing them with a further contact.... We made clear that in the absence of any further information from the victims indicating interest in the process, we would not proceed until either he was more certain, or something new had transpired to indicate victim interest in the program.

Then, out of nowhere, Ann's brother wrote to us, unaware that we had been in conversation with Charles, saying he had been informed Charles was incarcerated in our region, and wondering if we might be able to get a letter to him.... He had come to the conviction ... that in order to be completely freed from the last vestiges of his addiction, he needed to forgive Charles, and finally rid himself of the remaining animosity, anger and desire for vengeance that he had used to justify his own ... long-term addiction....

Within a few months, the next letter arrived from a member of the victim's family, this time from Ann. She wrote saying she ... hoped that an exchange of letters between them would culminate in ... a face-to-face dialogue which VOMP [Victim Offender Mediation Program] staff would facilitate. Charles needed some time to get his head around that notion, meeting with the institutional Elder and praying about it together.

> It didn't take long before he asked us to set the meeting up ... [He was] not certain what he could ever say that could be remotely adequate to the circumstance, yet [hoped] that whatever he might offer would help assuage her pain and increase a sense of peace....
>
> At the end of March, Ann flew into Abbotsford, where we met and spent some additional time with her to help prepare her for what the following day's meeting might bring. For two hours the next morning and two more in the afternoon these two met, sharing a simple format: the past (the impact of the crime and its aftermath for both); the present (what each was doing to heal and move on toward a more successful future); and the future (what hopes Charles held, given the length of sentence he had yet to serve, and what Ann hoped to accomplish, working with others, especially young women, from backgrounds and circumstances not dissimilar from her own). Toward the end of the afternoon, the institutional Elder, who had previously been invited, joined us. He commended both Charles and Ann for having done "this courageous thing," then, using the traditional drum that Charles had expertly painted with symbols deeply meaningful to Ann from her own Aboriginal tradition ... sang a song befitting their meeting ... then prayed a prayer of thanksgiving, a celebration of the new degree of healing they had witnessed....
>
> Source: David L. Gustafson, Community Justices Initiatives, Annual Report. Reprinted with permission of Community Justice Initiaitives.

they will not experience any further harm through the VOR or VOM process. Once this is established, preparation can begin, as the mediator works with the parties to give them an idea of what to expect from the encounter and to help them understand the ground rules for the meeting (such as, listen and do not interrupt others when they are speaking). The preparation stage can take as long as is necessary for the participants to feel ready to meet, since the mediator does not want to rush the parties toward an encounter. Throughout this preparation, and, indeed, throughout the entire restorative process, it is important the parties understand their participation is voluntary and they can withdraw at any time. If they feel in any way coerced into participation, it is possible the parties may come to feel (re)victimized and resentful, and these are not conditions that lend themselves to effective communication or restoration. Finally, once preparations are complete, the parties are ready for the meeting and it is here, with the assistance of the mediator, they will receive the opportunity to ask questions and work toward a resolution of the conflict.

In a VOR or VOM designed for purposes of sentencing, the initial discussion of the harmful event(s) will eventually need to transition into discussion of an agreement. An agreement of a sort may also be the goal of a post-sentencing VOR or VOM, although it functions less as an alternative sanction and more as a personal understanding between the participants. In either case, there are specific interventions the mediator might make to help the parties reach a mutual understanding of the event and a plan for its aftermath (these will be discussed later in the chapter). Even when an agreement is achieved, however, this does not spell the end of the VOR or VOM. Instead, a period of follow-up is required to ensure the parties are living up to their agreement, as well as to check to ensure their needs have been met and no renewed or new trauma has occurred. Within some versions of VOR and VOM, it may be necessary to hold a second meeting if the parties are not living up to the agreement, or if new issues have arisen that were not dealt with in the first meeting.

FAMILY GROUP CONFERENCING

[margin note: begining as a youth process → similar in Canada]

The traditional justice practices of the Māori people of New Zealand are often credited as the inspiration for family group conferencing, although this overstates the case. The 1989 Children, Young Persons and Their Families Act was instituted, in part, as an attempt to respond to concerns about the over-representation of Māori youth in New Zealand correctional institutions and to adapt justice processes to allow for the involvement of families (see Daly 2003). Through this legislation, family group conferences (FGCs) were designated the normal response for most youth crime violations, thereby bringing together victims and offenders, as well as their families and supporters, to resolve criminal incidents (see Consedine 1995, 2003). In the 1990s, the small Australian city of Wagga Wagga followed New Zealand's lead with the introduction of a police-cautioning scheme that combined the framework of New Zealand's FGCs with John Braithwaite's concept of reintegrative shaming. This resulted in the establishment of police-led conferences to deal with young offenders (see Moore and O'Connell 2003). The Wagga Wagga program further inspired similar projects in the mid-1990s, such as the one implemented by the Thames Valley Police (Pollard 2001).

Although these programs differ to various degrees, they all serve to bring the families of the victim and offender together to resolve the conflict. This occurs with the assistance of a state-appointed facilitator, in some cases a police officer, who is charged with the task of helping the families reach a consensual agreement (Raye and Warner Roberts 2007).

A more controversial variation of the FGC process is the family group decision-making (FGDM) program designed specifically for use in cases of family violence. According to the designers of this program, Joan Pennell and Gayle Burford (2002), FGDM employs a "feminist praxis" that attempts to "interrupt" gendered assumptions about male dominance and the roles of women and children within families, while also creating "links" between families and the resources they require to lead healthy and peaceful lives. The goal of FGDM is to give (immediate and extended) families ownership of their problems, but also to provide them with assistance to ensure family violence ceases. Indeed, unlike other restorative justice programs where there is a need to balance offender and victim needs, FGDM must place priority upon the victims' need for safety, given the dangerous stakes involved when re-offending occurs. So, when a case is referred to a FGDM program, a wide spectrum of family members are invited, although attention is given to ensure these family members do not in any way condone family violence. After this selection process, emphasis is placed on safety concerns, ensuring all family members feel protected within the FGDM meeting and are prepared to participate respectfully. At the onset of the meeting, a family ritual, such as a reading or a prayer, is used to symbolize the bond between family members. A statement from a protective authority, such as a police officer or caseworker, is then provided to relay the history of family violence events. Next, local or regional service providers are invited to speak and make the family aware of the resources available to them within the community. With this knowledge, the family is then left on its own to devise a plan. The facilitator and protective authorities are never too far removed from this meeting, but they give the family space to work through these matters. This is the most controversial component of this model, as there are obvious concerns about leaving a family struggling with abuse and violence unsupervised. Once the family has arrived at a plan, protective authorities review it to ensure that it meets safety requirements, and, if it does, the family is then responsible for carrying out its components. If, however, the plan fails, or elements of the plan are not being met, a meeting is convened.

CIRCLES

As noted in the previous chapter, contemporary restorative justice is often traced back to the traditional justice practices of Indigenous peoples. In particular, circles are regularly cited as a method used by several Indigenous groups who live in what is now North America. In the most basic terms, a circle is an occasion where a community is assembled to discuss matters related to and a possible resolution for an injustice that took place in their midst. All participants are given opportunities to speak, and their right to be heard is signified by the passing of a sacred object, such as an eagle feather, which, when held, communicates that all attention should be paid to that person.

Like VOR and VOM, there are several stages to circles:

- suitability;
- preparation;
- a full circle gathering; and
- follow up. (Stuart and Pranis 2006: n.p.)

very similar to VOM includes more people

The first step is to ensure the case is suitable to the circle process. Has the person who committed the wrong taken ownership of their actions? Is the community in a position to provide the support needed by the person harmed and the one who harmed them? Does the circle present any danger to the community? Once these and other issues are addressed, it becomes possible to begin preparing the parties for participation in the circle. Here, a facilitator will want to encourage the practices of respectful listening and dialogue, as was the case for VOR and VOM, but also to ready the parties for what those in attendance might have to say to them, anticipating how family and community members might react to the conflict. Certainly, it is not in the interests of the circle to have any participant go into a defensive shell if they feel the community assessment of their behaviour is too harsh. Only after these and other preparations have been made is it possible to initiate the circle. With so many potential participants present, circles can be time-consuming affairs. They require commitment from all parties, so the circles are not rushed or pushed forward in a quest for judicial expediency. Once the community has arrived at an appropriate sanction and it has been implemented, the circle facilitator needs to follow up with the victim and offender to ensure the agreement is being lived up to. This may also involve a ceremonial feast or other activity to symbolize the offender's progress through the terms of the agreement and to mark their full return to the community (see Ross 1996; Stuart 1996).

Contemporary circles take many forms. A style familiar to some Canadians is the sentencing circle, where a case may be diverted from the formal criminal justice system to be addressed within a (often Indigenous) community. The circle is comprised of the victim and offender, their support people (such as family and friends), Elders, a judge, and defence and crown attorneys, in addition to community members who have chosen to attend. Despite the presence of the judge and crown attorney as representatives of the state, these individuals do not occupy a privileged position within the circle meeting. They do not wear ceremonial attire or sit on a raised platform as they might in a regular courtroom, and they are not entitled to speak any more than other members of the circle. Their presence primarily serves to ensure the circle process, and the sanction achieved through the circle, meet the standards of Canadian law. In this sense, the judge's power over the proceedings is still evident in the fact that they must approve the community sanction arrived at through the circle process.

A controversial example of a sentencing circle is the case of Christopher Pauchay, an Indigenous man from the Yellow Quill reserve in Saskatchewan. On January 29, 2008, after drinking heavily, he left his two daughters out in -30° C weather (see Box 4.1). While some, such as *National Post* columnist Jonathan Kay, bristle at the idea that Pauchay was provided the option of a "traditional" justice response, such as a sentencing circle, former Crown prosecutor Pierre Rousseau points out that the sentencing circle process does not attempt to fully revive traditional Indigenous justice practices. This process would better be described as a hybrid combination of Indigenous healing circles with the Canadian criminal justice system, with the latter system still possessing the final authority over the sentencing decision. The judge in this case ruled in the end that Pauchay should serve a three-year prison term for his "reckless behaviour," despite the circle's recommendation Pauchay be given a conditional sentence to serve in his community.

The Diné in the US use peacemaking circles as a primary means of conflict resolution. According to Diné tradition, a person who has been harmed is permitted to demand reparative action from the offending party. A *Naat'aanii* (respected community leader) then assists the disputing parties, along with their families and other affected clan members, as they meet to discuss the harm. A prayer begins the meeting to focus all participants on the issues at hand, and subsequently, each party details their version of the events that transpired.

Box 4.2 The Folly of Native Sentencing Circles

Jonathan Kay

The facts surrounding Christopher Pauchay's crime were so memorably awful that even now, a year later, unbidden images of it still occasionally dart through my brain whenever I am dressing my own children in their winter clothing.

Pauchay was a father living on Saskatchewan's Yellow Quill reserve. On the night of Jan. 29, 2008, after a hard bout of drinking, he staggered out into a blizzard with his two girls — aged three and one — and blacked out. Pauchay survived. But his children, facing -30C weather in diapers and T-shirts, did not. In November, Pauchay pled guilty to criminal negligence causing death.

Aside from being horrific in its own right, the episode epitomized the lethal folly of a government mindset focused more on preserving aboriginal cultures than saving aboriginal lives. Yellow Quill — a geographically remote, economically destitute, politically dysfunctional, booze-addled 120-family hamlet — is an archetypal den of government-bankrolled Indian misery; the sort of place that would mercifully fold up shop within a matter of days if its residents were white instead of native.

Even in the very shadow of Yellow Quill's signature tragedy, our society's fixation on aboriginal cultural authenticity persists: This month, a judge declared that preliminary recommendations on Pauchay's punishment will be made by an aboriginal sentencing circle, a council led by "elders" in the Yellow Quill community.

One often hears sentencing circles spoken of as if they were an ancient feature of aboriginal civilization. In fact, the term was popularized only in the 1990s, when academics and government officials began blaming high rates of native criminality on a "white" criminal justice system that alienates natives with its focus on Western abstractions such as "justice," "guilt" and "punishment."

In 1996, the federal government began funding sentencing circles as part of its newly announced Aboriginal Justice Strategy, and amended the sentencing provisions of the Criminal Code to provide special treatment for aboriginals — later justified by the Supreme Court of Canada on the dubious basis that "many traditional aboriginal conceptions of sentence emphasize the notions of community-based sanction and restorative justice."

"[An] emphasis on healing rather than punishment is very much in harmony with traditional notions of native justice," wrote one academic in a typically earnest, award-winning report on the subject. "The aboriginal concept of the medicine wheel teaches that everything is interrelated and evolves in a circular pattern. An aboriginal community is a circle that is broken when a wrong is committed."

Like so much else that is written about natives, this is high-flown noble-savage nonsense — part of an ongoing intellectual campaign by white researchers and jurists to project their own utopian reveries on dimly understood native cultures. Not surprisingly, sentencing circles have done nothing to help alleviate native suffering: The order-of-magnitude over-representation of natives among Canada's criminal class is more or less unchanged since the adoption of reforms in the 1990s.

In fact, it is hard to think of anything more alien to native culture than a sentencing circle. The natives who populated what we now call Canada prior to First Contact — including Christopher Pauchay's own Ojibwa ancestors — were rugged hunter-gatherers who lived in small kin-based groups. As in all such societies, the mechanics of what we now loftily call "criminal justice" were necessarily based on the brutal principle of retribution.

The idea of applying a "traditional" model of native justice in Christopher Pauchay's case is particularly ridiculous — since even deliberate infanticide by natural exposure is generally condoned in hunter-gatherer cultures (and was common even in Europe until well into the Middle Ages). No pre-Contact Indian society would even have regarded what Pauchay did as a "crime" in the Western sense, since the children were his own. There was no aggrieved clan looking for retribution.

"Traditional" aboriginal teachings, it is also worth noting, are equally useless in respect to the sex crime epidemic that afflicts many native reserves — since patriarchal hunter-gatherer societies generally assign no sexual autonomy to women. When sentencing circles have been used in cases involving aboriginal rapists, the practice often has proven humiliating, and even dangerous, for the victims. As Frances Widdowson and Albert Howard describe in their groundbreaking new book, *Disrobing the Aboriginal Industry*, First Nations typically are dominated by one or two powerful families that coopt "community" sentencing procedures when one of their own stands accused. The last place a native rape victim should want to find herself is in a room full of tribal grandees circling the wagons around her rapist.

There is a certain sort of perverse symmetry at play here: We encourage natives to live in Third World hellholes under the theory that cultural empowerment trumps the need to integrate them into mainstream society. Then, when they start killing and abusing one another, our legal system follows the same "traditional" playbook. How many more children must die before we realize that the fairy tales we tell ourselves about native culture always come with a tragic ending?

Source: *National Post* January 20, 2009. Material republished with the express permission of *National Post*, as division of Postmedia Network, Inc.

The Truth About Sentencing Circles

Pierre Rousseau

After reading Jonathan Kay's article about Christopher Pauchay's criminal negligence on Saskatchewan's Yellow Quill reserve ("The folly of Native Sentencing Circles," Jan. 20), I realized that there is confusion about sentencing circles and aboriginal justice. I am a retired Crown prosecutor and spent many of my professional years working in aboriginal communities in northern Canada. I experienced first-hand the deficiencies of the criminal court system in those communities.

There is a misconception about sentencing circles. This is not an aboriginal process, but rather a process that was designed by judges who were concerned they had very little information about the communities they were sitting in and the people they were dealing with. A typical sentencing circle is composed of a judge, lawyers, the offender and, usually, the victim and members of the community that have an interest in the matter.

The purpose is to provide information to the court about the offender, the victims and the community, and to make recommendations about community resources to assist the court where there are possibilities of rehabilitation for the offender. The judge still decides on the sentence and has full latitude to impose a lengthy jail term. These circles, therefore, have no real impact on the suffering in the communities — they are only a consultation process used by the courts.

Sentencing circles were borrowed from the Plains' Healing Circles, and are an attempt by the mainstream system to co-opt aboriginal traditions in support of the court system. Except that a circle in aboriginal cultures is seen as a healing process, while here in Canada it is part of a punitive system.

Restorative justice is a concept that has been adopted in many countries, including Canada, and is based on restoring the relationships between an offender and his or her victim through a healing process. This better reflects aboriginal cultures that are very different from those of the dominant society. For aboriginal cultures, conflicts within the community should be resolved through restoring harmony and relationships, since those involved have to live together and punishment has little meaning.

When I was a prosecutor in the north, I saw numerous small-crime offenders sent to jail. When they came back to their communities after a number of weeks or months away, they were far more dangerous than they had been before being sent to jail. The courts had not contributed a bit in resolving the problems that were at the root of the crime. Jail terms were increasing, but so was violence and pain in the community.

Conversely, I also saw communities getting more involved in justice matters through justice committees that were taking responsibility for some minor crimes. I can attest to the fact that this approach works most of the time, and the rates of re-offending are far lower than the rates of recidivism for offenders who go through the main-stream court system.

A community-based aboriginal process has better chances of working in these communities than the mainstream system. And that's why the Aboriginal Justice Strategy (AJS) is effective. The AJS does not provide financial support to sentencing circles, but it provides funding to community-based programs that deal with criminal offences and other matters at the community level, some of which may assist the courts in holding sentencing circles.

Going back to Christopher Pauchay: His crimes are extremely serious and impacted his community in a way that is hard to imagine. Children are important in First Nations communities, and the Yellow Quill community was devastated by this awful crime.

The court got involved because this is how the government has decided justice should be rendered in these communities. The community did not request for the courts to get involved. But now the court wants to consult the community through a sentencing circle.

Once the court is informed of the impact of this crime on the community, and the circumstance of the offender, the victims and their families, then the judge will have the responsibility to apply the law to sentence this individual.

This is the judge's responsibility. Whatever the punishment handed to Christopher Pauchay, it will not be based on the decision of a sentencing circle.

— Pierre Rousseau lives in Sooke, B.C
Source: NP Editor February 2, 2009.

Next, everyone present is given the opportunity to speak about their thoughts and feelings with respect to the conflict and how it should be resolved (Yazzie and Zion 2003). Healing circles follow a similar path to those practiced in predominantly Indigenous settings, although they are typically more directed at establishing dialogue and fostering recovery than sentencing. As in the above two types of circles, healing circles are opportunities for the parties to come together in an inclusive environment and to hold an open discussion about a specific harmful event or series of harmful events. They can, in some cases, lead to subsequent sentencing circles if it is felt the discussion is positive enough to allow the parties to move toward cooperative settlement of the issue. However, they can also be used simply for healing or reintegrating particular stakeholders. For example, in some cases, "circles of support" may be formed around a victim or offender to help that person recover from their pain and reintegrate into their community. There are many Circle of Support and Accountability organizations across Canada doing this work with people who have been convicted of a sexual offence and are returning to the community after a period of incarceration (see COSA Canada for a listing of local organizations and to learn more about these programs). Such individuals, because they are perceived to still represent a threat, have great difficulty forming social networks, so "circles of support" are formed in lieu of such networks to ensure these ex-offenders have the assistance they need to avoid recidivism.

[margin note: helps builds networks and support systems]

In all circle types, a premium is placed upon the act of storytelling. The circle is an opportunity for multiple parties to present their own narratives of the events, but also to tell stories about the past that might offer some insight into current troubles (Pranis 2005). Through the sharing of stories, the parties can move toward an understanding of one another that has the potential to allow for either healing or consensual agreement, or both.

Though we delineate between the different styles here, in actually existing restorative justice, programs may not limit themselves to one particular form. Take the Nova Scotia Restorative Justice Program we discussed in Chapter 2. While the government retains key roles in the program, the actual restorative services are run by eight different community agencies and the Mi'kmaq Legal Support Network. The community agencies offer a variety of restorative programming that is delivered by both staff and volunteers. Each agency varies slightly in the type of programming they offer, often tailoring their programs to their community. For example, the Community Justice Society, the agency that serves the Halifax region, primarily uses talking circles. This agency also offers a youth night, an Options to Anger group, and other community programming. The Island Community Justice Society, in Sydney, NS, focuses on family group conferencing.

TRUTH AND RECONCILIATION COMMISSIONS

During periods of authoritarian rule and mass violence, the power of the state often allows it to disguise or deny the existence of human rights abuses. Families who lose loved ones, or individuals who experience torture, may find themselves up against a justice system that denies the harm, or even their existence. For this reason, truth is often seen as a vital objective in a post-authoritarian era. Once the authoritarian government is ousted and democratic rule has been established, or is in the process of taking root, these new regimes often establish truth commissions to sort through the lies of the past and to facilitate the transition toward the future (see Kritz 1995; Teitel 2000; Offe 1997; Osiel, 1999; Marchak 2008). We may typically associate the need for transition with regimes in the Global South, but the recent experience of the Truth and Reconciliation Commission of Canada shows this is not solely the case. Indigenous peoples in Canada have lived for over a century under an authoritarian Indian Act, which has governed the entirety of their existence, including who is and who is not considered an "Indian" and how resources located on reservations can be used. In 1920, the Act was revised to make mandatory the attendance of Indigenous children at residential schools. Though many of us perceive ourselves to live in a liberal democracy, it has not been experienced as such by all living within Canada's boundaries.

Truth commissions have long been used in such situations (see Hayner 2002), but it is the South African Truth and Reconciliation Commission (SATRC) that has inspired the clearest association between truth commissions and restorative justice (Minow 1999; Llewellyn 2007). The negotiated demise of the apartheid system in South Africa raised the question of what is to be done with the former perpetrators of violence. Many would have liked to have seen these people punished within a court of law or subject to vigilante retribution (Wilson 2001), but both of these responses raised the threat of civil war. The white minority that had long held power in South Africa still controlled many of the nation's vital institutions, such as the justice system and the military. It was deemed unlikely that they would just gracefully release power if they were faced with the threat of retribution. The SATRC was thus proposed as an alternative option. However, several of those who had been victimized under the previous regime were uncomfortable with the amnesty provisions that had typically accompanied truth commissions in Latin America. In Chile and Argentina, for example, blanket amnesties had been issued to release former perpetrators from all forms of civil and criminal prosecution, thus attempting to institute a complete letting-go of the past. The South African compromise offered that instead of a blanket amnesty, perpetrators would need to earn their amnesty. In short, they would need to stand before their fellow citizens and past victims and declare openly and honestly all that they had done. If they failed to tell the truth, their amnesty would be rejected, and they could potentially be subject to a civil suit or criminal charges.

This modified form of amnesty was still a difficult sell to South Africans who had been long oppressed by apartheid. To make it palatable, Bishop Desmond

Tutu, who had been an outspoken critic of the apartheid system and was now chair of the SATRC, made the link between the Commission and restorative justice. Tutu (1999) argued South Africa was heading toward a different type of justice, restorative justice, and, for the sake of individual and national healing, people needed to let go of their desires for retribution. For Tutu, South Africa had *No Future Without Forgiveness*, the title of his 1997 book about the SATRC, and in his view it was only by forgiving past enemies that the country could make a relatively smooth transition from an apartheid regime into a modern democratic state. Furthermore, Tutu singled out the Bantu notion of *ubuntu* to demonstrate a longstanding African culture of forgiveness. Roughly translated as "a person is a person through other people," *ubuntu* suggests we are all interconnected and, therefore, whatever hurts one of us, hurts all of us. This sense of human relationality means we all have an interest in repairing rifts and healing harms, since any scar left unattended will affect the humanity of each and every one of us.

But in what sense was this Commission a form of restorative justice? In its entirety, the SATRC consisted of three components. First, there were the Human Rights Committees that travelled the country so select victims and victims' family members could recount their suffering and request reparation. To be eligible for a Human Rights Committee, one had to be the victim of a gross violation of human rights, meaning that only the most serious offences, such as political murders and extreme forms of torture, were considered by the SATRC. At the hearings, the commissioners encouraged the victims to offer their stories and would acknowledge the bravery and strength of each speaker. Counsellors were also on hand to speak with the victims and to discuss their needs for healing. However, the Human Rights Committees did not involve a face-to-face meeting with the perpetrators of apartheid violence. Instead, this opportunity would come at the Amnesty Hearings, the second component of the SATRC. It was at these hearings that perpetrators of political crimes (and one had to prove that the crime had a political rather than criminal motivation) could reveal the full details of their actions in exchange for amnesty. These testimonies would then be vetted against the information gathered by the Human Rights Committees, as well as against the SATRC's own research into these past events. Victims were invited to attend the Amnesty Hearings and could, at times, be heard making sounds of admonishment when they felt a perpetrator was dissimulating or being less than truthful. However, an intensive discussion between perpetrators and victims was not facilitated by the SATRC.

Indeed, the roles of perpetrator and victim were not always sufficiently clear to allow one to imagine a discussion occurring between distinct actors. For example, it was not just members of the apartheid state who were called to task for gross human rights violations. Members of Black South African anti-apartheid groups were also complicit in these crimes. This included members of parties like the African National Congress or Inkatha Freedom, who used violence to eliminate or intimidate people suspected as informants, or who were members of competing organizations (see Wilson 2001; Krog 1998).

The testimony of Dirk Johannes Coetzee, from the Amnesty Hearings, illustrates the SATRC process. Here, a former South African hit squad commander is questioned by his counsel, Mr. C. R. Jansen, and discusses the murder of human rights lawyer, Griffiths Mxenge. The family of Griffiths Mxenge were upset that Coetzee and his co-conspirators were provided amnesty by the SATRC because they felt, for one thing, it was not clearly demonstrated that Coetzee had a political motive for the murder, and it was not simply a matter of individual discretion on the part of the killers.

The dissatisfaction expressed by the Mxenge family illustrates the intense challenges of dealing with such a brutal past. We also see that in the very law-like proceedings of the Amnesty Hearings, there was no clear-cut conversation between perpetrators and victims of apartheid-era harms. What was instead generated was a national discussion of the past. Daily reporting on the human rights violations exposed white South Africans more fully to the atrocities that had been committed in their name. This did not result in automatic societal reconciliation or consensus on the future, but it at least allowed Black, white, and other South Africans to begin a discussion of their common future, albeit a future that has proceeded in the presence of severe social problems, such as extremely high crime rates.

The final committee is the Reparations and Rehabilitation Committee, which was charged with the task of recommending forms of material and symbolic redress for the victims of apartheid-era violence. This Committee possessed no formal governmental power and was therefore only able to suggest certain responses in the hope the government would implement them. Unfortunately, even the meagre compensation payments recommended by this committee were more than the South African government felt it could afford, and the government eventually only made R571.5 million (approximately $71.7 million Canadian) available to victims of apartheid, in contrast to the R3 billion (approximately $376 million Canadian) recommended by the Reparations

Box 4.3 SATRC Amnesty Hearing of Dirk Johannes Coetzee (Griffiths Mxenge killing)

Mr Jansen: If we can turn to the Mxenge matter. I think it's a matter of public knowledge that Mr. Griffiths Mxenge was killed on the 19th of November 1981, is that correct?

DJC: That's correct, Mr. Chairman.

Mr Jansen: Now, were you involved in his murder?

DJC: I was involved in the murder, yes, Mr. Chairman.

Mr Jansen: Can you relate to the Committee your involvement in this Mxenge matter? I think if you'd start with your presence in Durban at the time.

DJC: Mr. Chairman, during November, early November — from early November onwards we were operating as a whole Vlakplaas team [note: this is a farm that served as the headquarters of the South African Police counterinsurgency unit C10]. All four teams were operating in the Durban area on instructions, and as usual I reported to Brigadier van Hoven's office as officer commanding every morning at half past seven, and every afternoon at 4 o'clock for debriefing and briefing. A few days before the 19th of November, on a morning briefing, he asked me to make a plan with Mr. Mxenge. He then in very short terms briefed me that he was an ex-Robben Island convict, that he was an attorney, that they were trying to build up a case against him, because he was an acting instructing attorney in all ANC cadres cases who were caught in the country, and that an amount something R200,000.00 went through his bank account. He then took me over to the office of then Captain Andy Taylor.

Mr De Jager: Did he add — sorry to interrupt. Did he add anything to the words, "You must make a plan with Mr. Mxenge"?

DJC: He did, Mr. Chairman, in the sense that he said we must not use guns or make him disappear, we must make it look like a robbery.

Mr Jansen: Can you continue. What happened thereafter?

DJC: He then took me across the passage to Captain Andy Taylor's office, the officer who handled the Mxenge case, who was on his specific case dealing with his surveillance, his phone tapping, etcetera, who then gave me a short description of his office and his house, of how many dogs he had on the premises. If I recall correctly he said it was four.... He then also went with us to show Mr. Mxenge's house, and the information was also given to us that he usually works late at night, and his wife usually leaves before him. I requested Brigadier van der Hoven at the time to arrange with Brigadier Skoon for him to send Joe Mamasela [note: Mamsala is an "askari" or former resistance member who now works for the apartheid government] down for me as I would pick him as one of my team members. At the time Joe Mamasela was actually working with West Rand Security, Captain Jan Coetzee, who succeeded me on the 31st of December 1981 as commander at Vlakplaas, but whenever Captain Jan Coetzee didn't have work for him he would work with us, or when I needed him it would be arrange with Captain Jan Coetzee. So Brigadier van der Hoven arranged and, according to my recollection, Sergeant Schutte brought Joe Mamasela down on the 17th of November during the night which the dogs were poisoned. He brought down with him from Vlakplaas a hunting knife and two Okapi knives. Four pieces of meat we got from the police single quarters kitchen, and I had a bottle of strychnine in the back of my car, green crystals which the farmers used in the earlier days for jackal, to kill jackal that caught their sheep. Small slits — I made four pieces of meat, small chunks of meat with four slits in it, and put knife point — only a small knife point of strychnine in each piece of meat. This was not for the dog to taste the strychnine, and if you put in too much the dog would vomit it out. We then, on the night of the 17th, gave the pieces of meat — went to Mr. Mxenge's house. Myself, and if I recollect, if my memory doesn't let me down, Captain Koos Vermeulen, Paul van Dyk, Almond Nofomela and Joe Mamasela drove to Mr. Mxenge's house, where Almond and Joe got out of the car and the meat was distributed in the yard of Mr. Mxenge. The next day some of the dogs got killed, I don't know exactly how many, and the idea was to leave it open for them to decide where they want to commit the murder, either at his place of work coming out, or on the road, or, if the situation might fall into their discretion as the right moment, at his house without being hampered by the dogs. Almond and Joe observed Mr. Mxenge's office and his movements. The murder took place a day or two, if not three, after the poisoning of the dogs, and in

> fact on the night of the 19th of November. I had an arrangement with them that I would meet them …
>
> *Mr Jansen*: If I may interrupt at that stage. Did you give the members of the team any instructions as far as the way in which the murder had to be committed?
>
> DJC: Yes, I did, Mr. Chairman. I said they should specifically not use guns, and must make it look like a robbery, and it was decided on knives, that Mr. Mxenge will be killed with knives.
>
> *Mr Jansen*: Did you give them any instructions as to how they should go about to conceal their involvement, or possible police involvement?
>
> DJC: Well, they should not leave any tracks at all at the scene …
>
> *Mr Jansen*: What is your present attitude towards what you did to the Mxenge family?
>
> DJC: An extreme mixed emotions of anger, for allowing me to get involved with this, all this nonsense, humiliation, embarrassment, and a helplessness of a pathetic, "I am sorry for what I've done," and I can do nothing else to them. What else can I offer them? A pathetic nothing, so in all honesty I don't expect the Mxenge family to forgive me, because I don't know how I ever in my life would be able to forgive a man like Dirk Coetzee if he's done to me what I've done to them. But I will hope that this will be the beginning of a new era in my life. I can just turn my back on it and walk on.…
>
> Source: Truth and Reconciliation Commission 1996.

and Rehabilitation Committee. The government also refused to implement a business tax on those companies that had profited from apartheid controls — a measure the Reparations and Rehabilitation Committee had recommended to redistribute wealth. In this sense, the outcomes of the SATRC have been, in many ways, less than restorative, but it is likely asking too much of any restorative justice process to achieve reconciliation so soon after a history of intense societal violence. rooted in their history.

The SATRC influenced the development of the Truth and Reconciliation Commission of Canada (TRC). Canada adapted this approach to create one better suited to the Canadian political and legal context. As part of a settlement for class action lawsuits filed by IRS Survivors against the government and the churches who ran the schools, the TRC did not seek to determine the amount of reparations to be paid, nor did it offer amnesties for perpetrators of physical and sexual violence within the schools. These matters were left to the settlement negotiations and the criminal courts respectively. The primary purpose of the TRC was to provide a comprehensive history of the IRS system, including Survivors' experiences of these institutions, as well as to increase public knowledge of the schools and provide a framework for working towards reconciliation, among other tasks. *their goal is not to repair the harms/injustice.*

RESTORATIVE JUSTICE AND REPARATIONS FOR CRIMES OF MASS VIOLENCE

The discussion of reparations brings us to another practice that is occasionally associated with restorative justice. With respect to crimes of mass violence, the term "reparations" is often used to refer to a wide variety of responses to an unsavoury past. Included within its ambit are truth commissions, but also compensation payments, restitution of stolen property, days of commemoration, memorial museums, lustration (the removal of members of a former regime from positions of power), and even tribunals (see Torpey 2001, 2003, 2006).

Prior to World War II, such reparations were more commonly associated with warring parties rather than with the victims of state violence. In the aftermath of war, a victor nation would typically demand war reparations from the defeated party. However, the scale and scope of Nazi atrocities during World War II changed this arrangement. During the War, Jewish groups began organizing for victim reparations. These groups were engaged in the process of resettling refugees from continental Europe in the UK, US, and what would become the nation of Israel. They noted these individuals, who had been forced to flee Europe to avoid either Nazi death camps or massacres, had also left behind them a great deal of wealth (see, for example, Goldschmidt 1945; Moses 1944; Robinson 1944). Indeed, the Nazi-orchestrated Holocaust was not only an operation of massive killing, it was also one of large-scale theft. Every piece of property their victims left behind was appropriated by the Nazi regime or stolen by Nazi soldiers and guards. As well, Jewish slave labour had been used to manufacture arms and other goods for Germany. For example, the car manufacturer Volkswagen, a key supplier of armaments and vehicles for the Nazis, used Jewish slave labour in its wartime efforts. Even in death, the victims were robbed, as everything from their clothes, to gold fillings, hair, and prosthetic limbs were appropriated and recycled by the Nazis. Under these circumstances, it is not surprising Jewish Survivors of the Holocaust felt they had a stake in reparations if and when the Allies won the War, especially considering the costs of Jewish resettlement they had to bear.

The lobbying efforts and negotiations engaged in by the Jewish groups that were soon under the Conference on Jewish Claims Against Germany (or Claims Conference) eventually achieved Allied support for Jewish reparations claims. Then, once the War ended, the American occupied zone of West Germany instituted a restitution policy (American Military Law no. 59) that was later adopted by the other Allied occupied zones. Efforts to achieve a broader reparations policy began in March 1952, in the Dutch town of Wassenaar, and culminated on September 10, 1952 in the Luxembourg Agreement, which featured a lump sum payment of DM3 billion (approximately $3 billion in 2018 Canadian dollars) to the fledgling nation of Israel (much of this in the form of goods). It also contained two settlements with respect to the Claims Conference: the first required West Germany to improve existing compensation and restitution legislation to make it more readily available to a wider group of claimants, and the second provided a payment of DM450 million (approximately $450 million Canadian) to the Claims Conference (Goschler 2004).

This reparations agreement did not end Jewish reparations claims once and for all. Despite the agreement's requirements that West Germany improve its reparations policy, new demands continued to arise with respect to its limitations. For example, the 1956 revised West German Federal Compensation Law improved on the narrow framework of American Military Law no. 59, moving West German reparations beyond merely returning stolen items, but still presented several problems for claimants. First, it restricted claims to those based upon racial, religious, or political persecutions, which raised challenges for Roma and Sinti (formerly Gypsies) claimants who had allegedly been persecuted as criminals because the Nazis associated their nomadic lifestyle with innate criminality (Puxon 1981). Second, only those who lived within the German borders as of December 1, 1937, or who moved to the Federal Republic within certain time limits, were permitted to apply, thus restricting reparations largely to those "who currently were German nationals or who had been German nationals at the time of their persecution by the Nazis" (Goschler 2004: 391). Finally, reparation was only available to claimants who lived in countries that held diplomatic relations with West Germany, thus excluding those victims from Eastern European nations or who had fled to them (Goschler 2004; Schrafstetter 2003). The continued efforts of the Claims Conference resulted in the 1965 Final Law, a law that was final only in name as victims excluded from this law pressed for further legislation that would recognize their claims. More recently, Germany has attempted to forge a "legal peace" with respect to reparations claims through the establishment of the "Remembrance, Responsibility and Future" foundation (2000), which is intended, in particular, to bring an end to US-based lawsuits against German corporations and the German government. As of 2019, this foundation is still operating. Moreover, in January 2018, the German government and the Claims Conference agreed to increase social welfare supports for Holocaust Survivors by US$88 million to provide better quality home care, food support, and other services.

Alongside paying individual and collective compensation, Germany has made efforts to encourage remembrance and historical understanding of the Nazi past. This has involved several efforts at commemoration, through memorials, museums, school curricula, and other vehicles (see Niven 2002). In addition, monies paid to the Claims Conference contributed to the spread of "Holocaust consciousness" (Novick 1999) worldwide, as funds were used to educate people internationally about the horrors of the Holocaust and the need to prevent similar events from ever happening again. This is not to suggest German responses to the past have always been accepted without criticism — this is certainly not the case. However, it does illustrate a family resemblance between the philosophy of restorative justice and the practice of reparations. Reparations are typically negotiated between representatives from both the perpetrating and surviving parties. The goal is to arrive at an agreement that will satisfy the claimants (to the extent that this is possible after such terrible events) and will foster a degree of social healing. In this manner, reparations are a victim-centred process focused upon the needs and suffering of victims, both as individuals and as part of a collective (Cunneen 2006). As well, as in the case of Germany, the offending nation or party may even be seeking reintegration within the international community, as it was often said that German reparations were directed toward bringing Germany back into the "family of nations" (Jelinek 1990). It was also an opportunity for German "national self-interrogation" (Maier 1988) through which Germans eventually came to reflect upon what it was about their national identity that allowed them to become perpetrators of such vile crimes.

It should be noted the term reparations is also often used for monetary disbursements in the aftermath of other collectively harmful events, such as the sale of unsafe products or environmental damage caused by corporate negligence. However, such compensatory agreements are of a different category than the reparations described here. These disbursements are better described as settlements, since they typically lack a significant symbolic component in the form of commemoration, public atonement, or apology (see Brooks 2003). Instead, they are more often than not monetary settlements designed to prevent more damaging civil lawsuits. In contrast, reparations for mass violence often carry much more significant symbolic weight, as they are meant to address victim concerns for material, cultural, and personal loss, as well as worries about the recurrence of the crimes. To this extent, such processes can have much overlap with restorative justice.

Table 4.1 Restorative Justice Styles

Restorative Justice Style	Typical Elements
Mediation and Community Mediation	• Local actors empowered to creatively resolve conflict • Deprofessionalized, deinstitutionalized local justice
VOR/VOM	• Safe environment, preparation, voluntary participation, face-to-face interaction and follow-up
Family Group Conferencing	• Bring the families of victim and offender together to resolve conflict • Family group decision making: feminist praxis that attempts to interrupt gendered assumptions about dominance
Circles	Occasion where a community is assembled to discuss matters related to and a possible resolution for a local injustice
Truth and Reconciliation Commission	Truth-seeking mechanisms that interrogate a nation's troubled past in order to reconcile former antagonists and transition nation toward a more peaceable future.
Reparations	Refers to a variety of justice mechanisms used in periods of societal transition. Includes truth commissions, compensation payments, restitution of stolen property, days of commemoration, memorial museums, and lustration.

GREY AREAS OF RESTORATIVE JUSTICE

In each of the styles there exist shades of grey in terms of the degree to which its actual practice lives up to the principles of restorative justice. For example, many of these practices are unable to realize the ideal of local empowerment propounded by many restorative advocates (Christie 1977; Zehr 1990). As much as many practitioners would like to see a restorative justice that is largely administered within local community settings (and therefore informal as opposed to being part of the formal criminal justice system), state resources and agents are often necessary to the functioning of a restorative justice program. We saw in circle sentencing, for example, the involvement of criminal justice figures (judges and lawyers) at crucial stages of the process, such as the judge's role in determining whether or not the community's sanction meets the standards of Canadian law. One can also see at work within the South African Truth and Reconciliation Commission a great deal of formal law. The SATRC tended toward legal interpretations of key events, such as in deciding what is a "gross human rights violation" or "crime against humanity." As well, it employed legalistic rules of evidence, used subpoenas to demand witness testimony, and followed a juridical rationale for determining whether or not perpetrators deserved amnesties (Christodoulidis 2000; see also Wilson 2001 and Meierhenrich 2008). Likewise, reparations often involve state-level negotiations rather than facilitated victim and perpetrator interactions.

But there exist other programs that borrow the label of restorative justice that are, perhaps, even more problematically situated within this category. For example, when conducting research on the practice of restorative justice in British Columbia, one of the authors came across several programs that used "community accountability panels," which were described as a form of restorative justice. These panels were locally operated and, in most cases, run by a group comprised largely of volunteer practitioners. They took referrals for cases of minor youth crimes that were diverted to them for sanctioning. Upon receiving a case, the program would assemble a panel of prominent members of the community with which the young offender would meet to discuss the crime. In rare instances, the victim may have also been present at the panel hearing, but this was hardly the norm. Instead, the youth would stand before the panel to listen to their advice and would be provided some limited opportunity for input into the sanction they were about to receive.

At the time, although it was not the focus of the research (Woolford and

Ratner 2003), this seemed like a potentially stigmatizing and punitive process, especially considering the very minor nature of some of the cases presented before such panels, which included acts such as thrown snowballs, shoplifting, and graffiti. Indeed, subsequent research suggests similar panels, like those used in England and Wales, are beset by potential problems such as "managerialism," in that they are used as an administrative means to speed minor cases through the court system. They also contribute to net widening by dealing with minor crimes that would otherwise be ignored by the criminal justice system. Finally, they are part of a process of reformalization, whereby lawyers are increasingly involved in these allegedly informal settings and the panels are facilitated in a legalistic manner. For example, they often use legal styles of questioning to obtain information from young persons (Crawford 2003; see also Crawford and Newburn 2002).

Panels such as these are in a grey area because they have a potential to be restorative, but they also violate some of our key expectations of restorative justice programs. They can be restorative as there is the possibility a very productive conversation will unfold between the community panel and the young offender, and this could have empowering consequences for the young person's life, helping reintegrate them into the community and halting what was potentially a path toward greater criminal involvement. However, there is also great risk that the panels will devolve into informal courts, where community members stand in judgment of a minor offender, enacting communal vengeance upon this young person. It also does not help matters that such panels are, in part, a repackaged form of diversion — a pre-restorative justice criminal justice reform that sought to direct youth away from the criminal justice system and toward community-based programs to spare young people the brunt of criminal stigmatization. Such diversion programs were roundly criticized by scholars like Stanley Cohen (1985), who saw them enabling an extension of the stigmatizing and social control powers of the state into everyday community life, especially with respect to providing increased state and social control over poor, minority youths.

This is but one example of a program that occupies this grey area of restorative justice. There are many criminal justice programs that pre-exist restorative justice, but which have been re-branded as restorative justice, since they are believed to aspire toward similar goals. Even offender literacy and job training programs are, at times, described as part of a larger restorative justice project, since such activities are integral to offender reintegration, especially if we wish

RJ comes in many forms, is done in different ways, and sometimes enters a grey area

RESTORATIVE JUSTICE STYLES 101

to provide restorative services for those who have been sentenced through the regular criminal justice system but seek a restorative immersion back into society upon their release from a correctional institution.

DOES RESTORATIVE JUSTICE WORK?

Given the ethos of restorative justice, some of the theories that animate it, and the various ways it is practiced, a common question is "Ok, but does it work?" Today, most government-funded restorative justice programs include an evaluative component. This involves measuring the degree to which the program has met its stated goals. A program that has the stated objectives of healing victims, rehabilitating offenders, and restoring communities may be evaluated on the basis of whether or not victims feel their needs have been met, whether or not offenders have committed further offences after participation in the program, and whether or not community members have become involved in the process.

With respect to evaluations of the role of restorative justice in helping victims of crime, several studies have shown positive results. For example, Heather Strang's (2001) research on crime victims in Canberra, Australia, compared court- and restorative-justice-assigned crime victims with respect to their desires for vengeance. She found that over half of those who used the courts longed for revenge, while this was true for only 7 percent of those who used restorative justice (cited in Braithwaite 2003). Those who were routed toward restorative justice were more likely to overcome some of their anger and vengefulness.

One of the most common measures for evaluating the experience of victims is whether or not they are satisfied with the process. Studies done in various countries have found that generally victims are satisfied. McCold and Wachtel's (1998) study in Bethlehem, Pennsylvania, showed that 94 percent of victims were satisfied with their conferences, and Strang's (2001) study in Wagga Wagga, Australia, revealed 90 percent were satisfied. Shapland et al.'s (2011) study of restorative justice in England and Wales asked several different questions, including "Do you think having the [conference/mediation] is a good way to deal with the offence which was committed against you?" to which 64 percent responded "a good way" or "a very good way," and "Would you recommend restorative justice to others?" to which 78 percent responded "probably" or "definitely." Studies have also shown that victims participating in restorative justice are more satisfied than those who go through the courts

(Latimer et al. 2001). There is some caution to be had here as it has also been noted in various studies that victims are, at times, the least satisfied participants in restorative conferences (Maxwell and Morris 1993). Overall, the evaluation literature suggests that at least some restorative justice programs have managed to offer victims a more satisfying justice.

Offenders typically have high levels of satisfaction and perceive restorative processes to be fair (Braithwaite 2003). This is particularly true for offenders who participate in programs that encourage a high degree of stakeholder participation (McCold and Wachtel 2002). Another common offender-related measure is recidivism. The question often asked by evaluations is whether or not restorative justice reduces re-offending. Recidivism is, like the other criteria we look at here, a complex one for any justice process to define and measure. Some evaluations define recidivism as any new arrest, some as new charges, others as new convictions. Are we interested in whether an offender committed the same offence again or a different one? For both restorative justice and criminal justice, recidivism is a complex measure. Reports on reductions in offender recidivism through restorative justice have been mixed, although some restorativists would argue recidivism is too blunt a measure and may not fully capture the gradual change an offender experiences after restorative intervention — a change that may include a few hurdles (or reoffences) along the way. Nonetheless, there are programs that show positive results on the recidivism front. For example, Restorative Resolutions, based out of the John Howard Society of Manitoba, was a program for adult offenders who had committed more serious crimes (crimes where the Crown is proposing a sentence of six months or more). In a study by Bonta et al. (1998), it was shown that participants in Restorative Resolutions had half the amount of recidivism as that exhibited by members of the control group, who were processed through the regular criminal justice system. Maxwell et al. (2006) also note that most studies show conferences have the potential to reduce recidivism, but this is not universally the case. In their view, the keys to success in preventing recidivism include active participation, consensual decision making, lack of stigmatizing shaming, and visible offender remorse (Maxwell et al. 2006). Bouffard, Cooper, and Bergseth (2017) looked specifically at young offenders and found that those who went through restorative justice reoffended less than those who went through the court process and that those who went through restorative justice and did reoffend refrained from offending for longer than those who went through the courts. In addition, a number of meta-analyses, such as Sherman and Strang (2007) and Sherman et al. (2015) have begun to see patterns of recidivism reduction as they look at multiple studies and sets of results.

The level to which restorative justice has benefited communities is still open to debate. Concerns that certain communities are unsuited to restorative justice, perhaps because they are perceived to be dysfunctional, appear unfounded, as even communities deeply troubled by cycles of violence and sexual abuse have been able to form positive helping networks through restorative justice programs. The example of Hollow Water, Manitoba, is revealing (see Box 4.3). Although there remain concerns about the levels of community pressure upon victims to accept the restorative justice process and the presence of offenders in their midst, the program has allowed this community to begin to come to terms with its intergenerational problems of physical, sexual, and emotional violence, as well as substance abuse. In contrast, the South African Truth and Reconciliation Commission, a process we described earlier as being primarily about societal healing or reconciliation, has seen a continued rise in criminal violence in the aftermath of its efforts. While a case can still be made that the SATRC has started South Africa on a path toward healing, several commentators suggest the SATRC was too legalistic and directed toward nation building (Wilson 2001), overlooked the structural problems created by apartheid by focusing solely on those who committed gross human rights violations and ignoring the many other beneficiaries of apartheid (Mamdani 2000), and left victims who did not buy into the quasi-religious philosophy of reconciliation unsatisfied and still seeking vengeance (Wilson 2001; Acorn 2004).

What remains is for more research to be conducted on the ways in which restorative justice contributes to strengthening community helping networks that act as a resource for individuals, providing them with relationships that can be relied upon in times of need (social capital). It is certainly reasonable to expect that people gathering to discuss a common concern will bond in a manner that will make them resources for one another in the future, but, so far, there is too little evidence to support this claim.

In all, restorative justice programs have been subject to a great deal of evaluation, and studies tend to support the claim that restorative justice offers benefits that are not typically or widely available through the regular criminal justice system. This very brief sampling of some of this research supports such a view (for more about the empirical results of restorative evaluations, see Sherman and Strang 2007; Elliott and Gordon 2005).

Thus far we have been discussing the evaluation of restorative justice as if

Box 4.4 Hollow Water Healing: Straightforward, Honest

A healing movement that has roots in British Columbia has successfully taken hold in Hollow Water, Manitoba and is reaching to other parts of the country.

Valdie Seymour and Berma Bushie are two of the founders of what is called the community holistic circle healing in Hollow Water, a First Nation of 700 people on the eastern shore of Lake Winnipeg.

It's a process that has successfully been used to deal with dozens of cases of sexual abuse. Eighty-four sexual abuse victims and 48 offenders have benefited from the circle healing in Hollow Water during the past 10 years. Nine out 10 offenders are taking responsibility for their actions and the pain they have caused, and seldom re-offend, said Bushie. Now others want to know how it's done.

… Bushie said Hollow Water's vision includes two basic values that sustained Hollow Water families in the past: children are looked upon as gifts from the Creator and women have a place of honor because the Creator has given them the gift of bringing life into the world.

The other key element was the four basic laws of the Anishinabe — honesty, kindness, sharing and respect.

In the mid-1980s, Hollow Water discovered a solution in the power of healing circles, beginning with a resource team of 24, the members of which openly shared their painful personal stories with each other.

A confidential survey in a workshop of 60 community members indicated that two-thirds of the participants had been sexually victimized as children, youth or adults, and one-third had sexually victimized others.

Bushie, a victim of incest and rape by the time she was 12, came to realize the silence regarding abuse would have to be broken if she wanted her community to live its vision.

"I lived in silence around these issues until I was 38," she said. "I came to know that the dynamics of silence in my community kept me from having a good life. I couldn't practise the laws of the Creator while I was trapped in that silence and rage."

The resource team heard its first sexual abuse disclosure from a child less than two years later, in 1996.

In search of help, 20 community members travelled to Alkali Lake, B.C. in 1988. By this time, Alkali Lake was renowned for having turned around an adult population of which 95 per cent were said to be abusing alcohol to the point where 95 per cent were considered "recovering" alcoholics.

When the Hollow Water group returned from Alkali Lake, it conducted a week-long stretch of workshops to share personal stories about victimization. Soon, there was a flood of 17 disclosures from children of current abuse cases.

"They were disclosing on uncles, aunts, grandfathers. It was a scary time for the community," Bushie remembers. As a child care worker, she was faced with the scary prospect of having to bring half of Hollow Water's child population into the care of its child welfare agency. Half of the adult population could have been reported to the criminal justice system.

"We felt such actions would escalate things, not bring order," she explained. "If you're an offender, the system will protect you every step of the way. The courts will do everything in their power to rip the victim apart to support your lie."

The offender, though, is faced with the prospect of jail, where, Bushie said, healing is unlikely.

Instead, Hollow Water concentrated on setting up an alternative. Two teams were formed, one to sit in circles with the victim, another for the offender, along with their respective families. Eventually, the two groups are brought together in a larger healing circle, and later a sentencing circle that also involves community members and the usual players that would be found in a court setting.

"Victims need to get out of the trap of shame and guilt and ... hear they're supported and celebrated for the things they've brought into the open," said Bushie.

Rupert Ross, an assistant Crown attorney in Kenora who travelled to Hollow Water as part of a three-year Aboriginal Justice Directorate project

> and wrote about it in his book Returning to the Teachings, knows the circles have a profound effect on the offenders.
>
> "I heard a woman say 20 years after being abused that she still feels so dirty that she can't have her grandchild sit on her knee because she doesn't want to contaminate him or that she can't stand to look at herself in the mirror," he said. "Statements like that have immense power over an offender because the truth is part of healing. Our justice system doesn't operate at that spiritual, emotional level."
>
> Bushie calls it a straightforward process that operates out of honesty. "There are no bargains of 'You do this and we'll do that.' Our way is not easy. To be honest is difficult."
>
> Source: Phlean 1998. Reprinted with permission.

it escapes the politics that we have argued are always operative for restorative justice. Yet even something as ostensibly objective as evaluation data is infused with politics. There are several different ways we must question that seemingly straightforward question, "does restorative justice work?"

First, we should ask, "work to do what?" Work is a relatively vague verb that can mean any number of things depending on how we define it. Take this book for example, we could ask of it, does this book work? Our answer, yes or no, is completely dependent on what we mean by "work." Does this book work to turn the two of us into authors? Yes. Does it work to teach students about restorative justice? We hope so. Does it work to change the justice system into a wholly restorative system? Most probably not, though we may console ourselves that it is but one small contribution to a broader movement toward transformation. Llewellyn et al. (2013) argue that, generally speaking, evaluations of restorative justice have been framing the things that restorative justice works to do incorrectly. They argue restorative justice evaluations have been using the criteria that the criminal justice system uses to assess whether or not it's working, a completely different paradigm of justice. They argue that instead of looking at recidivism, satisfaction, cost, or speediness we need to use criteria that are grounded in the theories of restorative justice. The criteria they propose draw from their conceptualization of restorative justice: relationship focused, holistic, contextual, inclusive, communicative, democratic, and forward focused. These are things we should be looking for. For example, does it include all the relevant stakeholders and allow them space to communicate their harm? If it does, it works. To conduct such an evaluation, one may also need to expand the notion of evaluation methodology. In this case, this would mean including observation-based research strategies that allow the researcher to observe the inclusivity and communicative practices within a particular restorative justice program.

A second pertinent question is, "who wants to know?" The ways in which we evaluate anything, including a restorative justice program, will change depending on the audience. Returning to our evaluation of this book, if we were trying to convince students that this was a book that "works," we might focus on criteria like number of pages (it's not a particularly long book) or price (it's not going to cost hundreds of dollars to purchase). If we were trying to convince scholars, we would use different criteria, such as its ability to synthesize a wide range of theorists or the clarity of the writing. The same holds true for restorative justice. Who wants to know whether or not it works will impact the criteria used in evaluation. Often, it is the funding body for the program that wants to see evidence that it is working, which is in many cases a government body. For government supporters of restorative justice, the desired outcomes may be described by a few key measures. Does restorative justice prevent offender recidivism? Does restorative justice reduce the costs of administering justice? Does restorative justice increase victim satisfaction? These are the matters that tend to have the best political optics for governments who are out to convince the general public they are bringing an end to the problem of crime, managing political coffers effectively, and meeting the demands of victims. However, the priority placed on questions such as these can lead to efforts at program evaluation in restorative justice that simply measure government interests rather than the actual restorative effects.

A third pertinent question is, "how do we know it works?" This question relates to the general difficulty in social science research of being sure that you are measuring the thing you want to be measuring. Again, we can use this book as an example. Were we to be asked if this book "works," there are several different measures we could try to use to answer that question. We could look at how many copies it has sold. If we sold a million copies we may confidently state that this is a good book. But perhaps it sold these many copies because students were forced to buy it, and after purchasing we don't even know if they read it. Instead we may try to measure whether readers of the book knew more about restorative justice after reading it, but how would we measure that? This problem becomes more complex with the type of conceptual outcomes

Llewellyn et al. (2013) argue we should be measuring: contextual, dialogic, forward focused. There is a growing trend for government and other funding bodies to demand quantitative results demonstrating the success of a given restorative justice program, and, while it is not impossible for some restorative justice programs to provide quantified measures to demonstrate their success, much of what restorative justice aims to achieve is not easily captured in straightforward numeric terms. For example, a goal such as healing may be reflected in survey question data about victim satisfaction and the degree to which the person feels healed at whatever point in time after the restorative meeting that the survey is conducted, but these are most certainly imperfect measures, since healing is a process and not an either/or characteristic of the self. One's sense of healing after a traumatic event will ebb and flow; there will be good days and bad days. Of course, this will be challenging to record even using a more qualitative approach. However, using a technique like interviews may allow participants to speak to the process of healing more so than a survey that asks whether they have a sense of closure at that point in time. A realistic achievement for restorative justice is to provide such persons with new frameworks for understanding the harm they experienced (or that they committed) so they may better negotiate their lives in the aftermath of the harmful event. Such frameworks are harder to gauge, especially when limited to quantitative analysis. It is also the case that there is no universally shared sense of healing (Braithwaite 2003). Experiences like healing and restoration are intensely individual, and it is difficult for a large survey to attend to all the various definitions of healing individuals might hold.

Beyond these more general questions about whether the tools of social scientific quantitative methodology can adequately capture the oftentimes ephemeral and deeply ontological experience of restorative justice are questions that arise in attempts to measure the success of restorative justice. Much early empirical restorative justice research was burdened by the problem that participants were not randomly assigned to either a restorative or retributive justice program, thereby allowing for measurement of the comparative success of the restorative justice program. This raised the concern that many of the participants in restorative justice may have been selected in a manner that included predominately those who are unlikely to recidivate and are more likely to feel satisfaction after participating in a restorative session. Indeed, offenders are often directed toward restorative justice programs because they are believed to be "promising" candidates, since they have admitted responsibility, volunteer to participate, and they may have a strong support network to help them with their reintegration (Latimer et al. 2001). For this reason, it is difficult to tell whether or not these offenders would have done equally well if their cases were processed through the regular criminal justice system. In addition to this problem of "selection bias," studies of restorative justice have also been criticized for lacking power in that they typically work with small sample sizes that prevent them from achieving statistical significance. These problems are common in program evaluations of all kinds; they are not limited to restorative justice. They are issues, however, that we need to be cognizant of when asking "does restorative justice work?"

Finally, we must ask, "does it work for whom?" We are all differently positioned in society based on things like race, class, and gender. Our experiences of crime, harm, and justice are likewise differently felt. A question that researchers and practitioners should be asking of restorative justice is how both victims and offenders may experience it differently based on their social positioning. Do queer participants feel safe enough to fully tell their story of victimization, and thus gain the empowerment restorative justice talks about, if they are surrounded by people who may be homophobic? Can Indigenous participants bring up the role of settler-colonialism, thus fulfilling the holistic promise of restorative justice, without being accused of offering excuses? Do women who have heard their partners apologize for their violence again and again experience an apology in restorative justice as healing? These are all questions that researchers and evaluators should be asking, and with the exception of some feminist work (see, for example, Miller and Iovanni 2013; Van Wormer 2009) they are generally silent on these issues. Sherman and Strang's (2007) meta-analysis is one of the few that does stress the need to examine for whom restorative justice works. One of their findings in particular re-enforces for us the need to interrogate how power differences mean that restorative works differently for different people. They found that going through a restorative justice process led to an increase in the subsequent frequency of arrests in Australia for Indigenous youth and in the US for Hispanic youth who committed property crimes. Like other aspects of restorative justice, evaluation results must be understood within these broader political contexts.

MICRO-POLITICS OF RESTORATIVE PRACTICES

When we talk about VOR, VOM, FGCs, circles, and even truth commissions, we often gloss over what we have stressed is the key component: the encounter. What actually occurs when people who have hurt and been hurt by each other get together? Harris, Walgrave, and Braithwaite (2004) identify what they call an ideal-typical scenario that illustrates how the process should occur. At the beginning of any restorative justice session, they argue, the offender will feel at the very least embarrassed about their behaviour and will more likely feel some shame and guilt. Victims may feel some shame themselves, some anger, and they will have a desire to resolve the harm that has been done to them. Victims may be torn, however, between wanting to resolve the harm by causing harm to the offender (in the traditional retributive way) and wanting to resolve it by diminishing their own suffering. The session will begin with the victim recounting their story, detailing the harm that has been done to them. The offender will, in the ideal-typical scenario, hear this story and feel compassion. They will recognize that their behaviour has caused this pain and they will feel remorse and shame. That shame can be accepted by the offender, it can be acknowledged, and the offender may then move to offering some sort of reparation. In doing so, the offender turns the power back to the victim, it is up to them to accept the apology or the restitution offered. The victim may feel empowered, that their dignity is restored and that their feelings of revenge are gone. All too often, however, restorative justice scholars theorize that this is probably what takes place and then try to measure various outcomes, but they do not engage in any analysis of what actually goes on during restorative encounters.

Rossner (2011, 2013) provides a more detailed and empirically grounded analysis of what happens in a successful restorative justice encounter. For her, restorative justice is best understood as a justice ritual, as not simply an open and spontaneous dialogue but a ceremonial act and process. We can think of all sorts of different justice rituals — processes that have a certain form and flow through which we attempt to come to a shared moral standard of right and wrong: court processes, arguments, and even public executions. Thinking of restorative justice in this way allows us to move from the vague ideal-typical scenario to more specifically outlining the interactional dynamics of a good restorative encounter. What makes for a "good" restorative encounter is, of course, up for debate. For Rossner, a good restorative justice ritual is one that is transformative for the participants: they come together and feel more connected to each other, they build empathy and solidarity and they carry that beyond the encounter. In order to identify the core aspects of the ritual that lead to this sort of outcome, Rossner engaged in in-depth observation of restorative justice encounters. She studied the emotional display of participants, their dialogue, monologues, and non-verbal cues. Through this analysis she says there are four important components of a successful interaction ritual in restorative justice:

1. *Shared focus through conversation rhythm.* Participants develop a rhythm to their conversation. There are fewer pauses, fewer long monologues, and they talk to each other rather than to the facilitator.
2. *Conversational and power balance.* All of the participants are able to contribute what they would like to the conversation. There is no one participant who dominates in time or energy. No one is left out or withdrawn.
3. *Turning point.* There is a moment in the encounter where emotions have built to the point where all participants are drawn in and begin to feel the empathy and solidarity that restorative justice strives to build.
4. *Public displays of solidarity.* After the emotional high point, participants engage in interactions that demonstrate the newly built connections: they maintain eye contact longer, they shake hands, they stay and chat after the formal close of the encounter.

This is not to suggest that these aspects of an encounter happen spontaneously. The magic of restorative justice (as proponents sometimes describe it) comes as a result of various strategies that participants use to intentionally manage and direct the encounter. A burgeoning body of research has used Erving Goffman's dramaturgical perspective to examine restorative justice encounters and analyze the social and political dynamics that occur at the micro level. Goffman (1993 c. 1959: xi) describes his dramaturgical approach as a "framework" for understanding any "concrete social establishment." A primary building block of this framework is Goffman's notion of the "definition of the situation." The definition of the situation describes the overarching or governing logic that guides social action. For example, a person laying down on a city sidewalk may be ignored as passers-by define the situation as a non-emergency by assuming the individual is simply resting after drinking too much or rationalizing that a qualified professional will soon be by to care for them. One person intervening, however, can shift the definition of the situation to an emergency, as that person's demonstrated concern can break others from their blasé disregard. A definition is thus never final or fully achieved. It is a matter of ongoing negotiation between actors located within a context. The creation or preservation of a definition of the situation requires work on the part of the actors engaged in this negotiation, and this work takes place both "back stage," or behind the scenes, and "front stage," or in front of an intended audience. Goffman (1993 c. 1959: 10) describes an actively maintained definition of the situation as a "working consensus," and the achievement of such a consensus can result in actors committing to a "line" as a way of preserving this consensus. In other words, they become invested in sustaining a performance that is intended to ensure the stability of the definition of the situation. This encourages players to commit to an accepted definition of the situation and its reproduction. The work actors engage in to maintain a definition of the situation also connects with "face," which is "the positive social value that a person effectively claims for himself by the line others assume he has taken during a particular interaction" (Goffman 1967: 5). Face is intimately entwined with one's sense of honour and dignity, hence the expression "saving face" to describe the lengths to which one might go to avoid embarrassment. Not surprisingly, in practice restorative justice works to create a definition of the situation whereby participants will commit to lines of action directed toward peaceable rather than conflictual presentations of self.

While all participants engage in impression management and performance during a restorative justice session, research has paid particularly close attention to the ways in which the process is directed by the facilitator (Rypi 2017, for example). In the pre-encounter preparation process, facilitators work backstage to prepare the participants and rehearse the encounter. Rypi (2017) found facilitators to be highly directive in the backstage preparations. They assisted offenders in visual impression management, encouraging them to change their clothing or cover tattoos in order to look less like a criminal. In one case, the facilitator cautions an offender from sharing their past struggles with drug addiction. While the offender wants to explain to the victim some of the problems that led to the crime, the facilitator suggests that the offender be vaguer about their troubles. Here, the facilitator stops the offender from ruining the performance (the encounter) by sharing information that reinforces a deviant self rather than a conforming, remorseful self-presentation. Facilitators also work to rehearse the encounter with participants beforehand. Facilitators would steer victims away from problematic questions (for example, those relating to whether or not the offender and their family are immigrants), and guide offenders towards suitable answers. Both of these were sometimes accomplished through role playing, a literal acting out of the encounter before it takes place.

Research has also highlighted the managing done by the facilitator in the front stage of the encounter. Most restorative justice sessions are comprised of several stages. These stages may not follow a discrete linear order, and there are other potential stages, but generally speaking each restorative justice session will feature an introduction, recital, transition, problem solving, and agreement building (Picard 1998). In the introduction the facilitator establishes a positive and productive atmosphere for the meeting by welcoming everyone and stressing the potential good that can evolve from their collective involvement in the justice process. The facilitator might also choose to remind the parties of the procedure for the session and the ground rules, such as by asking them not to interrupt one another. The facilitator chairs the session by setting the tone with the introduction and choosing who speaks first (Bruce 2013). Once this is accomplished, the recital unfolds through the victim and offender telling their versions of the events that transpired. Other members of the restorative meeting might also be invited to speak about what happened. Throughout the discussion the facilitator continues to chair by using a variety of prompts, such as, "Can you tell us more?" and "How did that make you feel?" They may have to manage any crises that occur, such as angry disagreements (Bruce 2013). It is key at this stage, however, that the facilitator help the participants move from discussing the event to discussing what to do about it. This can happen naturally without any influence from the facilitator, but the facilitator does have at their disposal some techniques for helping the participants along, focusing them on problem solving so they can eventually draw up an agreement (Picard 1998).

The first technique is to ask "open questions." Open questions are often "how" and "why" questions that allow respondents to explain themselves in their own terms, rather than nudging them toward a desired answer. So, rather than assuming the victim's feelings by asking, "What made you angry that day?" the facilitator would want to enquire more carefully, with a question like "How did that make you feel?" As well, the facilitator would want to avoid any line of questioning that may seem judgmental, such as "Why did you feel angry?" "Why" questions, in particular, have a tendency to sound accusatory and it would be preferable to provide room for the participant to describe their own feelings with a question like, "How did that make you feel?" (Picard 1998).

The second technique is to "summarize and paraphrase." When individuals are engaged in lengthy acts of storytelling, it is not uncommon for them to get overwhelmed by the details. A good summary helps to focus the parties on the major issues of contention, helping prevent unnecessary distraction. Summary is also helpful when a party repeats themself incessantly because it allows this person to know they have been heard. Similarly, a paraphrase is a briefer summary where a statement is rephrased to ensure clarity of meaning and to let the speaker know they have been heard (Picard 1998).

[margin note: this removes emotion and feeling.]

With both the paraphrase and the summary, there is the possibility of restating what has been said in more neutral terms. Thus, if a party puts something in positional and combative terms ("they're selfish and don't care about anyone other than themself"), the facilitator can hone in on the interest that is at stake in the statement ("so what I am hearing is that you feel a certain level of trust and generosity is important between neighbours") (see Fisher and Ury 1991 for further discussion of positions and interests). Once the statement is restated in this way, a new discussion can emerge as to how the parties might achieve the general interest (trust and generosity) rather than getting bogged down in the combative claim ("they are selfish"). This neutralized summary is, in fact, a third form of intervention, called "reframing." Through reframing, the conversation is shifted toward common interests that can be resolved, stressing what is positive and focusing the parties on issues that can be resolved (Picard 1998).

A final set of techniques is used for purposes of "acknowledging, validating, and normalizing" the feelings and sentiments of participants. For example, a facilitator may acknowledge the feelings of a speaker, as well as validate and normalize those feelings. In the aftermath of break-and-enter, it may be useful for the facilitator to acknowledge the fear one may feel after one's home has been broken into, and to validate that this is a normal feeling. Such an intervention would recognize a victim's sense of discomfort, help them put a name to their feelings, and perhaps allow them to move forward in the discussion (Picard 1998).

All of the techniques are designed to help parties transition from detailing the harm they suffered and laying blame (or providing excuses) toward finding a resolution. Facilitators also work as "brokers" of the resolution. They may bring a list of community resources with them to share with participants, nudging them toward using those resources as part of the agreement (Bruce 2013). Bruce (2013) also found that most facilitators in her study anticipated the agreements beforehand, discussing and negotiating potential outcomes with victims and offenders in the pre-encounter preparations, or in the backstage work. The goal is to subtly teach participants in the restorative justice session how to properly engage in conflict resolution. These soft technologies of power also serve as forms of modelling, with the facilitator providing the participants with a model they should follow (Woolford and Ratner 2008b). These techniques are also coupled with the efforts made to prepare participants for restorative justice encounters, which often involve tips on how to communicate and listen effectively.

More broadly, these techniques are part of the "staging" or "choreography" of restorative justice (Dignan et al. 2007: 12). These interventions combine with other facilitator efforts to script and design the restorative encounter in a way that better ensures its success. In some restorative programs, actual scripts are employed for facilitators to follow, so certain questions are asked and all participants receive their opportunity to speak. As well, facilitators are careful to arrange the chairs in the room to allow for effective face-to-face communication.

Recalling that restorative justice is meant to be an open and empowering process we might wonder to what degree this type of management by facilitators stifles these core values. There are concerns as well around the ways in which facilitators may replicate larger social inequalities in their direction of the encounters. If a mediator is too directive in paraphrasing or reframes in a manner that reinforces gendered or cultural stereotypes, the objective of an open and empowering dialogue may be compromised. Restorative justice encounters are not entirely spontaneous and unstructured. Although unscripted moments will likely arise, a great deal of planning is involved to try to produce restoration. But the balance between spontaneity and structure must be maintained so that the facilitator assists the parties in opening their restorative encounter to possible solutions rather than leading them to a pre-determined outcome.

THE EMBODIED POLITICS OF RESTORATIVE JUSTICE

Both the direct and indirect training of restorative justice participants aims to impart new dispositions in potential combatants. When we are in conflict, we often react in accordance with our conflict socialization. For example, a youngster who has observed family members being quick to anger may take on similar patterns. More broadly speaking, the entrenched position of adversarial law in our culture also means we almost automatically think in legal terms when confronted with conflict (Ewick and Silbey 1998). Recently, a mistake made by a roofing contractor led to rain getting into the walls of the house of one of the authors, destroying his paint and plaster in several rooms and presenting the risk of future mould and mildew. Although he and his partner sought to negotiate a reasonable solution with the contractor outside of the courts, they nonetheless did so in the "shadow of law" (Harrington 1985). The framework for their discussion included the legal rights they had as homeowners based upon the contract they had signed with the contractor. They did not assume this legal posture after a long period of deep strategic consideration. Instead, it came to them almost naturally, as though they could sense their leverage in this disagreement could be most readily found through recourse to legal thinking.

This sort of legal reflex is becoming a more regular feature of our societies. With movies, books, and television fixated on the drama of the courtroom, and with daily news stories of happenings in the courts, a legal rationality seeps deeper into our unconscious minds. It is also the case that legal terminology has become everyday parlance, with words like liability, moot, and tort in more frequent usage. In other cases, such as with the notion of justice, the term has become synonymous with its legal sense, thereby ignoring the long history of debate about justice that precedes the formation of the justice system as we know it today. In this manner, legalism has become a largely subconscious tool that we use to negotiate and make sense of our world.

The task for restorative justice is to challenge and disrupt this legal reflex. Embedded in legalism is a confrontational and adversarial sensibility that is much different than the restorative justice ethos described in Chapter 3. Although the legal ethos and the restorative justice ethos would be in agreement that conflicts are knowable, they would differ with respect to the question of how they are knowable. For restorative justice, they are knowable through open and cooperative interaction, whereas for the legal ethos, it is through adversarialism, with defence and prosecution presenting their competing versions of the truth. If we already inhabit a reality in which legalism is an almost automatic response to conflict, it is necessary for restorative justice to try to retrain us and discipline us according to the restorative standard. This may be less difficult for some individuals who have been socialized in accordance with spiritual or familial beliefs that stress cooperation over competition. But for others, restorative retraining will require a great deal of work. This may be especially true for some offenders who have learned to use violence as their reflex response to conflict.

Two notions drawn from the work of Michel Foucault can help us better understand the ways in which restorative justice seeks to retrain individuals and to fashion new subjects, in turn helping us to identify the ways in which the politics of restorative justice allows it to operate as a mode of governance, as a way to control people. These notions are "techniques of discipline" and "technologies of the self." Techniques of discipline are used to produce normality by creating normal individuals who are controlled rather than coerced in the sense that their behaviour is regulated by multiple techniques (such as time tables and traffic signals). For example, restorative justice practitioners educate participants in how to conduct themselves through the cues and interventions they use to remind participants of how they should be communicating. Through repetition of these actions, participants are drilled to become restorative rather than combative communicators. Through a great deal of preparation and frequent reminders, participants become disciplined to norms of effective listening and interest-based negotiation. Similarly, communities can play a role in disciplining their members to abide by a "harmony ideology" (Nader 1990) through which victims and offenders are coercively pressured to emulate passive, conciliatory behaviours, no matter how righteous their conflict(s) might be (see also Napoleon 2004 and Acorn 2004).

In contrast, technologies of the self rely on individuals' own self-regulation as they come to internalize societal controls and play an active role in monitoring their own conduct and being responsible for their activities (Burchell 1993; Pavlich 1996a). In Foucault's (1994: 225) words, technologies of the self

> permit individuals to effect by their own means, or with the help of others, a certain number of operations on their own bodies and souls, thoughts, conduct, and way of being, so as to transform themselves in order to attain a certain state of happiness, purity, wisdom, perfection or immortality.

This may be achieved through strategies that encourage individuals to accept responsibility for their own governance and to accept rationalities of self-governance as natural and unquestionable. Certain self-help programs, Alcoholics Anonymous or anger management programs for example, ask participants to police their own behaviour so they can halt practices of drinking and emotional displays that are perceived to be socially unacceptable. Likewise, restorative justice asks participants to become vigilant evaluators of the ways in which they approach conflicts so they might learn to walk the talk of restorative justice in their day-to-day lives.

This soft coercion employed by restorative justice practitioners may or may not seem problematic upon first glance, depending on your opinions on social control. It does, however, counter claims made by some advocates that restorative justice is "non-coercive" (Van Ness and Strong 2002). Moreover, it is necessary that we interrogate what sort of politics are at work when techniques of discipline and technologies of the self are put into practice. For example, some advocates have claimed that one of the strengths of restorative justice is that it is apolitical and can appeal to liberals and conservatives alike (Van Ness and Strong 2002).

In part, the adaptability of restorative justice to conservative and liberal contexts has to do with the vision restorative justice holds of the ideal citizen. In imparting its communicative techniques, restorative justice works to create individual citizens who are non-combative and peaceable resolvers of conflict. Such individuals are obviously appealing to governments that would like to have a passive citizenry more apt to engage in talk than to protest and undertake acts of civil disobedience. As such, restorative justice must not dogmatically seek to produce non-conflictive individuals. Indeed, there are times and places when restorative justice may feel it necessary to support combative relations, and it is only in ideal circumstances that cooperative communication should win out.

This conceptualization of the potential for governance to be administered through restorative justice should test any faith we had in the restorative justice encounter being a good thing in and of itself. The restorative encounter provides opportunities for empowerment and creative resolution, but it does not guarantee these or other desired outcomes of restorative justice (Johnstone and Van Ness 2007). Indeed, restorative justice can also be a venue for the renewal and strengthening of dominant power relations, using restorative techniques of discipline and technologies of the self to fashion a population ready-made to be ruled. Or, it can be used as a soft justice option for middle- and upper-class youth, while the resources of retributive justice are preserved for "risky" lower-class and minority youth. Both tendencies are examples of the potential for political manipulation of the practices of restorative justice. These are not inevitable outcomes of the use of restorative justice, but neither is the empowerment practitioners and theorists hold dear.

Our analysis of immediate context of restorative justice, its organizational styles, facilitative practices, and methods of evaluation, should make evident that restorative justice practices offer no certain protection against their political misuse. This fact becomes more worrisome when we look, as in the following chapter, more directly at the various participants in restorative justice, and the way in which their identities are shaped by the process — in some cases exhibiting a movement toward regulating rather than empowering these actors.

QUESTIONS FOR DISCUSSION

1. How would you evaluate a restorative justice program if you were using the ethos described in Chapter 1 as your starting point?
2. Should reduced recidivism be an indicator of restorative justice working?
3. How might the many political aspects of restorative justice change or disrupt Harris et al.'s ideal-typical scenario (pg. 110)?

5

CONSTRUCTING RESTORATIVE JUSTICE IDENTITIES

Who is involved in restorative justice? In Chapter 1, we described the various groups and actors that participate within the broader restorative justice social movement. But what of those who are present within actual restorative justice encounters or meetings: victims, offenders, facilitators, and community members? George Pavlich (2005) has demonstrated that these are all problematic identities in that they are, in part, socially constituted through the discourses of restorative justice. Put simply, none of these actors — victim, offender, facilitator, or community member — exists in a natural sense. This is not to say people are not harmed, that people do not commit harms, that individuals do not help to mediate these conflicts, or that these harms do not take place within specific social and geographic spaces. Rather, it is a reminder that the meanings we attach to the labels of victim, offender, facilitator, and community are socially constructed, built through social relations. Everyday life is often incredibly complex, with each situation allowing for discernment of a plurality of harms and wrongs. In making sense of these situations, social actors draw upon condensed narratives to marshal complex facts and to make difficult situations both understandable and actionable. Thus, the sense made of a criminal event is an interpretation that also plays a role in fashioning the identities of the actors involved in the event.

For example, it would appear on the surface that homicides would serve as relatively simple cases of the identities of the parties involved. Let's say a young person kills a parent after a heated argument (since most homicides are committed by someone known to the victim, this seems an appropriate example). Here, we have a seemingly clear-cut instance where the youth is the offender (or, at this stage, the accused) and the parent is the victim. The facilitator may be an individual called upon to conduct a post-sentencing mediation between the grieving spouse and their child, and the community is the neighbourhood in which the crime occurred. However, in assigning these identities, we have made several assumptions. First, we have treated the homicide as an isolated incident outside of a larger series of incidents — that is, all the events that came before and led up to the murder. If, in this case, the youth was subject to repeated abuse at the hands of the parent, their role as offender is complicated by their past victimization, and they are both victim and offender (a combination more frequent than the simplistic black-and-white media reporting of and political grandstanding around crime would suggest).

Second, we have assumed victimization begins and ends with the person who has experienced physical or material harm. However, as restorative justice proponents often remind us, there is, in fact, a wide circle of victims of this event, as the harm of crime ripples beyond the immediate stakeholders and the geographic space in which the crime occurred. The spouse is a victim, having lost their partner to homicide and child to prison. The community is victimized by the shock they feel that such a thing could occur in their seemingly safe neighbourhood, but there is a wider circle of suffering that may include the friends, uncles, aunts, cousins, and workmates of both the youth and victim/parent. Likewise, we also assume offending behaviour begins and ends with the actions of the youth, but what if the deceased person's spouse and the neighbours long turned a blind eye to the abuse the youth suffered? Are there degrees of responsibility that can be assessed and unpacked? Indeed, the example above is relatively straightforward with respect to responsibility in comparison to examples that involve family violence or violent assaults committed upon First Nations reserves. In such cases, the matrix of responsibility expands to include broader structural factors, such as patriarchy, race, class, and colonialism.

This brief discussion only scratches the surface of the assumptions that are at work when we try to make sense of traumatic situations through taken-for-granted criminal justice identities. The complexity of crime-based identity construction is more evident when we examine separately the identities of victim, perpetrator, facilitator, and community member. Each of these groups is fractured and inchoate. Identifying the processes by which they are given meaning allows for a critical understanding of crime-based identity construction. Doing so illustrates that the victim-offender dichotomy imported from the criminal justice system, for example, is a problematic basis on which to build restorative resolutions. Yet, restorative justice encounters have the potential to deconstruct these identities, showing that they are much more complicated than they seem. This is a task of great political import for restorative justice. Without such critical engagement, restorative justice is at risk of reproducing dominant criminal justice and political conditions (see Pavlich 2005).

VICTIMS

Restorative justice is often represented as a victim-centred approach to justice. This is because restorative justice does not marginalize the victim from the justice process while at the same time claiming to offer retribution on the victim's behalf. Instead, restorative justice recognizes the victim as a central stakeholder within the restorative process. It seeks to provide victims a prominent role in shaping the justice process and in deciding upon a just resolution to the conflict. The harm suffered by the victim and the needs of the victim in the aftermath of the criminal event are held to be of crucial importance. A restorative approach to crime requires an identification of victim needs, which may include the following:

1. Acknowledgment that the victim is blameless for the harm he or she suffered
2. Restitution of any stolen items
3. Monetary compensation for damaged or unrecoverable items or for hardship suffered as a result of the crime
4. Symbolic atonement in the form of an apology or statement of regret from the offender
5. A sense of safety and closure to assure the victim that he or she will not be similarly victimized by the offender again
6. An opportunity for the victim to voice his or her suffering
7. An opportunity to receive continued support from friends, community members, and/or counselors (adapted from Johnstone 2002: 64–67).

However, harm is not necessarily concentrated within a single individual or set of individuals. It can be broadly felt by all of those with some connection to the harmful event. As well, harmful events are not isolated instances and often rest in a larger series of harmful events. These are important points that are widely acknowledged within restorative justice, resulting in efforts to address the broader and rippling effects of criminal harm (see, for example,

Van Ness and Strong 2002). In contrast, there is an even more basic element of victimhood: its social and political construction.

Each of us is likely familiar with the difficulty experienced when trying to communicate a particularly painful experience. This frustration is perhaps most acute when we are very young and still learning the skills of language. A small bump or a minor disappointment can quickly cause us to unravel because of the exasperation felt when trying to express this hurt to our parent(s), who do not always fully understand our rudimentary language. These experiences continue even as we mature. Anyone who has experienced a major violation or loss has also experienced the challenge of trying to articulate this hurt and may have even felt quite upset at people who said too quickly or too easily, "Yes, I understand." This upset is caused by our sense that the person does not understand and cannot understand because the experience and our feelings about it are unique and cannot be reduced to simple words. In fact, we may not even fully understand the experience ourselves because it is associated with a confusing morass of sensations and memories.

In a similar way, the identity of victims is socially constituted through processes of verbal and symbolic communication. This means we require others to recognize our hurt so the label "victim" makes sense, otherwise we are completely alone in our victimhood, and it has no social relevance. Socially unrecognized victimhood can also result in one being deprived of (political) benefits and rights associated with this label. For instance, consider the period before various forms of family violence were fully recognized as public wrongs. Husbands and fathers were assumed to rule over their households, and therefore women and children who were subject to "moderate correction" at the hands of husbands/fathers were not considered victims of injustice, but rather the subjects of a legitimate form of control (see Box 5.1). These sufferers therefore faced an uncertain legal context with respect to what would and what would not be considered violence. In such situations, the power of the state to define who is and is not a victim often results in a competition among social actors to have their experiences of victimization officially recognized, as can be noted in mid- to late-twentieth-century feminist efforts to have courts take seriously the harms of domestic and family violence.

A stark example of the struggle over victim identities can be found in the case of Aubrey and Gus Lamm. When Randy Reeves killed Janet Mesner and her friend Vicki Zessin, Vicki's husband, Gus Lamm, and their daughter, two-year-old Aubrey, were left without a partner and mother. But eighteen

Box 5.1 William Blackstone on the Legal Rights of Husbands and Wives

By marriage, the husband and wife are one person in law: that is, the very being or legal existence of the woman is suspended during the marriage, or at least is incorporated and consolidated into that of the husband; under whose wing, protection, and *cover*, she performs every thing; and is therefore called in our law-French a *feme-covert, foemina viro co-operta*; is said to be *covert-baron*, or under the protection and influence of her husband, her *baron*, or lord; and her condition during her marriage is called her *coverture*. Upon this principle, of a union of person in husband and wife, depend almost all the legal rights, duties, and disabilities, that either of them acquire by the marriage. I speak not at present of the rights of property, but of such as are merely *personal*. For this reason, a man cannot grant anything to his wife, or enter into covenant with her: for the grant would be to suppose her separate existence; and to covenant with her, would be only to covenant with himself: and therefore it is also generally true, that all compacts made between husband and wife, when single, are voided by the intermarriage ...

The husband also, by the old law, <u>might give his wife moderate correction</u>. For, as he is to answer for her misbehaviour, the law thought it reasonable to intrust him with this power of restraining her, by domestic chastisement, in the same moderation that a man is allowed to correct his apprentices or children; for whom the master or parent is also liable in some cases to answer. But this power of correction was confined within reasonable bounds, and the husband was prohibited from using any violence to his wife ...

These are the chief legal effects of marriage during the coverture; upon which we may observe, that even the disabilities which the wife lies under are for the most part intended for her protection and benefit: so great a favourite is the female sex of the laws of England.

Source: Blackstone 1765: 442–445.

years later, when the Nebraska Board of Pardons was considering commuting Reeves' sentence, Aubrey and Gus were denied the opportunity to speak on his behalf, as well as to voice their views against the death penalty he had been served. Why? Upon a District Court Appeal of their exclusion, Aubrey and Gus were informed they were agents of Randy Reeves and not victims, since they advocated for mercy rather than retribution. In contrast, Vicki's sister, who supported the death penalty, was permitted to make a presentation before the Board of Pardons and was therefore officially acknowledged as a victim (Kay 2006; Acker 2006). This is a clear case of the state only allowing for a certain type of victimhood — a type supportive of punitive policies — and therefore playing a role in constituting what and who may be a victim.

It is, however, not just recognition by the state that is crucial to establishing a victim identity. We also seek social recognition so our friends and neighbours understand us as innocent sufferers undeserving of the harm we experienced, for victimization often carries with it an unfair stigma, as victim blaming is unfortunately too common in our society. In part, this is a protective mechanism we use to assure ourselves of our own security and to preserve our sense of existential certainty. To say, "They were harmed because they weren't careful," or "They were harmed because they associated with the wrong people," or "Look at the way they dressed," is also to say that such events are unlikely to befall us because we are not like the persons harmed. In this manner, victim claims to harm are made within a personal and emotional political context. This requires victims to articulate and fashion themselves as particular types of victims (for example, innocent and undeserving) so that they might gain broader public support. Christie (1986) refers to this victim identity as the "ideal victim," which he contrasts to those who are perceived to be deserving of harm because of their lifestyle.

To combat these tendencies, victims will often mobilize stories to communicate their hurt and to provide other people a sense of their experience, no matter how confusing and incommunicable this experience may seem. In order to establish their innocence and to socially proclaim victimhood, harmed individuals will often simplify their pain into an understandable narrative that engages their intended audience. In so doing, they will often draw upon culturally resonant tropes that highlight the theme of innocence: "There I was minding my own business ..."; "Unexpectedly ..."; or "To my surprise ...." Each such statement seeks to communicate that the victim is worthy and deserving of our empathy and support. Other statements might be used to illustrate that victims are good people who have been done wrong: "I had never imagined that anyone could be so cruel …"; "His actions caught me completely off guard …"; or "I had trusted him …." These examples are not to suggest that they do not contain a kernel of truth when they are used by people who have suffered harm. Instead, they show there are standard communicative tools available upon which victims can draw in their attempts to convince others of the legitimacy of their victimization claims.

The difficulty of communicating extreme harm is perhaps best illustrated through consideration of the Holocaust, and the intense challenges faced by memoirists and others trying to pass along to a contemporary audience their incredibly horrific experiences (see, for example, Levi 1989; Delbo 1995; Wiesel 2006). Even to speak of the Holocaust requires an act of historical construction, since the Holocaust is comprised of a vast range of events. Although the primary image we carry of the Holocaust is of the death camps, such as Auschwitz-Birkenau, where more than one million victims were sent to the gas chambers and their corpses burned within crematoriums, this is but one space of trauma in the broader Holocaust experience. The Holocaust was also comprised of forced deportations, state-imposed famine, slave labour, ghettoization, village massacres, sexual exploitation, rampant disease spread, and scientific and medical experimentation, to name but a few gross violations. In its totality, or even in but a fraction of its cruelty, the Holocaust is too much for one mind to process. However, people can gain some insight into its horrors through the narrativization of this complex experience. This is why generations of school children have been given *The Diary of a Young Girl* (Frank 1995 [1947]) as a first text on the Holocaust. Anne Frank's story provides an account of the everyday harms contained within an individual experience of the Holocaust, and therefore offers a point of connection in what is otherwise a seemingly incomprehensible period of mass suffering. It was also the case that many Germans first connected with the mass suffering of the Holocaust through viewing a 1978 American-made mini-series (titled *Holocaust*), which told the story of several families living through World War II and the Nazi-perpetrated atrocities (see Novick 1999; Cole 1999; Herf 1997). Such renderings of the Holocaust story ultimately receive criticism for being partial, but resonant narratives of the Holocaust can rarely tell more than a part of the story.

The key point here is that harm must be translated into a story to make it meaningful for others (see Alexander 2004). So, from the outset, an act of social construction is taking place in relation to the identity of the victim: the harmed individual(s) is being represented to an audience as someone worthy of their concern, and this requires that a comprehensible story be told about this harm. In addition, the construction of a socially recognized victim identity has further implications. Claims to victimization are mobilized for a variety of political purposes: to build support for harsher criminal justice policies; to encourage more resources for those harmed by crime; or to reaffirm shared social norms.

Historically speaking, it is important to remember our society did not always embrace the victim identity in the way that we do today. For years, people eschewed the label "victim," associating the term with weakness and powerlessness (Garland 2001). The victim identity emerged as a key nodal point for political mobilization in the midst of World War II. During this period, as noted in Chapter 4, Jewish organizations worldwide became aware of the atrocities being committed by the Nazis in Europe. As the Allies discussed what their post-War policy might be toward the Germans, these organizations lobbied for the restitution of stolen Jewish property and compensation for Jewish individuals and organizations. These organizations convinced the Allies — the Americans in particular — that the Nazi plundering of Jewish wealth, as well as the hardships faced by Jewish organizations seeking to resettle the refugees from Nazi slaughter, deserved post-War attention. Their efforts led to a novel reparations program through which money was paid by the defeated nation not to the victors of war, but rather to its victims and survivors (see Sagi 1980; Sebba 1980; Pross 1998; Goschler 1991; Kim 1999; Zweig 1987; Woolford and Wolejszo 2006). This period still represented a hesitant embrace of the victim identity, and individuals were less likely to broadcast their victimhood than they are today.

Identity movements in the late 1960s and early 1970s opened a new stage in the valuation of the victim identity. This was a period in which social activism was guided less by one's (class) position in the economic system (or relations of production) and more by forms of cultural identification. Marginalized groups more and more viewed their suffering and social dissatisfaction as a result not of their class position, but rather as a result of patriarchy, sexism, heterosexism, racism, and ethnocentrism, to name but a few. Identities based upon race, ethnicity, sexuality, and other cultural markers became increasingly prominent. Indeed, it was as an offshoot of the women's movement that the victim's movement began to gain its greatest ground. Feminist activists decried the lack of support offered to women who had been abused by their partners and loved ones and sought to increase services for, and advocacy on behalf of, abused women. The effort to establish shelters is one example of an emergent movement to recognize the needs of victims, not to mention to have females abused by their male partners recognized as victims. Moreover, an increased political voice for victims was found, as traumatic stories of violence and wrongdoing were drawn upon to illustrate the continuing power of patriarchy in society (Goodhand 2017).

Soon thereafter victims of other crimes began to organize to press government and society to more fully recognize their suffering and attend to their needs. This was a slow process that has, in recent years, produced victories in the form of the adoption of bills of victims' rights in many jurisdictions and the increased use of victim impact statements (Achilles and Stutzman-Amstutz 2006). Policies are also being created to ensure restitution and compensation made by offenders go to crime victims rather than the state. While these advances are certainly significant, most victims' groups would agree still more needs to be done. For example, the Manitoba Victims' Bill of Rights and provincial policy on victim impact statements are both restricted to those who are harmed by only the most serious crimes, which in this case means crimes of violence.

The creation of victim narratives to communicate complex victim experiences and the mobilization of victims as political actors does not, however, mean victims retain full control over the symbolism of victimhood. Nearly every day in the media and in the halls of government, the victim identity is drawn upon to relay some pressing matter. A heart-wrenching story of victimization may be employed by a journalist to show how cold and unfeeling contemporary society has become, or politicians may use a story of a needless death to suggest more needs to be done to fight crime. In short, once a group has successfully mobilized and achieved resonance (and even repair) through its trauma narrative, it is often the case that this narrative itself becomes an object or resource for personal and political application and manipulation. That is, the stories of suffering employed by the victims to forward their cause also become resources for other claims makers (both powerful and powerless) to use, and potentially misuse, for their own purposes.

This is a key point for understanding the reservations expressed by critical victimologists toward conservative victimology (see Miers 1989; Fattah 1992; Elias 1986; Walkate 1989), which advocates for increases in victim rights that do not challenge the assumptions about crime and punishment that dominate the criminal justice system. Conservative victim research takes for granted

state ICJS defined terms

state-defined notions of crime and victimhood, and state-sponsored means of criminal punishment. This allows for the co-optation of victim narratives by conservatives to promote retribution, since the trauma narrative becomes neatly embedded within the "common sense" of criminal justice and control (Garland 2001). Simply put, the only victims considered worthy of consideration are those harmed by street crime rather than state or corporate crime, and their post-victimization needs are viewed as synonymous with state punishment. This is not to deny that some victims may demand punitive and vengeful responses to their trauma, and their trauma narrative may be designed to elicit these sorts of responses, but victim movements are not unified and do not speak with one voice. For each victim, in fact, there may be multiple and competing trauma narratives about their suffering; however, certain narratives achieve broader resonance because they are consistent with or complementary to existing social and discursive conditions. Thus, a conservative and punitive victim image may provide greater resonance for those narratives that fit the overarching themes of conservative morality — such as vengeance and individual responsibility.

social construction around which crimes make you a victim

Alcoff and Gray (1993) note how survivor narratives can be subsumed by dominant discourses and retold in a manner non-threatening to the status quo; that is, suffering is negotiated between people but not in an equal way. They cite examples in which rape victims who make their stories public often face questions or statements (whether in a family, legal, or therapeutic context) that direct attention away from male responsibility for the acts toward gendered assumptions reflective of the patriarchal social order. Thus, in courtroom questioning, emphasis is placed on the emotional or allegedly hysteric nature of the survivor in that she was held to be in a fragile state of mind that left her susceptible to assault. The gendered order was also preserved by highlighting her passivity — she was vulnerable because she was without a male companion. The expectations of appropriate gender performativity were on striking display in the testimony of Christine Blasey Ford, when she came forward to accuse then-US Supreme Court nominee, Brett Kavanaugh, of raping her when they were teens. In addition to being required to dress in a professional manner and present herself as a reliable victim, *Guardian* columnist Emma Brockes (2018) recounts another conundrum Blasey Ford faced:

> Less talked about, perhaps, is the necessary editing down of the details of abuse. Christine Blasey Ford's ordeal was considered by some too trivial to matter, but there are dangers at the other end of the scale

too. An audience may sympathise with a victim up to a point, beyond which, rather than eliciting empathy, she risks triggering revulsion, or horror, with her account of what happened to her effectively placing her outside the reach of imagined experience.

In other cases, victim narratives might be useful tools for governments that want to encourage public fear as a way to drum up support for increased government controls (Walklate 2006). Certainly, in the aftermath of 9/11, we witnessed a Republican US administration that drew on the horrors of this event whenever its foreign policy decisions were called into question. In sum, the problem is one whereby trauma narratives can be used to empower the state or other already powerful actors and to reinforce structures of inequality rather than to empower victims.

This process creating narratives about a harmful experience is one that also feeds back into subsequent narratives of harmful events. The political use of victim narratives will often affect the way in which victim narratives of harm are subsequently created, such as when victims draw upon a "law and order" rhetoric to express their frustration with the criminal justice they have experienced and the lack of an adequate societal response.

So, what does this all mean for restorative justice? In its efforts to be victim-centred, restorative justice immediately enters into a field of competition over victim identity, and restorative justice practitioners must be aware of this and tread carefully. For example, restorative justice attempts to define more subtle notions of victimhood that allow for recognition of multiple levels of victimization (including the offender's suffering) that could potentially go awry in a political realm where "victim" and "offender" are assumed to be discreet and easily identified. Under these conditions, any mention of the past sufferings of the offender can be perceived as offender-centric and insensitive to the "true" victim. Yet it is by having participants in a restorative justice encounter consider each other's experiences and needs that practitioners seek to have them build mutual empathy. It is a tricky balance to ignore the wrongdoer's past experiences of victimization (such as family violence or living under the care of child and family services) without appearing to minimize the immediate suffering of the person wronged.

Some research has shown that restorative justice has failed to resist more dominant ways of imagining victims, instead reproducing dominant features. Maglione's (2017) analysis of restorative justice discourse found that the "ideal victim" is assumed to be emotional, disempowered, vulnerable, and a clearly distinct person from the offender. This can be problematic for two reasons: it may reinforce criminal justice images of the victim and limit restorative justice's capacity to offer new identities, and it may also restrict the restorative experience for people who have been harmed that do not fit these ideals. A victim who still feels in control, is not overly emotional, and who recognizes their own contributions to the harm may be found unsuitable for restorative justice or find facilitators pushing back on their narratives. It may be the case that the language of victim and offender is too corrupted by its frequent application in formal criminal justice systems that restorative justice must strike out and find a new language.

In fact, some restorative justice theorists and practitioners have done just that, referring to participants as "clients" or "agents." However, such refinements come with their own ideological baggage. The term "client," for example, suggests a consumer of justice services, who shops for an appropriate justice response. This fits all too snugly with a neoliberal definition of citizenship around consumerism and entrepreneurism. In the neoliberal ideal, the balance between citizen rights and responsibilities is shifted toward a notion of citizen responsibility, where the citizen is empowered to make choices, but these choices are circumscribed by an economic rationality and therefore not wholly free (Rose 1996, 1999). Thus, whatever gains are achieved by using the term client, such as an emphasis on individual choice and agency, are undone by the association of this term with an overly economistic model of choice.

It may well be that any alternative terminology is likely to be saddled with some ideological residue. Criminal harm is highly politicized, and there is no fully neutral wording that can take us beyond its reach. What may be more important, as we continue to grasp at terms and categorizations that allow us to narrativize harm, is that we do as Derrida recommends (see Chapter 3) and keep these calculations of justice open to deconstructive criticism and revision. This means reflecting upon the ways in which we imagine the victim: do we construct this person as an ideal victim? Do we exclude some members of our community from assuming the victim status? What are the political expectations and assumptions in our use of the term victim? In part, an adequate response to victim claims, as well as claims of a public or state failure to recognize victimhood, requires that we understand the victim identity as the result of social, legal, and political processes, and not as simply a by-product of the criminal or harmful act. Only through such a detailed approach can we understand the oftentimes arbitrary decisions that result in the elevation of certain victims, and certain types of victimhood, over others.

OFFENDERS

As can be seen above, the victim is a heavily politicized figure. But what about offenders? They are certainly politicized in our culture. A glance at most newspapers and news telecasts quickly confirms that few subjects cause more anxiety and consternation than offenders. For example, the issue of automobile theft in Winnipeg has long been a matter of great public concern. With Winnipeg ranked year after year as among the cities with the highest rates of automobile theft, people are legitimately fearful of having their cars stolen or damaged in the attempt. However, public panic reached a high pitch when stories appeared about deadly police car chases, stolen cars being sent unoccupied to crash into buildings, and car thieves terrorizing (and even hitting) joggers during their joyriding escapades. This perception of heightened danger combined with increased frustration as information came forward to suggest that a small group of young people were the perpetrators of a large percentage of Winnipeg automobile thefts and that, even when apprehended, these youths rarely spent more than a short time within correctional institutions. This resulted in opposition criticism of the formerly governing Manitoba NDP for their "catch and release" policies. The inability of the government to properly punish these young offenders was viewed by critics as evidence of their "soft on crime" policies.

In this example, young offenders guilty of automobile theft become a political football to be kicked around. In response to critics during legislative debate, the former NDP Minister of Justice would often cite the successes of NDP programs for dealing with automobile theft, and counter that the problem grew under the previous Tory government, leaving a huge problem with which the NDP had to contend. During such debates, however, the young automobile thief quickly disappears and, after some initial discussion of their home situations, or whether or not they suffer from Fetal Alcohol Spectrum Disorder, we hear little more about the broader motivations of these individuals. Why is it that they are attracted to automobile theft? Why has a culture of automobile theft become prominent in Winnipeg? What are the social and economic conditions of these young people? The offender is reduced to a simple mask of dangerousness and presented as someone who has little substance to their character, other than the fact that they are out to cause public harm and mischief. The young offender thus becomes a "risky" subject, someone to be managed and administered to rather than reformed and rehabilitated. Indeed, some young people need not even commit crimes to be considered "at risk," as they may possess specific qualities or characteristics, such as having attention deficit disorder or coming from a so-called broken family, that lead them to be considered "at risk" and therefore more likely than others to commit crimes (Hudson 2003; Hannah-Moffet and Shaw 2001). In this sense, they are criminalized because of who they are rather than actual criminal activities.

Thus, while victims' groups have at times succeeded in constructing resonant narratives to communicate their experiences, offenders and their advocates have had a tougher time reworking their image. In the reigning philosophy of liberal individualism that conditions much of our political thinking, offenders are viewed solely as individuals who have made poor choices and are lacking in moral character. Therefore, they must be held individually accountable for their actions. While our justice system admits more detailed information about the offender's background for consideration during sentencing, the court of public opinion does not necessarily go so far, as the public is often more content to view the offender as a dangerous Other with no real connection to the regular world. Such a rationale makes it much easier to support policies of exclusion and imprisonment, since these actions provide a sense of comfort that the source of harm — the offender — has been removed from community life.

Offender advocate groups have long wrestled with such views of offenders. For them, the societal response to offenders is often nothing short of paradoxical. The public fears and is encouraged to fear offenders. We come across a significant number of people who want nothing more than to see offenders placed in correctional institutions for as long as the law will allow. Yet, inadequate emphasis is placed on correction within such institutions, and offenders are released back into the community, more embittered, with more criminal contacts, and with fewer prospects for gainful employment and positive relationships. The system of punishment we desire, which is alleged to make us safer, in fact often makes us less safe. Indeed, the situation of offenders goes beyond the warnings of labelling theory (see Chapter 3). Recall that according to labelling theory, an individual who commits a primary act of deviance has not yet invested in a criminal identity. However, the criminal justice process can encourage them to make the transition from primary to secondary deviance — a stage at which criminal becomes their "master status" or primary form of identification. Correctional institutions can also contribute to a process of prisonization or institutionalization, whereby the offender's behaviour becomes shaped by the institution, making it very difficult for them to re-adapt to society upon release. They become accustomed to the schedules, sociability, and patterns of prison life, and find it very hard to resume a law-abiding life in the community. These problems are exacerbated by the difficulties offenders face on account of public stigmatization. Their status as offenders makes it very challenging to establish or re-establish non-criminal contacts, to secure gainful employment, or to find a positive living situation, away from the influences that might have contributed to their previous criminal behaviour (such as drugs and alcohol). This process has, in some cases, become more severe in contemporary prisons, where a programming vacuum has left inmates more susceptible to forces such as gang recruitment and drug addiction within prison walls. For those already stigmatized by the criminal justice process, gangs provide, in addition to immediate protection from other gang-affiliated prisoners, a seductive source of identification, providing a prisoner with a similarly situated cohort who will positively value the forms of capital (or wealth) the prisoner possesses in great abundance. That is to say, they can achieve status for their daring, for their toughness, and for the audacity of their criminal acts.

This pattern of revaluation of the criminal identity among gang members and other outcasts has long been the topic of great discussion among criminologists (see, for example, Cohen 1965) and is a persistent criminological phenomenon. However, it is important to recognize that at the root of this process of revaluation is a contest over the power to name and categorize in our society. Critical criminologists have often noted the "power to criminalize" (Comack and Balfour 2004) is unevenly distributed. In this view, law is not the natural and unproblematic reflection of our shared beliefs but, rather, the political creation of powerful actors. This is not to suggest we do not all, on some level, agree with many laws. We have been deeply socialized to hold dear the norms that are codified within our legal systems. Rather, laws, and our socialization into the normative system upon which they are based, are influenced by the values of dominant groups within our society. These values become so widespread, so second nature, that certain ways of seeing and knowing the world appear commonsense and almost unquestionable (Gramsci 1971). Thus, the fact that law reflects the interests of dominant groups is not so much a matter of individuals from these groups conspiring to create laws in their interests (although there are certainly historical instances of this), but more often a matter of law being made on the basis of certain assumptions about the world, or an orientation to the world, that is already tinged by power.

We see such biases at work in attempts at criminalization — the processes through which certain individuals are categorized as criminals while others are not. Consider for a moment who in your life you would brand as a criminal and who you would not. Do you know anyone who illegally downloads music or movies from the Internet? Do you know any casual users of drugs other than marijuana? Are these individuals who break the law criminals? If not, why? Is it because they have not been caught or sent to a correctional institution? Such questions begin to reveal the fact that the label of "criminal" or "offender" is not as clear-cut as we may like to believe. We are surrounded in our day-to-day lives by a whole cast of tax evaders, petty thieves, perpetrators of violence and other harms, who we do not brand criminal. In part, what appears to be at work here is that certain people are more able to resist the label than others. For the most powerful, the law often defines the harms they cause in other terms, such as regulatory offences. So, despite the fact we have seen some high-profile, white-collar offenders taken to task in recent years (such as global engineering firm SNC-Lavalin and their lobbying efforts to change the Criminal Code so that their bribes to and defrauding of Libyan organizations would not result in a ten-year ban on federal government contracts), these likely only represent the tip of the iceberg of such offences, some of which are still unrecognized as crimes (such as misleading advertising), or skillfully hid through offshore holdings, jurisdiction shopping, or through their diffusion within the practices of a large corporation. Others are able to use the resources at their disposal to spread the idea that their actions were accidental. Take, for instance, the way in which Michael McCain, CEO of Maple Leaf Foods, was able to present himself and his company after meat from his plants caused a listeriosis outbreak and the deaths of multiple Canadians in 2008. McCain is drawn as either a competent crisis manager or a sensitive human being (depending on one's perspective) rather than as someone potentially criminally liable for harming consumers — or as someone whose company helped lobby the federal government for greater privatization and deregulation of food inspection. McCain possesses the wealth, the language skills, and the socialization required to represent himself as a responsible person of integrity, and factors such as these make all the difference when it comes to resisting criminalization.

Even our friends and family often possess the resources needed to resist criminalization. We have access to exculpatory discourses that allow us to

Box 5.2 The Testing of Michael McCain

At the helm of Maple Leaf Foods, the golden boy of a great Canadian business family faces the ultimate public relations nightmare: Your products are killing

On Saturday, Aug. 23, the head-office lobby of Maple Leaf Foods in midtown Toronto should have been quiet — it was, after all, the middle of a sleepy summer weekend. Instead, the air was electric, the scene tumultuous. Maple Leaf, Canada's largest meat company, was facing the most serious crisis of its 100-year-plus history. It had been confirmed: Packaged meat from its Toronto plant was killing people.

It was the nightmare scenario for any consumer-products company. Maple Leaf's crisis plan was duly put into play. A camera crew was dispatched to the office lobby, where president and CEO Michael McCain, tall, lean and attired in an open-neck blue shirt with a white undershirt, taped a televised statement.

After announcing that he had closed down the plant and ordered a recall of its products, a grim-looking McCain apologized and expressed his sympathy for the victims of the nationwide listeriosis outbreak. He followed up with a press conference the next day. "Going through the crisis, there are two advisers I've paid no attention to," he told reporters. "The first are the lawyers, and the second are the accountants. It's not about money or legal liability — this is about our being accountable for providing consumers with safe food."

McCain's appearances and statements seemed perfectly natural to the public. To crisis management experts, they appeared to be expertly crafted. The contrite message resonated so strongly in public opinion that even as the number of deaths caused by listeriosis mounted and the entire Canadian food safety system came under attack, McCain seemed insulated by his statement that "the buck stops here." His sad, sober visage became standard fare on the evening news, on YouTube and in newspaper photos. He emerged as the human face of a company that cared about its customers.

Yet, when I met McCain in the fall, he made it clear he did not want to talk about himself, only about "the team." He refused to even call what he had done "crisis management." It was simply doing what was right; and doing what was right came directly from the company's ingrained values. "This is not about some contrived strategy," McCain said. "It's just about a tragic situation and an organization's desire to make it right." He insisted he could not even remember who had written the compelling words in the public statements — although Maple Leaf insiders say that the CEO's hand was in every deed and every word. "The core principle here was to first do what's in the interest of public health, and second to be open and transparent in taking accountability," McCain told me. "For the team, this was almost not a decision — it was obvious. It's just what we are."

… Maple Leaf experience one of those improbable, seemingly random events that start out on the edges of consciousness and suddenly threaten the existence of an organization. On Aug. 7, 2008, one of its distributors told Maple Leaf that a public health inquiry into some Maple Leaf brand meat products was in the works. Five days later, the Canadian Food Inspection Agency informed Maple Leaf that it had launched a formal investigation into three products from its Toronto meat plant. As the CFIA investigation got under way, Maple Leaf told its distributors to segregate the affected food. This was standard practice, and the news did not travel to the chief executive suite.

But McCain became entirely involved at about 10:30 on the evening of Saturday, Aug. 16, when he received a call at his cottage north of Toronto: The CFIA had confirmed the presence of listeria monocytogenes in two of its sliced meat products. Immediately, the identified product lines were recalled, and a press release to that effect was issued.

The following Tuesday, McCain was informed that the investigation had found more positive tests. Thus, the recall was widened. At that point, McCain says, "we didn't know what the nature of that investigation was, other than a) there was illness involved; b) there was possible death involved, a loss of life; and c) there was a possibility of a linkage to one of these items we had recalled."

Then came that fateful day of Aug. 23, when the possibility turned into reality. DNA linkage was established between some of the affected individuals and the two products. Maple Leaf launched a recall of 191 products, closed down the Toronto plant, unleashed its mass communication campaign and made its CEO accessible to the media.

Ken Wong, a marketing professor at Queen's University's school of business, admired McCain's public-service ad because it had the look of amateurishness. "The text was dull and dry," Wong wrote in a commentary. "McCain was clearly reading off a teleprompter, and his unpolished appearance gave every indication of being tired and weary. I don't know if it was intended, but the ultimate message was, 'We're concerned and this is not about advertising.' Interestingly, a non-ad was exactly what was needed to be the best ad."

The TV spot felt artless and genuine, right from the declaration of culpability to the un-slick presence of Michael McCain in his open-collar shirt. Yet Maple Leaf officials insist there was no premeditated attempt to make it look "real." "We never had the time to overthink anything," says Linda Smith, a communications consultant who has worked with the company for a dozen years. "We weren't that smart, believe me."

All of which is applauded by Christine Pearson, a crisis management specialist at Thunderbird School of Global Management in Phoenix. She says Maple Leaf's apology and accountability were up to the standards of the best reputation management she has ever seen, including Johnson & Johnson's response to the Tylenol tampering that killed seven people in the Chicago area in 1982. In Maple Leaf's case, "the communications piece seemed to me to be high-end boilerplate. He was doing all the right things — it was really good," says Pearson, who has taught at the Ivey School.

… McCain adds that brands and companies hit by product safety crises can come back stronger than ever before (Tylenol is a case in point). But it will not be easy, he admits. "It's like a golf game where you have one shot down the fairway and it's got to be right in the middle." Yet there is little comfort in the Tylenol example, because the manufacturer Johnson & Johnson was able to portray itself as having been as much the victim of the tampering as were the consumers. Johnson & Johnson could claim the deaths were not its fault — they were the product of sabotage. With Maple Leaf, the problem lay in its internal processes — in bacteria trapped in slicing machines — not an outside agent. It could not cloak itself as a victim.

... Now, Maple Leaf must move beyond communication tactics to a crisis-management strategy that sets people's minds at ease about eating its products. It started by announcing a program of continuous improvement in food safety. This includes establishing a food safety advisory council, made up of experts from around the world, and the creation of a new executive position, chief food safety officer (Randy Huffman, president of the American Meat Institute, was named to the position in November). And the company vows to work with government and other companies to enhance food safety across the entire industry.

... In a way, McCain is underlining his own dilemma. When he launched the product recall on Aug. 23, and put the full blame on himself, he was doing what was right for consumers, but also what was right for the brand. Whether it was the result of carefully organized strategy or just good instincts, it was textbook reputation management. Bob Kingston, the union leader, sees nothing heroic in Maple Leaf's performance — if McCain had not ordered a voluntary recall, he would have faced a mandatory recall by the food agency, Kingston points out. In that case, McCain could not have taken the high road and portrayed himself as a good corporate citizen. In Kingston's eyes, what was done was motivated by necessity, not altruism.

So McCain can't really win. The crisis management experts describe his action as "a textbook case" and "boiler-plate crisis management." It is faint praise, for it sounds like he is following a proven formula instead of acting from the heart. Yet surely he cannot be faulted for doing what was right to protect his company. In effect, the Maple Leaf case confirms what corporate reputation consultants say: Doing good is good business. Taking responsibility for a corporate failure is particularly laudable in an age when corporate executives shun accountability. You have only to look at the financial system, which was brought to its knees by executives driven by greed and heedless of the need to manage their organizations' risk. While McCain said his primary duty is to protect consumers, in truth, a CEO also has to consider the interests of employees and shareholders. He has certainly fought for the 300 jobs at his Toronto plant. As for the stock, it was battered down below $8 in late October, from $11 in early August, but

> it would have taken a bigger hit — particularly in the market meltdown — if he had not been so effective a communicator.
>
> For McCain, 2008 is the *annus horribilis*, a year when everything conspired against him. "It is certainly going to go down in my history book as one of the most difficult years ever," he says, "largely as a result of what I would call the compounding of obstacles."
>
> But he will be judged as much by what happens over the next few years as by the crisis of the past few months. Apart from class-action lawsuits, the tainted-meat crisis will spark investigations and calls for tighter regulation. (The CFIA proposed new testing standards in early November.) And the restructuring still faces challenges. It will be hard, at times, for McCain to manage his image — and his composure.
>
> Source: Pitts 2008/18. Reprinted with permission of *The Globe and Mail*.

explain away or rationalize our actions — "techniques of neutralization" (Sykes and Matza 1957). Techniques of neutralization are meaning frameworks designed to alleviate guilt and blame within a potentially stigmatizing context. For example, a person accused of a crime might offer a "denial of responsibility" ("it was an accident"), a "denial of injury" ("their insurance will cover it"), a "denial of victim" ("they got what they deserved"), a "condemnation of their condemners" ("who are you to judge me?"), or an "appeal to higher loyalties" ("I didn't do it for myself"). Statements such as these are used by individuals from all segments of society when they are accused of wrongdoing, but some have more power than others to make them stick — effectively employing them is differently possessed by different actors. A lawyer or corporate executive, for example, might cite the stresses of their high-pressure job as the source of their cocaine addiction (an "appeal to higher loyalties" since their drug use becomes less about their own desires and more about their commitment to their work), whereas as a crack or heroin addict living on the street has no such recourse. This power imbalance is often reflected in law. For example, in US drug law, punishments for cocaine use are much lower than those for crack, despite the similarities between the two substances (Stern 2006).

Criminals, therefore, often possess less power in terms of being able to resist categorization, and for this reason they are an easy population upon which we can heap many of our anxieties and fears. They are transformed into dangerous individuals, people who, because of their careless disregard for others, should themselves be removed from the community. As mentioned earlier, branding individuals with the indelible mark of criminal has the effect of excluding them from society, leading them to commit more strongly to the criminal lifestyle. Thus, through criminalization, we contribute to the creation of the very thing we fear.

Some restorativists accept the dominant constructions of offender. They typically respond to it by recommending we forge relationships with offenders to help them reintegrate into our societies and form positive ties with others. A first step in such a process is changing the way we apportion blame in reaction to harmful acts. Morally speaking, it makes little sense to pretend the harms did not occur or the behaviours were not harmful. Such a denial of harm would only serve to weaken our sense of self-respect as actors undeserving of harm (Hampton 1998; Murphy and Hampton 1988). However, the need to lay blame and to be tough on wrongdoing does not handcuff us to stigmatization. As John Braithwaite (1989) has long suggested, we can aspire toward a justice that is hard on the act, but not the actor. This is the foundational premise of his theory of reintegrative shaming. When we condemn the act and not the actor, we recognize the act does not entirely define a person. This allows them the opportunity to distance themselves from the act and to reintegrate into the harmed community. This view has become a central tenet of much restorative justice practice — opening a space for people who commit wrongs to prove themselves something other than criminals.

Restorativists are still engaged in the process of constructing the offender in manner that reproduces the governing rationality of the criminal justice system (Pavlich 2005). At the root of restorative notions of the offender is a harm-causing individual who needs to be reintegrated into the normative order. For Pavlich, this assumption must be unpacked. To begin, one could critically interrogate the notion that harm causation can be isolated within a single individual. Locating harm in individuals ignores that harm often has many sources, including structured patterns of social inequality that contribute to an individual's motivation to commit harm. As Robert Merton suggested long ago, the gap between one's culturally prescribed aspirations for success and the structural opportunities to achieve that success can lead an individual to "innovate," that is, to seek illegal means to achieve their aspirations (Merton 1938). Social inequality is also the source of grave harm, such as the structural violence committed against poor and working people in the name of preserving the capitalist system. For example, our capitalist economy depends upon unemployment so there will be competition for jobs that will keep wages low. This system and its supporters militate against ideas such as cost-of-living allowances and other substantive guarantees of general social welfare, thereby accepting the inevitability of child poverty, homelessness, and other social ills.

In addition, the construction of the offender helps create a subject who can then be the target of disciplinary governance. Through the techniques of restorative justice, offenders' behaviour is to be reshaped, re-making these wrongdoers as responsibilized (that is, as actors made responsible for their self-governance) and non-conflictive individuals. What this amounts to is a process that works in a very similar fashion to the regular criminal justice system in that its ultimate aim is to pacify and discipline those branded as offenders. For Pavlich, this is problematic since it contradicts restorative justice claims to be offering a justice that is distinct from, and even oppositional to, the criminal justice system. Even with concepts seemingly distinct and positive such as empowerment, offender subjects are made to actively participate in restorative justice, which easily leads them to participate in and be responsible for their self-governance (Richards 2011). For Pavlich, restorative justice too often reproduces and is very much a part of the system it claims to challenge. He hopes to push our thinking beyond the limits of our current justice horizons.

Following Pavlich, restorativists should be wary of the offender label and seek instead to understand the perpetrator of harm as an accountable individual situated in a broader context defined by forces and influences that play a role in shaping this individual's behaviour. Ideally, this would include adopting language with less baggage than the term "offender," which is something some programs do, using instead terms like "responsible person," "wrongdoer," or "person who did harm." This requires a degree of sociological sophistication, since the objective is to treat this harming actor both as an individual agent and as a person susceptible to/embedded in structural processes. The wrongdoer is directly responsible to their fellow citizen for causing them harm, but this harmful behaviour can only be fully corrected through a thorough analysis of the conditions that brought about the wrongful acts. How did the individual come to accept abusive behaviour toward women as normal? Why did the drive for corporate profit lead to the marketing of unsafe products? How did economic downturn and job loss contribute to the gambling addiction that was the motivator behind credit card fraud?

COMMUNITIES

When restorative justice practitioners claim community is an essential pillar of their practice, the obvious question to ask is, "what community?" Where do such communities exist? Certainly not in contemporary urban settings, some would argue, where a complex division of labour has deprived us of the most intensive bonding mechanisms of traditional community life (see Durkheim 1984 [1933]). We no longer possess shared belief systems, or depend as immediately upon one another for our daily survival, or remain settled in the same communities for extended periods of time, to list but a few of the changes that characterize contemporary urban life (Bottoms 2003; Kueneman 2008). This is particularly applicable in those urban settings most prone to crime: inner cities. Here, urban deindustrialization has moved decent-paying, working-class employment opportunities from city centres to the outskirts, creating a vacuum of poverty within the inner city. Bereft of opportunity, inner-city communities have in some cases become more fractured (see Anderson 1999). Drugs, violence, vandalism, prostitution, and the other social ills are conditions better suited for the formation of illicit subcultural communities than the sort promoted by restorative justice practitioners. This is not to suggest that such communities do not rally and show resilience in the face of challenges, but they often have a steeper slope to climb than is true for others.

Other critics wonder if the concept of community is itself problematic. When we place ourselves within a community, we are presuming that there are others who do not belong to this community. Indeed, the identity of a given community, or an "us," is often dependent upon a notion of those who do not belong to this community, or a "them" (see Pavlich 2001). They are essentially excluded from our communal world. More severely, they are potentially excluded from our "universe of moral obligation" (Fein 1993), in that we only feel responsibility toward those with whom we share communal ties. Nazi fascism is often used as an example of exclusionary community formation. The Nazi vision of Germany (and later Europe) was built upon the exclusion of Jews, Roma, Slavs, homosexuals, and Others not perceived to meet the criteria of their Aryan community ideal. Potential danger lies within the idea of community: it promotes an ethics whereby within the community, like looks after like (that is, I watch out for my neighbour and vice versa) (see Koontz 2003), while at the same time placing limits upon this ethics, drawing a line beyond which all obligations of caring stop (that is, I no longer need/feel responsible for those outside of my community).

The restorative justice response to these criticisms has been to redefine community or, at least, to redefine the purpose of community within restorative justice. Some restorativists, for instance, prefer to speak of micro-communities, or "communities of care," by which they mean our close relationships to family, friends, and other significant persons who possess the moral force needed to influence our behaviour (McCold and Wachtel 1998). It is often presumed we all possess such connections to positive support persons who can come to our assistance and stand beside us at a restorative justice meeting. This is, perhaps, overly optimistic. As Johnstone (2002) notes, we cannot discount the possibility that there are people who are largely deprived of positive social relations. Rather than presume the existence of such networks, others have used Robert Putnam's (2000) notion of "social capital" to argue restorative justice is more about building communities and creating networks. A person who possesses a high degree of social capital, for example, will find their job search much easier, since they will be able to use their network of friends and family to learn about openings and to gather glowing references. In contrast, a person with low social capital may be able to enter the workforce at only the most menial levels, since they will not be able to rely on their social network as a resource. Social capital is, therefore, a form of social power that can be cultivated in community settings through the formation of helping networks. Applying this notion to restorative justice, it is not necessary that the community exist fully formed at the initiation of a restorative justice process. In fact, it may be possible to build such a community through restorative justice, as people form relationships with one another through addressing local injustices. By offering opportunities for the creation of social relationships, restorative justice enables social networking that will ideally continue to function long after specific restorative meetings have reached a conclusion.

The problem here is that all of these notions of community lack anthropological specificity. That is, they have not fully grappled with the notion of community as an "essentially contested" subject possessed of a variety of meanings (Johnstone 2004). Put in the most basic of terms, community is something defined by communities. We are part of a community because we share some common qualities with our fellow members (such as a location and/or culture), but also because we identify ourselves as part of that community. Community, therefore, is an active process of identification with others. This process can take an exclusionary form, as suggested by critics of restorative justice. However, this is not necessarily the case. While there has been a tendency for communities to form through an us/them binary, not all communities follow this strategy. There are indeed some communities that fit what some would refer to as "becoming communities" (Nancy 1991; Agamban 1993). This form of community life entails a sense of common identity that is not bound by rigid borders. Here, community represents something much more fluid, definable only in the experience of it.

Indeed, there are examples of community life that are defined by guidelines of hospitality and mobility rather than in stark contrast with an external Other. For example, some Coast Salish communities in British Columbia remain open to membership of individuals from other cultures and, in fact, encourage inter-marriages between their members and members from other communities as a means for creating inter-group ties. Moreover, the borderlands between these communities were traditionally not defined by fixed boundary lines, but rather by spaces that were shared territories, as much under the stewardship of one community as another. As Thom (2006: 21–22) states, Coast Salish members

> see boundaries and borders as arbitrary and artificial at best, and at worst a part of a recurring colonial mechanism of government to create division between communities and kin and weaken the potential strength of the Coast Salish people as a Nation. These people are concerned that the power of such maps and terms will have the effect of severing their connections to place, framing the future of engagements with the land exercised as rights negotiated under land claims settlements firmly in western ontological terms.

In these cases, the identification with the community does not necessitate an exclusion of others, since there exists recognition that the boundaries of the group are fuzzy and permeable.

This form of open community does not simply reflect a romanticized view of Indigenous peoples. Rather, it recognizes that notions of collective and community identity have often allowed for a certain degree of play. In some communities, one can shift ethnic identity. Prior to colonization, this was possible in Rwanda. A person could go from Hutu to Tutsi identity by acquiring certain goods (in particular, cattle), and these identities only became rigidified and exclusionary through the imposition of colonial racial science and the subsequent politicization of identity (Mamdani 2001). In such cases, identity is not an essential quality of the person, but rather a marker of certain material attachments (either to economic wealth or the land).

What this suggests is that community is not necessarily exclusionary. We can conceive of community rather as dynamic process that takes place within particular social, cultural, economic, political, and historical circumstances. Within these contexts, the process of community negotiation can indeed turn exclusionary, particularly when specific forms of community identity are politicized and prioritized. Take, for example, the politicization of identity in Bosnia-Herzegovina. Sarajevo, the largest city in this region, was a multicultural and cosmopolitan metropolis before the dissolution of Yugoslavia. After the death of former president Josip Broz Tito and the fall of communism, the many ethnicities of Yugoslavia lost these two key sources of political solidarity. This resulted in some provinces within Yugoslavia, namely Croatia and Slovenia, seeking independence. The breaking away of these two republics left Bosnia-Herzegovina on a precipice. Would it, too, secede? During this period, Yugoslav president, Slobodan Milosevic had been instigating the ideology of Serbian nationalism in order to secure his rule. This left non-Serb populations, such as Muslim and Croat Bosnians, feeling insecure. Ethnic communities then became more rigidly bound, and longstanding grievances that had been forgotten or placed aside in the day-to-day life of cosmopolitan Sarajevo re-emerged with a vengeance. Terrible stories of the Bosnian War abound: neighbour turning violently upon neighbour, when only weeks before they sat in the same cafes and shared a conversation (Power 2002).

Community closure and exclusionary politics are not necessary facts of community life. Community identity does not have to define itself in opposition to an always excluded Other. Instead, it can be defined through relations, and the strength of these relations allows one to identify oneself as part of several communities, each of varying and shifting intensity. These identifications become dangerous and exclusionary when they are politicized and made exclusionary; that is, when they are treated as an essential difference between one group and another.

It is clear that restorative justice must aspire to a different ideal of community life. The goal is not to draw upon or to fashion fixed, static communities of support; rather, community is the process of relations through which we negotiate our identities. Restorativists must be extremely careful in the image of community life they construct when advancing their programs. There is an inherent appeal to selling restorative justice on the basis of it being community centred, but whatever is gained by such an appeal is quickly lost if restorative notions of community lead to the drawing of strict social or spatial boundaries.

If the community of restorative justice is thought to be a specific town or neighbourhood, exclusionary principles are likely to obtain, and a restorative justice program could become tempted to restrictively define their potential participants. As well, it is important to recognize that service providing and not-for-profit organizations currently operate in "quasi-market" conditions (Bartlett and LeGrand 1993), in which they are required to compete with other organizations for funding and resources (see Chapter 6). Under these political conditions, one could imagine a situation in which restorative justice programs, and their corresponding communities, compete with one another, each vying for a larger share of a perceived limited pool of public resources. The well-being of one restorative justice program/community could therefore be perceived to be at the expense of another program/community. This can be seen more broadly in the social services when a "silo" mentality takes over and each social service organization works primarily to protect their specific piece of turf rather than cooperating with other organizations for the benefit of those using their services. In conditions of perceived resource scarcity, restorative justice programs in the same region can also feel the impulse to compete rather than coordinate with like services. Again, restorative justice must work with a notion of community that is open, multiple, and flexible.

FACILITATORS

The traditional image of the restorative justice facilitator is that of the community notable — a person of some standing within a group who has the moral authority to help guide others in their decision making. In contemporary restorative justice practice, there are some such figures who still reside within communities, such as trusted elders or religious leaders. Indeed, the initial renewal of informal justice practices was designed to empower such figures to serve as facilitators in neighbourhood justice programs (see Chapter 4), but modernization has taken a toll on the forms of legitimation required for the exercise of power in our societies (and, it must be noted, facilitation *is* a modality of power). As Max Weber (1946: 78–79) outlines, the ideal-typical legitimations for power are "traditional," "charismatic," and "rational-legal." Traditional legitimacy belongs to those whose power stems from the traditions and customs of a specific society. Thus, an elder may be granted special status because of their connection to and knowledge of the group's traditions. Charismatic authority is based upon the personal qualities of the individual, such that they are able to appear a legitimate authority because they exude a magnetism that attracts the engagement and obedience of others. We often think of figures like Martin Luther King Jr., whose name is almost synonymous with the US Civil Rights Movement he represents. Many such figures have come to fill roles within restorative justice programs, relying on their charisma to ensure the participation of the disputing parties. Finally, rational-legal authority is the product of official process or qualification, and it is this form of legitimacy that is becoming more commonly sought in restorative justice programs. Under this authority, there is less reliance on the personality of the leader, and more focus on the rules and procedures of governance to ensure stability within the movement or organization.

As Weber (1946) notes, charismatic authority is often short lived. Once the charismatic figure dies or retires, their followers must seek other means to ensure the regular operation of their projects. This often results in recourse to rational-legal authority, since such authority can be formalized to ensure certain standards of practice are maintained. In the case of restorative justice, we increasingly see more emphasis placed upon facilitator training and qualifications. It is no longer assumed any community member is competent enough to help their fellow members negotiate their conflicts. Instead, such a person requires a specific education to prepare them to facilitate in potentially difficult situations. For example, when facilitating a conflict between two intimate partners, where family violence may be evident or suspected, a lay facilitator may not be sufficiently attuned to the subtle intimidations an abuser might use to ensure they get their way and therefore may not do enough to advocate for the wronged party in the meeting. It is also the case that community facilitators may not be fully aware of the programs and services available within their community. If this is so, the restorative meeting may result in a recommendation for addiction counselling or anger management training, only to discover these services do not exist or are overbooked. Therefore, many restorativists now claim that it is to the advantage of all parties if the facilitator is a trained professional.

It is also true that facilitators are no longer necessarily assumed to be trustworthy based upon their status within the community. Given the fractured nature of modern urban communities, interpersonal trust has come to be replaced by contractual trust, meaning that what makes a facilitator seem trustworthy is not the product of a longstanding relationship but, rather, built upon their contractual guarantee that they will facilitate the conflict in a fair and equitable manner (see Durkheim 1984 [1933]). For this reason, more and more restorative justice agencies are investing time and energy in developing facilitator codes of ethics that provide a set of behavioural expectations to which facilitators must abide. Of course, since there are seldom national or regional licensing bodies for facilitators, there is still some question of whether or not such codes carry any weight. A centralized licensing body would be able to withdraw the professional credential of a facilitator after an instance of ethical violation but, at the moment, no such body exists in Canada, or in most other jurisdictions.

These and other factors speak to the professionalization of restorative justice. Indeed, restorative justice can no longer be seen solely as a lay practice, since it is now the subject of countless training programs and practitioner guides. For state-supported restorative justice programs, restorative practitioners are often expected to have training in victim-offender mediation, risk assessment, motivational interviewing, trauma counselling, and other such skills. But what are the consequences of the professionalization of restorative justice?

The image of the facilitator as a lay practitioner has much different connotations than the facilitator as a conflict resolution professional. The lay practitioner is someone who is reasonably familiar with you and your family. Their lack of professional status means the process is more informal in the sense that the problem of the injustice(s) is worked through by people who know one another. However, this changes when the facilitator becomes a conflict resolution professional. The involvement of this person, unfamiliar and yet to be trusted because of their experience and training, results in the conflict appearing more closely connected to the field of formal law. The conflict resolution professional then becomes perceived as a potential competitor with those professionals who have traditionally possessed monopoly control over the field of law: lawyers and judges (Bourdieu 1987). Also, as restorative justice competes for clients and resources within this broader field of law, it tends to model itself on other professional groups, most notably lawyers and doctors, to make itself seem serious.

The construction of the restorative facilitator as a professional presents the danger that restorative justice will lose its local and informal roots and become more fully part of the formal criminal justice system. Such has been the case with the practice of mediation in civil law. Mediation was first touted as a community-based process for resolving conflicts between neighbours, whereby lay mediators would help people negotiate the conflicts that interfere with civility and sociability in community life (see Chapter 4). For example, neighbours in a dispute over a contested property line could talk things out with the help of a respected community member rather than pursuing their case in the courts. However, the state came to view mediation as a cost-effective means for reducing backlog in the courts (Burger 1979). Once the state lent its support to mediation, its practice became potentially more profitable. A mediation market thus emerged, with lawyers and other justice professionals adding mediation to their skill sets in advertising their services. In a relatively short period of time, community-based mediation became less prominent, largely eclipsed by a growing cadre of professional mediators, who could charge upwards of $200 per hour for their services (Woolford and Ratner 2005).

There is also the risk that formalized restorative justice training will reduce restorative justice to a technical practice, offering practitioners very pragmatic tools for preparing for and intervening during facilitated meetings, but not preparing them for understanding the broader context of the conflict. Thus, a facilitator could be trained to possess a large toolbox of tactics they would apply to a crime involving an Indigenous offender who has found themself drawn toward gang involvement. However, the facilitator may have little understanding of the forces of colonialism, the difficult transition from reserve to city life, and the racism experienced by Indigenous peoples in the inner city.

Given the complexity of the injustices with which restorative justice practitioners must deal, it would be naïve to expect them to work within this field without training. However, restorative justice must resist the course taken by other professions, and not make training and credentials the primary source of legitimacy for facilitators. Instead, even trained facilitators should derive their sense of legitimacy from the satisfaction and empowerment they provide to participants in restorative justice, as well as from their ability to plot the linkages between private troubles and public issues (Mills 1959).

OPENING RESTORATIVE IDENTITIES

Restorative justice has typically been defined as a process that involves victim(s), offender(s), and community member(s) in resolving the harm caused by a criminal event. However, buried in such definitions are assumptions about these so-called stakeholders. Victim, offender, community member, and facilitator are not unproblematic identities, and the assumptions we make about each have distinct political consequences for the practice of restorative justice. The argument presented in this chapter is that each of these identities must be held open for reconsideration. It is less a matter of doing away with the language of victim, offender, community, and facilitator (though this is a reasonable start restorative justice programs may make to opening these identities) than it is of broadening our sense of what we mean by these terms. These are not fully formed identities, since each is the result of a socio-political process through which the label is given meaning. As well, these are not distinct identities since it is possible for actors to fill more than one role.

Keeping these identities open and even allowing them to be potential topics of discussion within restorative justice meetings would enable restorative justice participants to address and challenge their own preconceptions of these terms. If the person who has committed an injustice is not reduced and individualized by the label "offender," there is then the possibility of speaking more broadly about the structural factors that are the wider context of injustice. Only in this way can a community contemplate transformative action, taking the private trouble of the crime and transforming it into a public issue to address.

In addition, the restorative justice meeting could then serve as a venue in which each of these identities is broadened and complicated. A community member could also be understood as a victim of injustice, since they now live in an environment that seems more dangerous. The offender, although responsible and accountable, could also be understood as a victim of personal and structural injustices that have left them with little opportunity, or with an overwhelming sense of anger. Thus, by keeping these identities more fluid and open, restorative justice can help participants negotiate what these terms might mean at the local level, rather than to have these statuses imposed through a quasi-criminal justice process.

QUESTIONS FOR DISCUSSION

1. Should restorative justice continue to use the language of "victim" and "offender"? What alternatives could it use?
2. What are some practical strategies a restorative justice program could use in order to prevent defining community in an exclusionary way?
3. What are the benefits and drawbacks to lay practitioner versus trained professional facilitators? Should restorative justice only be led by trained professionals?

6

RESTORATIVE JUSTICE CONTEXTS

Restorative practices are directed toward a variety of injustices, ranging from petty theft and zoning disputes to murder and mass violence. How does the social and political context in which it is practiced condition restorative justice, including its practices and outcomes? Of primary concern here is the role of power in shaping how restorative justice is promoted, funded, implemented, integrated into existing institutions, and experienced by participants. What are the ways in which various forms of structural domination (such as those related to race, class, gender, sexual identity, and their intersections) influence restorative justice? Specific modes of political economy and governance present both possibilities and perils for restorative justice. Here, the place of restorative justice within neoliberal capitalist democracies will be of particular concern. What goals of state and governance are served by restorative justice in this context? What pressures does neoliberalism place on the values and practices of restorative justice? Answering these questions will allow us to begin to consider some of the social and political limitations, which is essential for purposes of developing a transformative restorative justice political strategy.

LEVEL OF ANALYSIS

In assessing restorative justice, our attention is often fixed on individuals. As noted in Chapter 4, evaluations of restorative justice programs typically examine levels of participant satisfaction or whether or not offenders are less likely to recidivate after taking part in a restorative justice encounter. Because restorative justice aims to better engage victims, offenders, and community members in justice processes, and to improve outcomes for all of these parties, these measures make a certain amount of sense. However, to fully understand how restorative justice works, we must also zoom out and identify the macro- and meso-level factors that influence its delivery. Structural (macro) patterns of power, as well as institutional (meso) practices, provide the conditions under which individual outcomes are made possible.

Remaining at the micro-level for a moment, it is important to acknowledge that restorative justice can produce impressive results for individuals. Its potential to direct emotion toward the creation of an experience of justice that is unavailable from the formal criminal justice system can be powerful (Dietrich 2018). In the immediacy of a meeting between individuals who come together to discuss a harmful incident, there are several hard-to-define yet socially meaningful qualities that allow for the seeming magic of restorative justice to unfold. We look to our fellow participants and make interpersonal assessments, and sometimes we do this intuitively without realizing we are doing so. Do they show "integrity?" Are they "trustworthy?" Are they "sincere" in what they say? These and other human characteristics are difficult to operationalize in a social scientific manner, but we nonetheless tend to believe they are discernable within interactive contexts. In evaluating them, we often seek out clues. We examine body posture (are they sitting upright and being attentive?), tone of voice (does their voice communicate deeply felt sentiments?), a willingness to take ownership for their deeds (does the person make excuses or take responsibility?), and, perhaps afterwards, their actions (are their subsequent actions consistent with their representation of self within the restorative meeting?). Through this examination, we gain either a sense of trust or distrust for the speaker, as well as an opinion on their level of sincerity (see Tavuchis 1991). Thus, in a restorative justice meeting between individuals, part of the facilitator's work is to encourage honesty and openness, to invite people to express their feelings, and to make sure they remain actively engaged in the discussion. In this manner, the facilitator hopes to build trust between potential combatants. This need for trust also speaks to the strategic reason for using tools such as ice breakers or humour at certain points in the meeting, or perhaps a prayer or opening song. Whereas ice breakers and humour might help relax the parties and make them feel more at ease (and therefore more willing to expose their "true" selves within the meeting), a prayer or opening song can help remind participants they are all members of a common community with shared norms and values.

None of these aspects of interpersonal relations are simply micro-level interactions, however. They connect to the meso-level patterns, or structural contexts. A person's trustworthiness or integrity, for example, is often read through structuring cues of race, class, and gender. We habitually assess if individuals whom we assume to belong in one or more of these identity categories are performing their role as expected. And because of reigning patterns of prejudice, some may view an apparently cis-gendered woman who wears their hair short and dresses in masculine clothes, and therefore does not perform their femininity in accordance with dominant normative standards, as less trustworthy in her claims to have experienced sexual violence. An angry or silent racialized minority or Indigenous person may also be assumed to be hostile and threatening rather than exhibiting a defensive posture developed after multiple negative interactions with mainstream social institutions. How we see and react to one another, while not entirely determined by these structures, is certainly textured by their force.

If the goal is to encourage societal transformation through restorative justice, a potential negative consequence of focusing exclusively on individual needs and the outcomes of meetings is the risk that we might restrict our focus to personal differences without connecting these differences to wider structural inequities. For example, much transformative potential would be lost if a conflict between two youths from different ethnic backgrounds that has resulted in a violent assault was addressed solely as an interpersonal issue rather than an intergroup conflict emanating from broader ethnic tensions in the community. If transformation is indeed the goal, it is necessary that facilitators and community participants make attempts to connect such conflicts to their structural conditions so the restorative justice meeting does not merely ameliorate the immediate problem while leaving the broader conflict unaddressed.

The point is that seldom are problems simply interpersonal. Instead, they connect to broader collective experiences. Injustices committed through everyday harms are often the result of patterned behaviours — as is evident in examples such as hate crimes and bullying, where individuals seen as members of specific groups (such as ethnic minorities or individuals who do not fit a cis-gendered, heterosexual norm) are targeted. In such cases, the restorative justice meeting is clearly required to address matters that extend beyond interpersonal relations by discussing how it is that bullying or hate crimes came to be problems in these communities. Even though such conflicts may be tricky and require greater time commitments, the payoff is that such meetings have better potential to link with injustices of broader public concern.

Individual conflicts may also be manifestations of broader intergroup conflicts. Such conflicts are not uncommon in our society and can take a variety of forms: Indigenous peoples and city police officers may be in dispute over perceptions that racial profiling practices are resulting in Indigenous mass incarceration; tenants of an apartment complex may be in conflict with the owners of the complex, as well as the architects who designed it, the contractors who built it, and the municipal inspectors who failed to notice the many code violations apparent in the building's construction; or two ethnic communities who share a common neighbourhood may discover their children are engaging in an ongoing turf war that results in multiple acts of violence and aggression. Any of these cases could spark individual incidents that are referred to restorative justice, but they will only be superficially addressed if they limit discussion to the micro-criminal or harmful event and not larger patterns of conflict and domination.

It must be stressed that although structural patterns of power are persistent, they are not static. What this means is that they do not stay the same in all times and places. The purpose of an intersectional analysis is to direct our attention to the particular configurations of power that take shape in specific temporal and spatial, social and political, and institutional and affective circumstances. We need to consider some of the broader structural patterns and where restorative justice might fit in addressing their resultant harms. But these structural patterns are not hammers designed to turn every restorative justice system into a nail — that is, we cannot get beyond the empirical responsibility to assess each context of injustice on its own terms to get at the specific shape structural power takes in a particular locality at a particular time.

RESTORATIVE JUSTICE AND GENDER

Feminist scholars have long noted that criminal justice is a gendered process (Adelberg and Currie 1987; Naffine 1987; Chunn and LaCombe 2000; Balfour and Comack 2014). In other words, one's experiences within the criminal justice system, whether as the accused, victim, volunteer, or one of the many system employees, is contoured by one's gender and the role expectations assigned based on others' perceptions of that gender. In particular, the formal criminal justice system tends to be male-centred and does not respond well to the specific justice concerns and needs of women as both victims and perpetrators of crime (Comack 2014; Johnson and Rodgers 1993). For example, prisons and other carceral institutions impact women in unique ways. Separation from children, especially for women who are single caregivers, can result in loss of custody. As well, strip searches and other intrusive measures against incarcerated women's bodies are traumatizing for those who have been sexually assaulted (Kilty 2014). Likewise, as victims of crime, women's experiences are also unique. This is particularly true in relation to gendered crimes such as sexual violence, where women can find their performance of femininity (such as whether they dress and present themselves in a manner that makes them appear desirable, and yet not complicit in their own violation) on trial as defence attorneys seek to prove the innocence of their (mostly male) clients.

Give these negative experiences, one would hope restorative justice might provide options that better address the specific justice concerns of women. Indeed, Barbara Hudson's work, discussed in Chapter 3, shows the points of overlap between restorative justice and a feminist intersectional approach, allowing us to see some potential for a feminist practice of restorative justice. Feminist scholars and advocates have thus far focused mainly on the use of restorative justice in cases of gendered violence such as sexual assault and intimate partner violence. Earlier analyses were quite hesitant about the use of restorative justice. Questions are raised about the risk of re-victimization through such processes, as well as with respect to how restorative justice practices in a patriarchal context may reproduce this context and even condone its violence (Cameron 2006; Curtis-Fawley and Daly 2005; Daly and Stubbs 2006; Lewis, Dobash, Dobash, and Cavanagh 2001; Stubbs 2002). Consider, for example, a circle intended to address intimate partner violence taking place in a community where it is generally believed wives should be subservient to their husbands. Is such a circle likely to find a transformative solution that ends not only the violence but the husband's controlling behaviour? And what about the strides feminists have made in criminalizing intimate partner violence, which for too much of human history has been considered the right of husbands? Are these advances lost when such violence is directed away from the courts toward a seemingly gentler alternative justice?

In recent years feminist frustration with the failure of the criminal justice system for survivors has led them to re-think and re-assess the use of restorative justice. Some see great potential in restorative justice to empower victims and provide them with space to both speak and have their voices heard (McGlynn, Westmarland, and Godden 2012). Sexual assault is a crime that is often met with disbelief so the opportunity to have the harm recognized by the offender, family members, and others is a restorative justice process could have tremendous benefit for survivors (McGlynn, Downes, and Westmarland 2017). The process may also provide women with the social and material supports they require to cope with or end an abusive relationship (Gaarder 2015).

This is a rich and ongoing discussion (see Zinsstag and Kennan 2017; Ptacek 2010). These scholars do note that restorative justice is an alternative that will still be subject to the same patriarchal conditions that have shaped our criminal justice response. For that reason, they tend to focus more attention on transformative justice, a topic we discuss in the final chapter.

Beyond cases of gendered violence, we also need to consider whether or not restorative justice is itself a space in which gender is performatively constructed and governed. Judith Butler (1990) argues that gender is performative in the sense that it is through the way we present our gender in our day-to-day lives that we construct ourselves as gendered individuals. These gendered identities can be subsequently used to govern us, such as when our perceived guilt or innocence in a conflict is understood, in part, through the adequacy with which we meet socially prescribed gender expectations. Society consists of a variety of frames that regulate appropriate expressions of gender and by which we abide, though some people also disrupt these norms by refusing or subverting expected performances. Given the overarching structuring power of gender performativity, it is very possible for restorative programs to become enlisted in the work of reproducing a gendered order. Restorative justice meetings could, for example, turn toward proposing self-help measures, time-management skills, and mothering programs to a stressed-out and criminalized mother who has resorted to crime to combat the feminization of poverty. In such a case, restorative justice would be seeking to correct her (mis)performance of gender, to persuade her to accept her role without complaint, rather than countering the forces that increase her likelihood of poverty. Again, this is also a problem within the criminal justice system, but, given its promises of openness and empowerment, it is fair to ask even more of restorative justice.

In this sense, restorative justice cannot simply be assumed to align with feminist principles. Such principles must be kept active by reflecting on the gendered dimensions of the case at hand. Because restorative justice offers a venue where gender domination can be discussed and considered in relation to experiences of injustice, it holds more potential than criminal justice for opening discussion to the intersecting challenges faced by various women in the gendered context of the law. The tools are in place for discussion of gender domination to occur through restorative justice. It is up to practitioners and participants to commit to such discussion and to challenge their own gender presumptions.

RESTORATIVE JUSTICE AND RACE

A key and oft-noted failing of North American criminal justice systems is their production of racialized injustices. Racialized individuals are more likely to be caught within the criminal justice system and held within its grasp for longer periods of time. At every stage of the criminal justice process, from arrest to bail hearings through sentencing and parole, Indigenous peoples, Black Canadians, and African Americans are more likely to be under police surveillance, arrested, sentenced, identified as a high risk to reoffend, and subsequently captured within the criminal justice system when compared to those who present as white (Delgado and Stefancik 2017; Maynard 2017; Tauri 2014; Wacquant 2009).

Critical race theory has emerged as a distinctive approach in socio-legal studies to counter those theoretical perspectives that ignore the racialized character of the law. Drawing on intersectionality, critical race theorists recognize that race is experienced differentially across any given society, and these experiences also vary depending on other identity characteristics held by an individual (for example, a Black woman's experience of racialized injustice will differ from that of a Black man, and each of these experiences may also vary depending on the time and space in which they are situated). For this reason, critical race theory places great emphasis on storytelling as a means to capture unique experiences of intersecting structural oppressions.

It is also important to note that race is not defined by biology. Race is a product of social relations rather than merely a function of skin colour. It is how we imagine racial difference that is key, rather than anything inherently connected to the level of melanin pigmentation of one's skin. Critical race theorists argue that although racial prejudice is ubiquitous, it is not natural, meaning it can be addressed. Addressing such inequality requires a practical politics and not just theoretical deconstruction. It is not enough to simply criticize structures of racial privilege. Workable legal strategies for meeting the everyday needs of racialized peoples are promoted in the meantime, while work continues toward building a more just society. This means that existing legal tools, such as constitutional rights, are used to advance the needs of racialized people, even if such rights may be based largely on a Eurocentric and individualistic understanding of the world. Despite this foundation, they can be used to support the needs of racialized people, whose basic human rights may be violated by overzealous state surveillance or policing. Working with such individualistic mechanisms is preferable to suggestions that the legal system simply need to operate in a "colourblind" fashion, since colourblindness tends to bury both subtle and explicit racial biases rather than remove them. It treats racism as though it is a problem that can simply be ignored by pretending it does not exist, and thereby does not address how racism is structured into our daily lives (see Delgado and Stefancik 2017).

The question arises as to whether or not restorative justice might play a role in meeting both the day-to-day and overarching social justice needs of racialized people. Given the long history of state-based justice mechanisms controlling racialized and Indigenous peoples, it is no surprise that some might be skeptical of the potential of restorative justice to break this historical pattern (Agozino 2004; Tauri 2014). For scholars like Tauri (2014), restorative justice remains part of a state system that has, in neoliberal times, sought less direct means of violence to carry out the settler colonial project of eliminating Indigenous peoples and their territorial claims to the North American continent. When restorative justice is a top-down, state-driven process, it can be used to try to assimilate Indigenous peoples to European justice norms and pacify Indigenous resistance.

On the other hand, some do see in restorative justice the potential to meet some of the criteria of critical race theory (Gavrielides 2014; Williams 2013). As was the case with feminism, the relationality and narrative richness of restorative justice holds the potential to allow the unique voices of racialized peoples to be brought forward in restorative justice meetings. However, scholars are also cautious in recommending that such restorative justice processes need to take place under local, community control, and in culturally appropriate settings, so that state objectives do not override the transformative potential of restorative justice (Williams 2013).

RESTORATIVE JUSTICE AND LGBTQ COMMUNITIES

LGBTQ communities and issues have largely been invisible within the wider criminal justice research. Restorative justice is no different in this regard. LGBTQ people are overrepresented in the criminal justice system, and this is particularly true for LGBTQ youth, racialized LGBTQ people, transgender and gender non-conforming people, and homeless LGBTQ individuals. The reasons for this overrepresentation are manifold, including intolerance and discrimination, which manifests in these individuals being excluded from their families and schools, denied job opportunities, restricted in their housing options, and faced with other consequences of our society's continuing hostility to LGBTQ people. This discrimination is further evidenced in how LGBTQ people are policed and punished. Some US state indecency laws, for example, target consensual sex between LGBTQ people, but also racialized people, including racialized LGBTQ people, for drug use (Center for American Progress 2016).

Incarceration presents a particular threat to LGBTQ people, as they are more likely to be treated harshly and abused while in a correctional institution, including being more likely to be placed in solitary confinement and subject to high rates of sexual assault by their fellow inmates. As reported by the Center for American Progress (2016), in the US, where 2 percent of the general inmate population reports experience of sexual assault at the hands of another inmate, this is the case for 24 percent of transgender people. Such injustices are in addition to other humiliations, including insults and incorrect pronoun use.

Again, there is potential in the communicative and relational dynamics of restorative justice for fostering greater understanding of LGBTQ experiences. However, this is not a guaranteed outcome. Because restorative justice is based in the community, one cannot simply assume that the communities that have rejected, harmed, humiliated, and isolated LGBTQ individuals will provide a safe and productive space for addressing their experiences as both offenders and victims. Given that too many LGBTQ people have experienced family and community rejection, it is unlikely restorative justice will contribute to LGBTQ healing and reintegration unless ground work is done to ensure that those who have rejected their LGBTQ family and neighbours are educated in acceptance and support. Of course, fostering acceptance stops short of the material needs of LGBTQ people, who also need to be able to interact with employers and landlords free from discrimination, so that they do not continue to suffer joblessness and homelessness as a consequence of prejudice. Restorative justice could play an important role in encouraging and strengthening the community networks of LGBTQ people and can do so if practitioners and proponents better familiarize themselves with the distinct challenges faced by these individuals.

RESTORATIVE JUSTICE AND CLASS

The criticism is often made that the term restorative assumes there is something to restore, but what can be restored in a situation where one's entire social network is beset by crushing poverty and structural violence rather than existing within a middle-class ideal of harmony?

In economically stable communities, where a network of relations connects neighbours and families because there is less in-and-out migration, an offender is perhaps more likely to be able to rely not only upon their family to help walk a more positive path, but also on their neighbours to assist in reforming their behaviour. But what about a community where economic opportunity lies more in the drug trade than permanent jobs? Of course, such communities include many people who are models of resilience and strength, and these communities still exhibit strong networks (as is the case for Indigenous reserves). Yet, the structural violence of economic disenfranchisement and ghettoization still take a toll in terms of limiting crime-free pathways to well-being (see Anderson 1999; Wacquant 2001). In such situations, an offender may not possess the social networks, resources, or time to ease their reintegration. And economic inequality can make reintegration even more difficult, as employment and housing challenges face a former offender who does not have the social capital — that is, the power of social networks — to help them remain crime free. This context makes the focus on recidivism as a measure of whether restorative justice works or not particularly fraught. Someone may commit a crime out of economic necessity, breaking into garages to steal goods that they sell, perhaps, or selling drugs in order to make money. That person may go through restorative justice, understand the harm they have caused the victim and feel real remorse and shame for their actions. But if that person is then left in the same economic position we should not be surprised if they reoffend. Rather than demonstrate the failure of restorative justice, this re-offending points to the failure of our economic system to provide resources for all community members.

This brings us to consider the broader class context that has the potential to shape the delivery of restorative justice. Given the challenges presented to restorative justice programs in so-called disorderly communities, there is the risk that restorative justice gatekeepers will instead direct their services toward middle- and upper-class offenders. Indeed, the criteria of what makes a person suitable for restorative justice is weighted upon factors that advantage people of higher economic standing, in that, for example, these people are more likely to have the social networks and resources that make them seem like good candidates for restoration. Therefore, middle-class and upper-class youth may appear more redeemable in the eyes of those who refer people to restorative justice programs (such as judges, lawyers, and police officers), since they not only possess the economic resources to pay for any damage they may have caused, but also class dispositions that make them appear ready for redemption. For instance, they may have internalized mannerisms of politeness and practices of speech that make them seem more outwardly remorseful for their actions.

A class dimension can also be identified in the move to use restorative justice for white-collar crimes like breach of trust or embezzlement offences. Such cases seem quite attractive on several levels. First, restorative justice can be presented to businesses as a practical way for them to recoup some of the money or goods stolen. Second, employees who have stolen from their employers typically possess skill sets that allow them to earn money and to pay off their debts. Finally, these offenders are viewed as being less of a risk to the public, since their white-collar status gives them the appearance of being less dangerous because their crimes took place outside of the public limelight. When such cases become prominent parts of a restorative justice program, they could contribute to a two-tiered justice system where the poor offenders get prison while the white-collar offenders receive restorative justice.

A class-conscious restorative justice is nonetheless possible so long as the various advantages of economic privilege, or its absence, are also made part of the consideration for referring cases to restorative justice, as well as for discussing how the wrongdoing came to pass and how it may be resolved. For example, restorative justice programs, at times, offer employment training or entrepreneurial opportunities so that those branded offenders can start to rebuild their lives. Such programs, however, cannot simply seek to place individuals in menial jobs, or ignore intersecting racial, age, class, and sexual identity barriers to employment. They need to address the real barriers presented by structural economic violence by offering the individual skills to meet their subsistence needs, and not to simply force-fit the individual into the lowest and most precarious positions within this system. Such class awareness is also important in recognizing that the needs of healing and personal reform have personal costs that we are not all equally positioned to pay, but also in thinking about the overarching violence of structural inequality in our society and its likelihood to produce future injustices.

RESTORATIVE JUSTICE AND AGE

Age, like class, is an overarching context of restorative justice. Once again, the most disadvantaged in this hierarchy, namely, young people, receive differential treatment through existing restorative justice programs.

The category of youth is itself a social invention (Cote and Allahar 1995).

There is no biological category that necessitates a clear distinction between those with ages ranging from twelve to eighteen years (and this range may vary according to region) and those who are younger or older. Youth is a purgatory in between the supposed innocence of our younger years ("childhood") and the workaday world we will be immersed into thereafter. It is liminal in the sense that it is a space of transition, when we are said to seek out our identities, to experiment, to drift, but hopefully come out on the other side properly socialized into the normative world.

Youth is the primary terrain upon which restorative justice operates. When restorative justice is considered in most political jurisdictions, youth are typically its first intended targets. Why is that? Some suggest the transitional nature of youth makes young people ideally suited for restorative interventions. Since young people are still in a process of formation, they are considered malleable and open to change. It is at this point we can seek to halt their initial drift (Matza 1990) into deviance and return them to a law-abiding lifecourse, preventing their movement from acts of "primary deviance" toward accepting a criminal "master status" and entering the realm of "secondary deviance" (see Chapters 3 and 5).

At work in this seemingly logical rationale for youth-based restorative justice are several assumptions about youth. To begin, the category of youth is essentialized — that is, it is treated as a foundational essence or truth about individuals rather than something that is socially constructed. Thus, the implementation of youth restorative justice plays a role in reproducing the category of youth, and thus of reproducing a category of people who can be targeted with specific forms of governance. We must always be wary of attempts to construct a population for governance, since these efforts of categorization are means by which social control can be established to target certain individuals more than others. Indeed, youth have been increasingly criminalized in recent years, as moral panics about youth crime have painted a broad stretch of the youth population as "at risk" (see Hogeveen and Minaker 2008). The language of describing young people as "at risk" serves to extend the reach of the criminal justice system beyond the world of actual offences and into the realm of potential offences, making heretofore law-abiding members of society into subjects of criminal justice concern. Even programs intended for children, such as "head start" or "healthy child" programs directed toward helping parents bond with and socialize their children, are often justified through a criminal justice rationale that views young people as potential future criminals before they have even entered elementary school.

Second, too many restorative justice programs still treat youth as passive objects within their justice processes. Young people typically enter the restorative justice programs surrounded by adults. Adults refer them to the programs, adults facilitate the meetings, and adults attend as the support persons for young offenders. In the worst case of community accountability panels (see Chapter 5), the young offender comes face-to-face with a panel of community notables who are meant to advise the youth on their wrongdoing and how they might make amends. Whatever the rules of inclusion and participation are in these processes, the young person is likely to feel intimidated and pressured by the "moral scolding" they receive at the hands of the panel (Crawford 2003). The young person is also likely to look to the adults for clues as to how they should and should not act. In this sense, the intergenerational character of most youth restorative justice leads to imbalances of power that cannot be easily masked through rhetoric of open and non-coercive participation.

A more youth-centred approach to restorative justice is offered by programs like the Youth Restorative Action Project (YRAP) in Edmonton, Alberta. Run by youth, for youth, YRAP seeks to empower young people rather than adults. Although YRAP is reliant on the criminal justice system for referrals and needs judge approval for the agreements it achieves, it still provides young people with a great deal of autonomy with respect to how they deal with the conflicts in their midst. It does so by making youth the primary decision makers in the everyday practices of YRAP.

The young people at YRAP have committed to selecting cases that reflect broader challenges within their communities, such as racism and sexism. For example:

> Riff, a relatively recent addition to the YRAP team, suggests that: "I vote to include a case when it is something that I feel is a racially motivated crime, something with abuse. Usually, I will try to vote yes for that because I think it is important to get that issue in the forefront." By mobilizing their resources around such forms of social injustice, members see themselves providing a forum for the education and reconciliation of troubled youth. (Hogeveen 2006: 59)

YRAP empowers young people to not only be agents with respect to specific conflicts, but also in relation to prominent issues that trouble the places in which they live. This also allows YRAP to serve as a space in which young people can challenge and contest a wide variety of issues, including the social construction of the category of youth, as well as racialized and class-based assumptions about crime and victimization (Hogeveen 2006).

Although youth crime appears, on the surface, a natural target for the practice of restorative justice, it is necessary that this be denaturalized and criticized so restorative justice can achieve a broader empowerment, which includes the empowerment of young people, as illustrated by YRAP, rather than simply offering new tools for targeting and criminalizing youth.

INTERSECTING STRUCTURES OF DOMINATION

Gender, race, sexual identity, class, and age all represent structures of domination under which the injustices addressed by restorative justice are experienced. Each on its own is a challenge for a restorative justice practitioner seeking to ensure a transformative resolution to a specific injustice. They are not, however, faced independent of one another. As individuals we don't simply have a gender, but no sexuality, class position, race, or age. Instead we are positioned at the intersection of these structures. Some people may be positioned with privilege in some structures and oppression in others: a white man is privileged in terms of his race and gender positioning, but if he is young and living on the street he is marginalized as well. This is why we use the term "intersectionality." The larger task is to refine our theories and practices so we can attend to these structures in their overlaps and entanglements. This is especially true when thinking about harm and justice, as many people who come into contact with the criminal justice system as offenders or victims are marginalized on a variety of axes.

In coining the term intersectionality, Kimberlé Crenshaw (1991) selected her metaphor very deliberately. She likened the experience of an African-American woman to sitting at the intersection between two roads, one patriarchy and the other racial domination. What developed at this intersection was a novel and distinct experience that could be explained by neither the theories developed for white women or Black men. The combined forces of patriarchy and racism shaped the lives of African-American women in a unique manner. Similarly, nearly each restorative justice encounter will take place at the centre of a complex intersection. In interviews that Amanda conducted with restorative/alternative justice staff members in Winnipeg, a key theme that came up again and again was flexibility. Case workers believed strongly that their processes needed to be flexible to account for the different circumstances of participants.

Often, the programs responded to the differing structural positioning of participants. For example, Onashowewin is an agency in Winnipeg that provides restorative justice practices to Indigenous peoples facing criminal charges. Rather than simply provide the same process for everyone, case workers tailor it to each person. They offer workshops specifically for men and women, and they have workers who are particularly knowledgeable about the conditions for Indigenous young people. Staff consistently understood and discussed the people they work with as being positioned at the intersections of a variety of structures, as one staff noted, "If you're looking at someone who's living in poverty, single mom, whatever, these are the challenges. Housing, education, employment. Sometimes its addictions, sometimes it's not, parental skills. All these different types of things" (Nelund 2016). The restorative and alternative justice programs Amanda studied tried to address these inequalities through their justice practice and their focus on empowerment assisted in highlighting them. The degree to which any program could address the structural conditions of oppression they identified however, was constrained by the larger political context (Nelund 2016).

RESTORATION AND NEOLIBERAL POLITICS

With respect to the economic and political context of restorative justice, the most salient tendency governing contemporary economic and political life is neoliberalism. Neoliberalism is a wide-reaching phenomenon. To fully understand the consequences of this political-economic context for restorative justice, it is necessary that some care be taken to describe exactly what neoliberalism is, since it is a contested notion.

Over the past thirty years, corporate power has become more mobile or globalized, pressuring regions to create regulatory conditions inviting investment. As well, a "neoliberal international" (Wacquant 2004: 100), with its institutions (such as the World Trade Organization and the International Monetary Fund, which work toward advancing neoliberal monetary policies) and think tanks (for example, internationally, the Organization for Economic Cooperation and Development, the Heritage Foundation, and the American Enterprise Institute; in Canada, the Conference Board, the CD Howe Institute, and the Canadian Council of Chief Executives), has spread the economic and political principles of neoliberalism to the furthest reaches of the planet. This movement is argued to represent something distinct from liberalism, the political philosophy that has dominated Western governments for some time. Under liberalism, emphasis was placed upon *laissez faire* governance, a call that inspired earlier attempts to roll back state involvement in economic and social relations. However, in the late twentieth century, this philosophy shifted to challenge welfare-state provisions of health care, education, unemployment, retirement, housing, and other benefits that had been won by the working classes through their demands that the state address the hardships brought by unregulated capitalism. These welfare-state provisions were dominant in Western nations following World War II, and they demonstrated that the state could play a vital role in directing capitalist production by offering workers the security and spending power required for them to contribute to a stable national economy (see Tickell and Peck 1995). However, in the 1970s, these policies were perceived to be in crisis, as the social programs of the welfare state appeared cumbersome and attempts by nation-states to regulate matters such as labour or environmental policy came to be viewed as a burden by increasingly mobile and globalizing corporations and investors. Moreover, with the fall of the Berlin Wall and the rise of Glasnost in the USSR, the demise of the communist alternative led a triumphant capitalism to take an even more aggressive stance against state involvement in the economy. Thus, neoliberalism, a political rationality often seen as originating in the economic policies of former British Prime Minister Margaret Thatcher and former US President Ronald Reagan, became the new reigning philosophy. Other economic systems, it was argued, had fallen onto the scrap heap of history, leading to the neoliberal mantra, "there is no alternative" (TINA).

Neoliberalism is not a simplistic concept, as it is a flexible approach to economic and political policy that adapts to specific regional contexts. Despite there being multiple "neoliberalisms," one can discern a neoliberal ethos, just as we spoke in Chapter 3 of a restorative ethos. Within the neoliberal ethos, neoliberalism refers to a collectivity of discourses and practices that serve to monitor and regulate the capitalist system in a manner that encourages free mobility and maximal profit for capitalists (Hardt and Negri 2004). Political neoliberalism is intertwined with economic globalization (Jessop 2002). Neoliberalism provides globalization with a political strategy directed toward toppling labour, environmental, and other regulations that are viewed as prohibitive to investment. It also suggests a strategy of governance (or governmentality) that operates by shifting responsibility from the state onto individual and community actors, so as to remove from the state some of the expense and demands of governing the day-to-day lives of individuals. As Rose (1996: 41) writes:

> [Neoliberal] rule ... seeks to degovernmentalize the State and to destatize practices of government, to detach the substantive authority of expertise from the apparatuses of political rule, relocating experts within a market governed by the rationalities of competition, accountability and consumer demand.... "Community" emerges as a new way of conceptualizing and administering moral relations amongst persons.

In addition to calling upon states to reduce their levels of regulation (particularly with respect to regulations that hamper corporate profit making), the neoliberal ethos inspires broader self-regulation and so-called responsibilization amongst citizens and communities, enlisting these actors into the neoliberal economic project, while allowing the state to retreat into a role of merely managing and more subtly directing the national economy. For example, communities and individuals are asked to help manage and police the consequences of neoliberal rollbacks — that is, as social security is removed and more people find themselves without adequate financial or health support, individual community members are encouraged to care for their neighbours, to "look out for one another," to form neighbourhood watch groups, and to participate in community policing and community justice.

Despite the rhetoric of neoliberalism, which suggests an opening of and a freeing of the economy and society, the neoliberal ethos is often coercive in its application. In this regard, states and actors do not, in all cases, simply volunteer to privatize state-run industries or to expand the realm of private ownership to include more and more public goods. Governments that stubbornly cling to socialized businesses (such as state-owned energy utilities) or services (such as housing), or that resist the patenting of traditional knowledges or genetic material, will find themselves facing the full brunt of neoliberal power. "Developing world" countries in particular face austerity programs imposed by the International Monetary Fund that require privatization of state-run social services in exchange for aid, or through a growing body of trade agreements designed to push open the door to global commodification. In terms of the latter, we see the emergence of the Agreement on Trade Related Aspects of Intellectual Property Rights (TRIPS), the Agreement on Trade Related Investment Measures (TRIMS), and General Agreement on Trade in Services (GATS), which all play a part in restricting the ability of governments to control the patenting of products (including biological life forms), to insure foreign investment brings with it some benefit to the nation (through employment or technology transfer strategies) and to protect national services from foreign competition (such as socialized medicine) (Hart-Landsberg 2006). Even a nation such as Canada might find itself forced to bend toward corporate interests under the terms of the North America Free Trade Agreement (at the time of writing, renegotiated as the Canada-United States-Mexico Agreement and awaiting domestic ratification), as its provisions allow corporations to sue the signatory nations for their procurement policies, environmental regulations, or other interventions perceived to threaten the free pursuit of profit.

In addition, the neoliberal ethos is sufficiently malleable that it can even assimilate seemingly contradictory political philosophies into its operations. In this regard, the neoliberal ethos represents, to some degree, only a partial assault on the welfare state that does not necessarily amount to its absolute disappearance. Instead, some welfare state protections are maintained under the direction of the "left hand" of the state (Bourdieu 1998), although they are reconfigured so emphasis is placed on the responsibilized obligations rather than entitlement of citizens (Hartman 2005). In this manner, for example, forms of unemployment benefits are likely to continue under neoliberal systems because they play an important role in allowing for greater worker flexibility, especially for those workers whose employment is irregular, temporary, or casual. However, these benefits are then coupled with workfare or similar programs that reinforce the message that the citizen has an obligation to work, no matter how insecure or low-paying their job (Hartman 2005), or unemployment benefits might be reduced to insufficient levels so they no longer provide an adequate safety net and compel people toward poverty-level wage jobs. In part, the dregs of the welfare state are preserved to mitigate the contradictions, crisis tendencies, and consequences of neoliberalism for everyday life. These include:

- Growing rates of un- and underemployment, vast increases in precarious work, as well as numbers of those who have dropped out of the workforce altogether;
- A worsening of unregulated environmental devastation, resulting in loss of habitat and a decline in global liveability, including the spread of new diseases and the intensification of others that accompany ecological destruction;
- Zero-sum competition between regions, as they lower regulations to

attract investment, resulting in greater inter- and intra-national geographical disparities;
- Growing volatility and instability within the global financial system, as well as the fact that downward economic cycles and crises spread rapidly across the globe;
- The power of the nation-state to regulate its territory is further undermined at the hands of supranational institutions and agreements;
- Individualizing tendencies of neoliberal governmentality, largely through the discourse of "responsibility" whereby each individual is held accountable for their own well-being, resulting in a further erosion of social cohesion;
- A magnification of the divide between the rich and the poor;
- A commodification of heretofore untouched areas of our lives and worlds, including life forms, plants, and seeds;
- A stepping-up of global policing operations and an intensification of war, as the terrain of war shifts toward a greater frequency of attacks on non-combatants (and the line between combatants and non-combatants becomes more blurred);
- Greater corporate/capitalist influence in electoral politics, causing wider cynicism with regard to democratic representation and lower political participation amongst the citizenry;
- The mobility of corporations is not coupled with a mobility of people, which, along with the growing ferocity of war, leads to larger numbers of refugees (economic and political), *sans papiers*, boat people, and others seeking the right of movement;
- Previously secure groups who find themselves suddenly prone to economic or social exclusionary policies that detract from their former, more stable, social status (such as beneficiaries of welfare state policies in the Western world).

This list could go on, but these tendencies illustrate the "ontological insecurity" (Giddens 1991) that is provoked by neoliberal-inspired harms. Such insecurity is likely to produce greater social instability unless neoliberalism can attach itself to a mode of social regulation that allows for the effective management of potentially unruly populations caught within and reacting to these dangerous and very uncertain circumstances. For instance, as people become more desperate for sustenance, but also for all the goods and services sold to them through the capitalist marketplace, they may be increasingly drawn to crime when other legitimate avenues are closed off. To address such risks at both the global and local level, new forms of social control are emerging (Fraser 2003). On the one hand, the International Criminal Court, the United Nations, NATO, and other such bodies are increasingly involved in global policing. On the other hand, local community justice programs, alternative dispute resolution, and similar projects are being designed to enlist community members in the mediation and resolution of justice issues (Fraser 2003; Hardt and Negri 2000).

Critical criminologists and socio-legal scholars have often noted the coincidence between the ascendancy of neoliberalism and the rise of restorative justice. Moreover, they have pointed to overlaps between the two (see Pavlich 1996b; Woolford and Ratner 2003). For example, restorative justice promotes the devolution and decentring of state criminal justice powers in a way that fits the neoliberal rhetoric of reducing state infrastructure and involvement. Responsibilizing citizens to attend to their own criminal justice problems through "technologies of self" helps fashion docile citizens. Social projects, such as restorative justice, potentially serve as much to reinforce the logic of criminal justice and adapt individuals to the neoliberal era as they do to challenge the dominance of so-called retributive justice (Pavlich 2005). Directing people to focus on resolving local conflicts and coping with structural inequalities can do much to mask the source of the injustices that cause hardship in their day-to-day lives.

Once again, however, like most aspects of neoliberalism, its position on criminal justice is flexible and multifaceted. For, although neoliberalism makes room for restorative-type practices, especially when they appear to have some practical value in terms of managing minor offenders, it does not forsake punishment. Indeed, punishment is intensified under neoliberalism, since retribution continues to have positive value. This is not a value in terms of reforming offenders, as imprisonment and harsh sentences have rarely achieved this goal. Rather, the value stems from warehousing those who are viewed to be incorrigible, removing them as potential risks to law-abiding society (Wacquant 2009). As well, the value is a symbolic one, since it allows neoliberal politicians to demonstrate their tough-on-crime mettle, and with this, politicians can make the populist claim to represent the everyday interests of citizens, who are represented in political discourses as being ever fearful of crime. Moreover, the sensationalism of crime comes as a welcome distraction from the deeper and more widespread harms produced by neoliberal economic and social neglect.

Finally, retribution is itself a neoliberal growth industry, evidenced by the rise of for-profit prisons in the US (Stern 2006). In 2016, US private prisons have grown at a rate of 47 percent since 2000, a rate that easily surpasses the 9 percent growth rate across all prison types. Rates were highest in the growth of private federal facilities, as well as the exponential growth (442 percent) in private immigrant detention centres, which was not included in the calculation of the 47 percent growth rate (The Sentencing Project 2018). The trend toward having states outsource punishment to private industries is consistent with a neoliberal philosophy that seeks to reduce the size of government.

These criticisms of restorative justice and its relationship to neoliberalism will receive greater attention in the next chapter. What is important here is that we recognize that restorative justice operates in a distinct political and economic environment, and that this has implications for how restorative justice goes about its business. How restorative justice agencies work illustrates this point. As noted earlier, such agencies may be run by not-for-profit or non-governmental organizations, or they may be state-run. Whatever the case, the agency is dependent on government resources, primarily in the form of funding and case referrals. To ensure a steady and reliable flow of funding and referrals, it is important for restorative justice agencies to speak in a language that makes sense to, and appeals to, those in power. Restorative justice advocates looking to promote their work may decide to focus less on the idealistic aspects of their philosophy and more on how to market themselves in terms that will appeal to the neoliberal palate. For example, the word "accountability" has great currency in contemporary neoliberal times. Everyone and everything must be accountable, from governments and their sub-agencies to citizens. We find restorative justice agencies emphasizing to government that their programs offer accountability in the sense that having the offender face their victim is a way of holding that person accountable for the harm they have caused. Having the offender make reparation to the victim is a more far-reaching form of accountability than that achieved through the regular criminal justice system, and it also fits the compensatory logic of neoliberalism by translating an injustice into monetary terms, thereby, in part, transforming justice into an economic transaction. As well, a restorative justice program might highlight the fact that it can save the government time and money through its use of volunteer workers and community resources to address the problem of crime. Sales pitches like these have become increasingly necessary in the field of not-for-profit agencies because there are a great number of such agencies competing for a limited pool of government funding. In this context, a "quasi-market" (Bartlett and Le Grand 1993) structure unfolds, meaning agencies must seek to outbid their competitors to ensure they receive and maintain their piece of the pie. This makes it increasingly difficult for agencies to hold a principled stance in relation to the services they provide and leads many to adapt so as to better serve the desires of government.

What this all means for restorative justice is that practitioners must be very savvy in terms of what sort of compromises they are willing to make in order to ensure the well-being of their agency. For some, the principles and practice of restorative justice may appear so crucial to the needs of victims, offenders, and communities that compromising some restorative justice principles may be a necessary trade-off for exposing a greater number of people to a form of justice that is still widely unknown. For others, these compromises will appear little more than a selling out or appropriation of restorative justice, which redirects the transformative potential of restorative justice toward the task of increasing social control and further solidifying neoliberal domination. In other words, restorative justice cannot just accept the downloaded task of making communities responsible for their own crime control — it must also initiate discussions and actions that have the potential to influence wider social change. It should not be beyond the reach of a restorative justice movement to counter neoliberal policies — for example, to advocate for liveable wages and adequate levels of welfare payment since the lack of these elementary protections is often a primary source of community insecurity.

CULTURE, MEANING, AND THE POLITICS OF RESTORATIVE JUSTICE

Frederic Jameson (1991), the literary critic and social theorist, famously spoke of the "cultural logic" of late capitalism — a term he used to articulate how the cultural conditions of postmodernism provided a meaning framework for a globalizing capitalist system. Critical scholars have long studied how culture plays a role in the preservation and reproduction of social domination. Culture provides us with a source of meaning making, with ways of seeing and interpreting the world. Therefore, we must not ignore the cultural context of restorative justice.

Culture, however, should not be understood here in an essentialized and bounded sense. Following Clifford (1988), culture is a "deeply compromised" notion that has been used to place limits on what is, in truth, a complex set of relationships. Culture is not a thing, but, rather, a loose assemblage of values, practices, and behaviours that are never wholly fixed, but, rather, always in interaction with historical processes of "appropriation, compromise, subversion, masking, invention, and revival" (Clifford 1988: 338). Our cultures are never unitary because members of a cultural group will have different views and interpretations of their practices and values. And these practices and values may also change with time as the cultural group faces new challenges or is exposed to new influences. We must treat culture as something that is in process and changing. However, despite its dynamism, culture also provides us with a persistent means for making sense of the world — it offers us a store of meanings upon which we can draw to understand and interpret the unfamiliar present. While what it means to be Canadian in 2019 may be different from what it meant in 1919, we can still draw on our history (contested as it might be), shared reference points, and artistic and cultural life, among other factors, to try to understand our position in a broader global society. For some in Canada, this store of meaning may allow for expression of values of tolerance and human rights, while for others it may mean learning from mistakes of settler colonialism and racism. In either case, the dynamism of Canadian culture provides resources for making sense of our world.

It is culture as a system of meaning making that is most important for proponents of restorative justice. Contemporary Western societies are often characterized by anger, suspicion, and heightened intolerance. This atmosphere fits well with Bottoms' (1995) notion of "popular punitiveness" whereby politicians tap into public concern about crime to gain support. In the wake of sensationalized crimes, it is not uncommon to hear media pundits and radio callers demanding only the harshest of punishments. These sentiments appear to have increased in the Trump era, as the atmosphere of distrust and fear has become more pronounced, and a wall across the border is presented as a prophylactic measure to prevent the entry of gangs and murderers into the US. In these cultural conditions, crime and the criminal have come to occupy a special place in our growing list of anxieties. Politicians and the media understand this. They capitalize on these anxieties by feeding us stories to confirm and exacerbate our fears, following the dictum "if it bleeds, it leads." Politicians also profit off our anxieties, laying the risks of contemporary life at the feet of their political adversaries and promising to offer us a tough response.

How can restorative justice counter this cultural atmosphere of fear and put minds at ease? In part, restorative justice attempts to alter the climate of fear by providing opportunities for victims and community members to meet with offenders and to recognize their common humanity. However, restorative justice needs to find opportunities to broaden its efforts toward cultural change. This attempt is already occurring through charismatic speakers, documentary films, media stories, emotional engagement in actual restorative justice sessions, and other venues through which public awareness of restorative justice is generated. Rene Durocher's story, which was presented at the beginning of this book, is one such example. For years after he successfully reintegrated back into society, Mr. Durocher spoke to numerous school groups, conferences, organizations, and at public events to try to connect the general public with the life and humanity of an "offender." Such efforts are important and need to be expanded and linked to broader movements for peace and social justice that are seeking to sponsor a more tolerant cultural world.

RESTORATIVE JUSTICE AND OTHER-THAN-HUMAN ACTORS

In Chapter 2, we argued that harm is too broad a foundation for restorative justice, using the example of the harm caused by an earthquake and suggesting that a restorative justice encounter could not be established between the earthquake and its victims. However, this is not to suggest that other-than-human entities have no part in restorative justice. Too often in our thinking about justice, and criminal justice in particular, we proceed as though the worlds of nature and those of society and its constituent cultures are entirely separate. French philosopher of science, Bruno Latour (1991), has noted that it is only with so-called modernity that European-based societies began to draw a sharp distinction between culture and nature. In what he refers to as an act of purification, we imagined our cultural worlds as separate from our natural worlds, rather than integrally entwined. We do this despite the fact that we are constantly confronted with hybrids of our cultures and natures. Phenomena such as HIV/AIDS cannot be understood as belonging solely on the natural side of this equation, for example, because it is not solely biological. Rather, its spread, as well as our efforts to contend with it, depend also on cultural networks and actors who perceive the natural world through a distinctively cultural lens. For example, fears about the spread of HIV/AIDS in Vancouver's Downtown Eastside could not simply grapple with the problem as a natural one, tracing the movement of the pathogen through the population of intravenous drug users. Instead, more knowledge was required about how intravenous drug users interacted and shared their supplies with one another. The social and the natural aspects of this problem were significantly entwined, and realistic interventions, such as needle exchanges and safe injection sites, could only emerge from thinking about the two together.

In March 2017, the New Zealand government recognized the Whanganui River on North Island as having the same legal rights as a human being. The Whanganui iwi, the Māori groups in the region, have long understood the river to be an ancestor and its protection to be one and the same as their protection (Roy 2017). The river is not protected because it is perceived to be owned by the Māori, nor is it protected simply because its existence helps sustain the existence of those Māori who reside near to its shores. It is protected in its own right, and for its multifaceted relationship with the Māori (see Box 6.1). As the lead negotiator for the Whanganui iwi stated:

> We have fought to find an approximation in law so that all others can understand that from our perspective treating the river as a living entity is the correct way to approach it, as an indivisible whole, instead of the traditional model for the last 100 years of treating it from a perspective of ownership and management. (quoted in Roy 2017: n.p.)

The move toward recognizing ecological rights in law is growing. Such rights to a safe and sustainable environment, it is argued, allow citizens to sue their government and industries in instances where ecological rights are violated. In one example, one million Argentines living near the Riachuelo-Matanza, one of South America's most polluted rivers, were able to win access to clean water.

Such ecological rights have been established in over one hundred countries, making Canada an international laggard on this score. As a space of legal pluralism, however, meaning that Canada is defined by many legal jurisdictions, including the Indigenous legal traditions that preceded colonization, Canadians can turn to Indigenous understandings for guidance on thinking ourselves in relation with nature. The work of Tasha Hubbard (2014) on relationships between Indigenous peoples on the Great Plains and the buffalo is but one example. The Indigenous peoples of the Great Plains often describe the buffalo as the first people — a valued group defined by their own personhood. The notion of personhood here, whether applied to buffalo, a river, or salmon, is not intended to individualize and anthropomorphize these entities, but rather to recognize their sacredness as part of a crucial set of mutually sustaining relations.

Recognizing nature as a participant in social relations attributes to it an active role, one that acknowledges it as comprised of a set of entities that exist independent of the human world, but also entangled with this world. Restorative justice, as a relational approach to justice, will be found lacking if it is unable to attend to human and other-than-human relationships in its practices. This is especially so in the era of the Anthropocene, when humans have physically altered the environment in a manner that presents a global threat. The question thus arises as to what sort of standing might other-than-human entities have in a restorative justice meeting.

Because restorative justice concerns itself not just with individuals but with associations or communities, it is important to acknowledge that the other-than-human world is part of our communities. When conflict threatens to disrupt human associations, there are often also other-than-human interests at stake. For example, a conflict between an industrial plant and residents worried about the pollution of a local creek may be settled if the plant's owner promises to provide training and jobs for the residents, providing them with compensation for the threat to the creek they enjoy and have traditionally viewed as central to their collective life. But in such an instance of restorative justice, no one has spoken for the creek or the other-than-human flora and fauna that also rely on its waters. Here, restorative justice might do well to implement a "Lorax principle" whereby by a designate is assigned responsibility for speaking on behalf of the other-than-human parties impacted by the conflict resolution process.

Conflicts concerning the right to city space also involve other-than-human aspects. Consider the issue of camping in public parks. In Victoria, BC, the challenge of homelessness, combined with the relatively mild climate of the city, resulted in numerous peoples camping overnight in public parks. This brought complaints from some members of the general public about the danger and disorder represented by having homeless people sheltering in parks. We can see here, different groups within the same society had different visions of, and relations to, these natural settings. For some, parks were a shelter and safe place to sleep away from the noisier and busier city streets. For others, the parks were places of refuge and reflection where they went walk their dogs and exercise. City Hall responded to this conflict by creating a Parks Regulation Bylaw, which permits camping in certain parks between 8:00 p.m. and 7:00 a.m. during the warmer months, so long as tents are not placed along paths and are removed from the park by the end of the allowed period. This is a reasonable attempt to negotiate competing culture/nature entanglements, but how might the conflict

Box 6.1 New Zealand River Granted Same Legal Rights as Human Being

After 140 years of negotiation, Māori tribe wins recognition for Whanganui river, meaning it must be treated as a living entity.

In a world-first a New Zealand river has been granted the same legal rights as a human being.

The local Māori tribe of Whanganui in the North Island has fought for the recognition of their river — the third-largest in New Zealand — as an ancestor for 140 years.

On Wednesday, hundreds of tribal representatives wept with joy when their bid to have their kin awarded legal status as a living entity was passed into law.

"The reason we have taken this approach is because we consider the river an ancestor and always have," said Gerrard Albert, the lead negotiator for the Whanganui iwi [tribe].

"We have fought to find an approximation in law so that all others can understand that from our perspective treating the river as a living entity is the correct way to approach it, as in indivisible whole, instead of the traditional model for the last 100 years of treating it from a perspective of ownership and management."

The new status of the river means if someone abused or harmed it the law now sees no differentiation between harming the tribe or harming the river because they are one and the same.

Chris Finlayson, the minister for the treaty of Waitangi negotiations, said the decision brought the longest-running litigation in New Zealand's history to an end. "Te Awa Tupua will have its own legal identity with all the corresponding rights, duties and liabilities of a legal person," said Finlayson in a statement.

"The approach of granting legal personality to a river is unique ... it responds to the view of the iwi of the Whanganui river which has long recognised Te Awa Tupua through its traditions, customs and practice."

> Two guardians will be appointed to act on behalf of the Whanganui river, one from the crown and one from the Whanganui iwi.
>
> Albert said all Māori tribes regarded themselves as part of the universe, at one with and equal to the mountains, the rivers and the seas.
>
> The new law now honoured and reflected their worldview, he said, and could set a precedent for other Māori tribes in New Zealand to follow in Whanganui's footsteps.
>
> "We can trace our genealogy to the origins of the universe," said Albert. "And therefore rather than us being masters of the natural world, we are part of it. We want to live like that as our starting point. And that is not an anti-development, or anti-economic use of the river but to begin with the view that it is a living being, and then consider its future from that central belief."
>
> Financial redress of NZ$80m is included in the settlement, as well as an additional NZ$1m contribution towards establishing the legal framework for the river.
>
> Source: Roy 2017. Reprinted with permission of *Guardian News and Media*.

have been resolved if handled in an eco-sensitive restorative justice meeting? The park is a hybrid space marked by human intervention on the natural world that shapes lines of trees, pathways, bodies of water, and other features of this shared space. It is contested by its human visitors, but also a space of sanctuary for other-than-human animals. In resolving the conflict, it seems some of these parks' denizens were not fully represented.

There are, then, a number of contextual factors that must be taken into consideration when promoting and implementing restorative justice. There are severe structural challenges faced by any project concerned with changing our justice practices. Imbalances related to questions of identity, class, politics, culture, and ecology are just some of the considerations faced when thinking about how restorative justice might participate in a politics of transformation. However, before we consider this transformative potential, we must first look honestly and closely at the limitations of restorative justice.

QUESTIONS FOR DISCUSSION

1. What are some practical strategies a restorative justice program could implement in order to address the ways gender, sexual identity, race, or class impact participants?
2. We argue that restorative justice agencies that rely on government funding can be constrained within a neoliberal ethos and ultimately contribute to it. Do you agree or disagree? What would it look like if agencies did not rely on governments for funding and referrals?
3. Should restorative justice include other-than-human actors? What are scenarios in which it would be important to do so? How might a restorative justice process change to accommodate these actors and how would it change because of their participation?

7

RESTORATIVE JUSTICE CRITICISMS

Restorative justice, despite its broad support, has received a great deal of critical attention over the years. In typical restorative justice fashion, restorativists have often embraced criticism and self-criticism as part of a necessary dialogue about how to improve justice in our communities. They even go so far as to invite some of their most avid critics to attend restorative justice conferences and to debate key concerns in writing. Restorative justice cannot be accused of being an insular movement afraid to look its critics square in the eye. It is also the case that some of the criticisms of restorative justice are more damning than others and require some deep rethinking rather than a mere tinkering with restorative justice concepts and procedures. There are, what have been here termed, both technical and substantive criticisms. The technical criticisms illustrate oversights and errors in restorative justice thinking that are correctable through minor adaptation and revision. In contrast, substantive criticisms attack the broader ethos of restorative justice, exposing contradictions and dangers at its very roots. To address these latter criticisms, restorative justice must engage in an intensive project of re-evaluation and re-invention.

In its initial stages, restorative justice was prone to defining itself through a series of stark oppositions. As seen in Howard Zehr's (1985) early work (see Chapter 3), listing the characteristics that distinguish restorative from retributive justice was a common practice for restorativists seeking to clarify the restorative vision of justice. This is certainly not an uncommon practice for any new movement, or for any process of identity formation, for that matter. We often strive toward an understanding of who we are through an exercise in establishing what we are not. How often, for example, do Canadians assert their national identity by portraying themselves as "not like Americans?"

This tendency in restorative justice thinking, however, has led to both technical and substantive critiques of restorative justice. Indeed, it speaks to the larger question of the degree to which restorative justice is, or should be, attached to the formal criminal justice system (CJS).

TECHNICAL CRITICISMS

Kathleen Daly's (2003) criticisms of restorative justice can be viewed as technical rather than substantive because they are aimed at refining restorative justice thought rather than pointing out its irresolvable errors (see also Walgrave 2004; Roche 2007). Indeed, Daly's primary concern is to foster a more realistic understanding of restorative justice that avoids a stark and inaccurate differentiation from the formal CJS. To begin, Daly notes that what often happens when restorative justice is compared to the formal CJS is the ideal of restorative justice is set in contrast to the reality of retributive justice. For example, the punishment of imprisonment — with its tendency to institutionalize the offender and expose him or her to greater violence and pro-criminal attitudes — is cast against the ideal of community reintegration — where a caring community helps direct an offender onto the right path. Of course, the latter is an ideal vision of how restorative justice will work rather than an empirical comment on its current reality, where reintegration may prove to be an uneven and slow process, especially if community members do not step forward to offer their support.

Ideal visions of alternative justice forms often look very different when implemented. Indeed, when forced to operate within or alongside the CJS, these visions are often prone to corruption. Reform-oriented spiritual groups like the Quakers once supported imprisonment because they believed that, in its ideal form, prison would offer a quiet place for personal contemplation that would allow offenders the opportunity needed to foster personal change (Toews and Zehr 2004). In their wildest dreams, spiritual advocates of imprisonment could not have imagined these institutions would become massive warehouses for poor and minority groups in our societies (Stern 2006).

By focusing on the worst truths of the formal CJS, the restorative portrayal of the CJS also oversimplifies how it actually works. For example, it is erroneous to represent the CJS as entirely formalistic and authoritative. Plea bargaining shows (see Chapter 2) lawyers and their clients can negotiate a settlement on the steps of the courthouse. The CJS does offer opportunities for informal negotiation and compromise. As well, judges can deliver sanctions that involve punishments other than imprisonment, such as probationary or conditional sentences, that allow offenders to remain in their communities so long as they abide by the conditions of their sentences.

The wrongful portrayal of the CJS, as well as the presentation of an overly idealized version of restorative justice, has in the long run done a disservice to the restorative justice movement (Daly 2003). In actuality, restorative and retributive justices often work together. As has been demonstrated throughout this book, there are several points in the restorative justice process where assistance or input from representatives from the CJS is required. From the gatekeeper referrals that initiate the process, to the funding that supports the agencies that run the program, to the judges who review the restorative agreement and decide whether or not it meets prevailing judicial standards, we often witness a partnership between the two justices rather than direct contestation. Indeed, much of restorative justice operates, to once again use Christine Harrington's (1985) terminology, "in the shadow of the law."

For instance, let's return to the example of the Community Holistic Circles of Healing (CHCH) program in Hollow Water, Manitoba (see Box 4.3). Hollow Water was a community beset with long-running cycles of violence that were the residue of the harm wrought by Canadian residential schools. With generations of young people removed from their communities and raised in the cold and harsh environment of the residential schools, many Anishinaabe children did not receive the socialization and cultural training they would have from living with their families, which would have better prepared them to be parents. The lingering trauma of the residential school experience, combined with the broader impact of colonization (see Ross 1996), also contributed to substance addictions within the community. To address the epidemic of sexual and family violence within the community, Hollow Water launched a circle program to help reintegrate "victimizers" back into the community, ensuring they would no longer be a danger to their loved ones or neighbours. The program involves first getting victimizers to take responsibility and admit to their actions. If they own up, or if the CHCH team believes they can convince them to own up, then the judge for their case will assign a probationary sentence that allows the victimizer to remain in the community for a combination of traditional Indigenous and contemporary treatments. If, at any point, the victimizer fails to live up to their probation order, which mandates participation in CHCH, they are returned to the CJS for formal processing (Lajeunesse 1996). Throughout the process, the CJS looms as a means for coercing CHCH participation. In the National Film Board of Canada documentary, *Hollow Water* (Dickie 2000), we see the case of Richard Kennedy, who was assigned a probationary sentence within his community on the condition that he takes responsibility for his crime of sexually molesting his daughters and that he participates in CHCH programming. Kennedy only admits to his crimes after two years within the CHCH program, nearing the time when his probation period is about to end and he would likely be returned to the CJS for further processing. Although an offender might have difficulty in coming to terms with their past and this can be a lengthy process, it is likely that the threat of criminal justice played some role in swaying Richard Kennedy's decision to take responsibility. Nevertheless, there was a hybrid combination of formal and informal justice, with both community and state actors playing important roles.

For Daly, restorative justice misrepresenting itself and failing to adequately show its intersections and overlaps with the CJS makes it very difficult to convince an already wary public of the merits of this new justice option. This is also the case when restorativists claim restorative justice is non-punitive. The reasonableness of this claim hinges upon what exactly we mean by punishment and retribution. Is it, or is it not, a form of punishment to stand before one's community and admit to wrongdoing? It certainly causes discomfort and potential humiliation and embarrassment, so, if what we mean by punishment is an act that causes the wrongdoer a degree of discomfort, restorative justice is, in many cases, punitive. What differentiates restorative from retributive punishment in the minds of some restorativists is the fact the offender is given a say in what shape the sanction will take, whereas in the CJS penalties are imposed. This, however, does not take away from the fact that some form of inconvenience is decided upon and delivered to the offender, even if in a different form, such as a public apology or community work. If this were not the case, victims would be more likely to leave restorative meetings unsatisfied because of a sense that the wrongdoer has done nothing to atone for the harm caused.

R.A. Duff (2003) takes this point further to argue restorative justice can only be properly achieved through retributive punishment. For Duff, criminal wrongs upset normative relationships in our societies. Our shared values of "mutual trust, concern, and respect" are disrupted and challenged by the acts of the wrongdoer, and justice is an opportunity to recommit to these values. This can only occur if the offender recognizes the importance of these shared values through an apology that expresses their "repentant recognition and desire for reconciliation" (Duff 2003: 389). The severity of the breach of the normative order may also demand some other burdensome efforts on the part of the wrongdoer, such as participation in community work. In Duff's vision, then, restorative justice is not to be a feel-good environment defined solely by positive cooperation amongst the stakeholders to a wrong. It is a space of moral censure in which the facilitator must take pains to communicate to the wrongdoer the grievous nature of their violation and to encourage remorse from this individual.

With both Duff (2003) and Daly (2003), we see criticisms designed not to evidence the sheer poverty of the idea of restorative justice but, rather, to make restorativists reconsider some of their grander claims. Only by redressing such overstatements, it is argued, will restorative justice be able to present an honest reflection of itself to the general public. Practitioners and proponents of restorative justice have, in many cases, taken this advice to heart. Indeed, a common refrain upon the introduction of any new restorative justice program is that it is not soft on crime. In saying this, the restorativist is communicating to the public that the offender will, in fact, experience discomfort through the restorative process and will have to bear a heavy burden of shame and responsibility. As well, fewer programs attempt to remain distant from the CJS and instead have accepted there will be a certain amount of judicial oversight, especially with respect to judges having the final authority to accept or reject community-recommended sanctions. They also recognize they cannot operate without some level of cooperation from the state, especially if they want to continue to receive case referrals.

Other technical criticisms are aimed less at showing the connection between restorative and retributive justice and more at pointing out occasions where restorative justice has jettisoned elements of the CJS that serve important purposes. For example, several scholars have worried about the loss of due process rights within restorative justice (for example, Levrant et al. 1999; Skelton and Frank 2004). In particular, the maxim that one is "innocent until proven guilty" is sacrificed in restorative justice programs in which accused persons are asked to admit responsibility up front in order to guarantee their admission into the restorative process. This could present a grave problem if an accused person admits to charges they might otherwise be able to defend because they fear the courts and are willing to sacrifice their rights to ensure participation in a more benign-seeming restorative justice program.

Other concerns include that restorative justice will lead to net widening (Van Ness and Strong 2002; Umbreit and Zehr 1996; Wright 1991). Past diversion programs that sought to remove offenders from the criminal docket have been criticized for extending the reach of the state by processing through criminal justice programs harms that might otherwise have been dealt with informally (Cohen 1985). A contrast between Andrew's usually law-abiding siblings might help illustrate this point. When his older brother, then but a boy, was caught shoplifting at the local corner store, the police were called merely to scare him. The officer who came to the store gave him a stern lecture and then brought him home to his parents, who were told of the incident with the expectation they would take care of matters. Only a few years later, however, his sister was found shoplifting small items from a department store. The security guard called the police, and the arresting officer diverted her to a local anti-shoplifting program through which she performed some minimal community service tasks and met with other light-fingered girls to discuss the temptations of theft. Besides illustrating how well Andrew has turned out in comparison to his reprobate siblings, this example shows that diversion, as a supposed informal response to wrongdoing, in fact resulted in a ramping up of the criminal justice response to petty crimes.

Restorative justice has presented the same danger in that it can be used as a less resource-dependent alternative for dealing with low-level crimes, widening the net of social control to capture graffiti scribblers, petty shoplifters, and even snowball throwers. This is not to say these individuals have not committed harms; rather, it is a question of whether the degree of harm they committed merits a state-supported response. One worry with mobilizing restorative justice for these infractions is that it will, despite its best intentions, stigmatize young individuals by offering an excessive response to minor forms of acting out, especially considering the tendency of most youth to drift or age out of these sorts of activities (Matza 1990). All too frequently, overzealous responses to minor offences result in increased risk of the offender embracing a criminal identity, or simply becoming more likely to violate the conditions of their sentence, since the restorative process places them under greater surveillance and therefore greater risk of getting caught again (see Levrant et al. 1999).

A final technical criticism worth considering is that restorative justice leads to disproportionate sentencing (Ashworth 2003). Since the interventions of the classical school of criminology, and in particular Cesare Beccaria's principle that the "punishment should fit the crime," we have an expectation there will be a relationship between the seriousness of the act committed and the sentence received. Moreover, we expect this relationship to hold true across the entirety of our society. Here, a hypothetical example might best illustrate.

Imagine identical twins who have been raised in the exact same circumstances. At different points in time, approximately a year apart from one another, each twin embezzles $2000 from their employer to pay off gambling debts. In their separate trials, we would not expect one twin to receive time in prison while the other receives community work and counselling for their gambling addiction. Indeed, if there were a difference between the sentences, we would expect the second judge to provide a rationale for why sentencing differed from that of the colleague who saw the previous case. Restorative justice, however, does not typically limit itself to sentencing guidelines or to past precedent. Its emphasis is instead on the collective efforts of the stakeholders to creatively resolve the particular harm (Sharpe 2007; Wright and Masters 2002), and creativity is not a recipe for ensuring regularity of sentencing. In the example of the twins, it is conceivable each twin would receive very different sanctions from each restorative justice conference.

None of these criticisms is intended as the final nail in the coffin of restorative justice and some, such as disproportionate sentencing, can also be problems in our current justice system. These criticisms simply point to oversights in restorative theorizing and practice that need to be addressed. The stark distinction between restorative and retributive justice can be resolved by a more nuanced understanding of the intersections between these two systems and by reconceptualizing what we mean by punishment. Greater attention to due process rights could be given by requiring that accused persons speak with a defence lawyer prior to entering the restorative program so they are fully apprised of their rights. Net widening is addressed in some cases by programs restricting their clientele to only those clients who would receive prison time for their crimes, but in others by distancing the program from the state so it no longer gives the perception it is doing the state's work. Finally, differential sentencing can be addressed by having judges review restorative justice sanctions, although in some cases, restorativists prefer to argue differential sentencing is a reflection of the very particular circumstances of each crime and should not be problematized (Braithwaite 1994).

Potential restorative justice responses to technical criticisms serve primarily to reiterate that restorative justice and its guiding ethos are adaptable in the face of injustices, and criticisms, such as those discussed above, provide restorative justice the opportunity to improve its justice delivery and refine its practices. This is more difficult in the case of the substantive criticisms that are directed at the very heart of restorative justice.

SUBSTANTIVE CRITICISMS

Substantive criticisms challenge the substance or content of restorative justice. In this sense, such criticisms strike at the core presuppositions of restorative justice theory and practice, arguing these are unworkable or even dangerous offerings under current social circumstances. For example, expanding on the net widening criticism, some scholars have wondered whether or not an expansion of state control is inevitable through restorative justice. The restorative justice process is viewed to be too thoroughly entrenched within the formal CJS, as it is dependent on this system for referrals, funds, and even its terminology (terms like victim, offender, and crime). Moreover, the neoliberal conditions, described in the previous chapter, lead the state to seek out new ways to govern populations without relying solely upon the cumbersome machinery of the state, namely courts and prisons. These factors combine with the previously noted "quasi-market" conditions in which a rolled-back welfare state offers less funding for not-for-profit service providing agencies (see Chapter 6), requiring that surviving agencies struggle and compete for existing funds. Such conditions tend to provoke these agencies to make compromises in their programming and idealism so they might appeal to the needs and ideological leanings of people in power. For example, in research on restorative justice in British Columbia, Woolford and Ratner (2003) came across one restorative justice agency that had attached itself to its local Great Canadian Superstore, acting as their preferred program for dealing with shoplifters. The agency was even considering taking the further step of allowing Superstore to advertise on agency pamphlets in order to ensure their continued relationship. This agency, like many other community justice groups in British Columbia, had begun its program with a small provincial government grant, but the challenges of sustaining their work was seen as difficult without increased government and corporate support. With these sorts of pressures at play, the core principles and practices of restorative justice are likely to drift toward corruption, or to be wholly or partially co-opted by state agents (Levrant et al. 1999; Mika and Zehr 2003).

Others suggest that, even prior to co-optation, restorative justice is complicit in social control. Many such scholars are influenced by the work of Michel Foucault, the French philosopher and social historian, who, late in his career, developed the idea of governmentality, which refers to "a way of problematizing life and seeking to act upon it" (Rose 1993: 288), to describe the sixteenth-century rise in arts of governance that were directed toward shaping the will and behaviour of individuals (Foucault 1991, 1994). Governmentality involves "any attempt to shape with some degree of deliberation aspects of our behaviour according to particular sets of norms and for a variety of ends" (Dean 1999: 10). Governance, according to Foucault, therefore, occurs not simply through the might of the state, but, rather, through the proliferation of ways of thinking that serve as background assumptions to guide our individual choices. That is, governance narrows the boundaries of what is thinkable so our individual decisions fit within a limited set of normative options. Thus, the logic of governmental rule takes shape within individual mentalities and circumscribes thought and action, thereby effecting a "responsibilisation corresponding to the new forms in which the governed are encouraged, freely and rationally, to conduct themselves" (Burchell 1993: 276). For example, public education around issues of crime and risk prevention has been directed at preparing citizens to better safeguard their property and well-being. Through this education, it becomes a matter of common sense that a person should purchase a car alarm, a house alarm, and avoid certain areas of the city at specific times, alongside other acts of personal protection. Through this training, we become more responsible for governing our own self-management and safety and, more importantly, begin to think about our lives in terms of crime and risk prevention. We no longer ask the state to act as the guarantor of our safety; instead, this becomes the obligation of the self-governing citizen. At the same time, the offenders apprehended for committing petty crimes that require us to be more prudent in our safety measures may be subject to critical thinking errors and addictions programming so that they, too, are trained to be less "risky" members of society. Governance is thereby no longer solely the remit of the government and its police force; it is also a local, individual matter.

George Pavlich (2005) has described restorative justice as participating in several governmentalities. The first restorative justice governmentality encourages participants in restorative justice meetings to examine and reshape their conduct in relation to their experiences of crime and justice. For example, offenders are asked to take responsibility for their actions, victims are asked to express how the crime has affected them and to present reasonable demands for repair, and community members are asked to participate in the reintegration of the offender and the healing of the victim. This governmentality works not only upon their behaviour in the actual meeting but is also intended as a guide for their future behaviour. This goal of individual self-governance has additional benefits for the state, since individuals who accept and internalize restorative values and practices free the state of this responsibility, thereby lessening the costs and reducing the work of governance. For example, if a neighbourhood can deal with its youth vandalism problem through community meetings, neighbourhood watch programs, and volunteer-run after-school programs, the state is not on the hook for such services.

The second mode of restorative justice governmentality fashions a way of understanding the world (and crime in particular) that makes the pursuit of restorative justice appear more rational and understandable to those involved. If restorative justice is to govern our behaviour, it must first change how we think about crime and criminal justice. It does this by reframing or redefining core components of criminal justice. For Pavlich, this involves providing answers to the questions:

1. *What is governed?* Unlike formal criminal justice, restorative justice claims to govern harm rather than crime, since it is not the violations of the state's law but, rather, the harms suffered by individuals and communities that are of primary concern.
2. *Who is governed?* Those who are to be governed are all of those who have a stake in the crime and its effects — victim, offender, and community members — rather than just the offender.
3. *Who governs?* Whereas judges and lawyers are the individuals empowered through the practice of criminal justice, restorative justice seeks to give greater agency to victims, offenders, and community members.
4. *What is appropriate governing?* Instead of focusing on the past, restorative governance should be directed toward the future. It is therefore less a question of punishing a wrongdoer and more an issue of creating a dialogue among stakeholders so they can work out how to avoid repetition of the crime.

For Pavlich, the problem with these restorative justice governmentalities is they do not represent a true alternative to the CJS. They still govern "crime" as defined in our CJS, target marginalized populations, empower criminal justice gatekeepers and professionals, and seek a future that seems little more than a more peaceful version of the status quo state of affairs. Pavlich argues that restorative justice is thus fundamentally dependent on the CJS and criminal law. This amounts to more than the problem that restorative justice tends to misrepresent both its relationship with and the workings of the CJS. More importantly, it means restorative justice is locked into the conceptual and practical tendencies of the CJS and therefore fails to provide a true alternative to its dominance. For example, although restorative justice shifts our attention to the harm suffered by victims and community members, it nonetheless relies on criminal law to define the acts that are to be considered harmful. Therefore, it prevents itself from addressing harms that are not specified within criminal codes, as well as structural harms.

If restorative justice does not avoid the narrowing definitions of criminal law, it is likely to remain silent with respect to serious injustices that threaten to cause a great deal of harm. For instance, the Alberta Tar Sands have had a staggering effect on the Albertan and Canadian economies, but also on environmental conditions in northern Alberta. One of the most troubling cases of environmental damage has occurred in the village of Fort Chipewyan, 260 kilometres north of Fort McMurray, where doctors have confirmed the Indigenous population suffers from a higher than expected rate of cancer, including rare bile-duct cancers. Fort Chipewyan rests on the shores of Lake Athabasca, which is fed by the Athabasca River and has been found to contain unsafe levels of arsenic, mercury, and polycyclic aromatic hydrocarbon. While there is not yet absolute proof the problems faced in this community are the result of the conversion of the Tar Sands' bitumen into crude oil, processing this crude oil does produce large amounts of contaminated water, all of which may not be properly contained. Does restorative justice not have a place in such a conflict? A restorative justice that sought to be a significant alternative to the formal criminal justice system, especially one geared toward transformative ends, would need to address such potentially disastrous injustices, given their terrible toll on human lives, even (or especially) if the law has not yet seen fit to criminalize them.

Likewise, restorative justice must be able to address structured inequalities that entail great levels of social harm. The continuing disparity between men's and women's wages, as well as the increasing feminization of poverty through the neoliberal rollback of social assistance, have left many mothers struggling to make ends meet and to support their children. When dealing with cases of fraud or other crimes committed by these desperately poor mothers, should restorative justice simply focus on the criminal act and ignore gendered disadvantages? Or, more ambitiously, can restorative justice not provide a space for discussion of and activism for state subsidized childcare, minimum incomes, and other policies that would assist lone parent families?

Pavlich (2001) also takes issue with restorative justice notions of community and justice. For Pavlich, the restorative justice notion of community, even with the more nuanced concepts of "communities of care" or "micro-communities," has the potential to be exclusionary. This is because the term "community" suggests a bounded physical or symbolic space, whereby those not belonging to this space are placed beyond its boundaries, so even in the case of a "community of care" that is defined around familial and friendship relations, a limit is set with respect to which only a select few can claim inclusion. Ethically speaking, Pavlich finds this a problematic beginning for restorative justice, since it is still predicated on us/them thinking: *we* are members of this community of care and therefore share responsibilities to and for one another; *they* are not part of our community and therefore we owe them no sense of obligation. Pavlich recommends, in contrast, a notion of hospitality instead of community. This is because the good host is one who welcomes and seeks to get to know their guest and therefore remains open to those who are different or unknown, an idea Pavlich (2001, 2007) finds much more promising for relationship-building than the closed space of community.

Pavlich also alerts restorative justice advocates to the dangers of a justice alternative built upon compromised foundations. As noted above, he finds the restorative notion of justice too dependent on criminal justice reasoning, and he proposes instead that restorativists aspire toward a sense of justice that pushes beyond criminal justice's "conceptual horizons" and "calculates" justice in a manner free from criminal justice precepts (Pavlich 2005: 106, 116). In this sense, Pavlich's ambition is to provide critical deconstructive tools to help us truly think beyond the contemporary configuration of criminal justice. Pavlich does not, nor does he wish to, spell out what these new justice horizons might look like. Because Pavlich's critical project is directed toward removing limitations upon our thought and action, and toward opening our discussions to different justice possibilities, he is reluctant to prescribe exactly what the future justice should look like. Instead, in keeping with the spirit of Derrida's deconstruction, he proposes responses to injustice should take into account the specific and local circumstances of that injustice. If a person suffers an injustice at the hands of another, for example, in the form of a violent assault, we would not enter into this conflict with preconceived notions about who is the victim and who is the offender or what criminal code violation has occurred. Rather, an effort would be made to, like the good host, understand the particularity of each of these individuals and their situations. What initiated the violence? How did the two parties experience it? What are the cultural, economic, social, or political factors that contributed to this act of violence? Such questions are not entirely different from those that might be asked by restorative justice practitioners, but they are here removed from the discursive limits of the formal cjs, which has the unfortunate tendency to shape the meanings drawn from and interpretations applied to specific cases of injustice.

Table 7.1 **Criticisms of Restorative Justice**

Technical Criticisms	Substantive Criticisms
• By focusing on the worst truths of the formal cjs, the restorative portrayal of the cjs also simplifies how the cjs actually works	• Too thoroughly entrenched within formal cjs
• RJ can only be properly achieved through retributive justice	• Neoliberal conditions lead the state to seek out new ways to govern populations without relying solely upon courts and prisons
• Jettisoning elements of the cjs such as due process	• RJ is complicit in project of social control
• Net widening	• Participates in several governmentalities
• Leads to disproportionate sentencing	• Locked into conceptual and practical tendencies of cjs and therefore fails to provide a true alternative to its dominance
	• Issues with the notion of community in its potential to be exclusionary

CRITICISM AND THE POLITICS OF RESTORATIVE JUSTICE

Criticisms of restorative justice — only a handful of which have been considered here — are crucial to understanding and redirecting the politics of restorative justice. Not only do these criticisms help us to identify the current political barriers to effective restorative justice practice and the practical and technical oversights of existing restorative justice practice, they also encourage us to interrogate the foundational assumptions of restorative justice.

We learn, for example, from net widening critics that restorative justice rests in a precarious political position that leaves it constantly at risk of co-optation. This is a technical criticism that demands a great deal of practitioner attention to the pressures faced in the day-to-day operations of a restorative justice agency, and to resist those that might corrupt or compromise the agency. However, when net widening is expanded upon as a substantive criticism that identifies the structural tendencies toward co-optation, the matter is not so easily resolved through the good intentions of restorativists. What is then required is a broader social movement assault on the social and political conditions that prevent a fuller realization of restorative justice. Under current conditions, this means first and foremost an oppositional struggle against the structures of domination covered in the previous chapter. This asks a lot of practitioners and proponents of restorative justice, since their daily work is set against the pain, hardship, and immediate needs of those with whom they work. And yet they will always be working in a state of triage if the deeper causes of injustice remain unaddressed.

We also learn from critics of the stark division between restorative and retributive justice that the representation of restorative justice as an alternative and polar opposite to the CJS is disingenuous at best. However, if we follow Pavlich's more substantive critique, the solution to this problem is more radical than simply being honest about the retributive debts of restorative justice. Pavlich's work demands a thorough re-imagining of justice that is not foreclosed by the limitations of the CJS. We must think beyond criminal justice and hegemonic conceptualizations of victims and offenders, criminal law and practices, and the like if restorative justice is to become transformative. Following Pavlich's lead entails a rigorous critical opening up of restorative justice thinking — to the point where restorativists show a willingness to interrogate even the grounding assumptions of the restorative ethos.

QUESTIONS FOR DISCUSSION

1. We outline a number of technical criticisms here, what are others?
2. Consider Duff's argument. Must restorative justice include punishment? Or is it an alternative to punishment?
3. Do you agree with Pavlich? Is restorative justice fundamentally dependent on the CJS? Defend your response.

8

TRANSFORMATION AND THE POLITICS OF RESTORATIVE JUSTICE

Taking the criticisms of restorative justice seriously, and responding to the intersectional, neoliberal, anthropocentric, and retributive context in which restorative justice currently operates, the question is: how might restorative justice mobilize itself politically to combat the co-optation and full governmentalization of its justice philosophy and practices? Also, how might restorative justice participate in a broader transformative political project that works with and alongside other groups concerned with matters of social justice and the goal of overcoming injustices (such as anti-poverty groups, feminists, environmentalists, Indigenous activists, Black Lives Matter, the labour movement, and anti-neoliberalism groups)?

While Sullivan and Tifft (2006: 5) present restorative justice as "subversive" and as an "insurgency" because it competes with the state over the question of how to approach issues of social harm, they also recognize this subversive quality can be dampened or diluted. Indeed, the adaptability of restorative justice can lend it to application within a very conservative politics. Restorative justice can be, and is often, focused on street crime, on youth, and toward holding offenders accountable for crimes that are perceived to be solely the result of their individual choice. In this respect, it can serve the ideological purpose of individualizing criminal activity and victimization with little regard for the structural conditions that make crime possible (White 2008).

For some restorativists, the apolitical potential of restorative justice is one of its strengths. Van Ness and Strong (2002: 156) suggest that "restorative justice is neither a conservative nor a liberal agenda." Daly and Immarigeon (1998: 31) also note, "Restorative justice as a social movement can embrace both 'neo-liberalism,' with its focus on economic rationality, entrepreneurial activity, and concern to 'empower the consumer,' and grass-roots forms of democratic socialism." In fact, restorative justice has been frequently embraced by neoliberal nations concerned with fiscal conservatism and reducing the machinery of the state (Braithwaite 2003) but who still want to implement potent societal regulation strategies. Most recently, the Manitoba Conservative Government has publicly stated its intention to promote the use of restorative justice (Taylor 2018). But with this announcement no promise was made to add to the anti-poverty and decolonizing work that would be necessary for a transformative restorative justice to address the roots of crime and not just its symptoms. Nor were any details included about increasing funding for the social services required to make restorative justice programs work. Moreover, in the aftermath of the same government cutting the successful Restorative Resolutions program, which operated out of the John Howard Society of Manitoba working with adult offenders, one might wonder if the new commitment to restorative justice will be aimed more at youth and low-level offenders.

It could be argued that the political adaptability of restorative justice is a sign of weakness rather than strength. While one can appreciate the ways in which restorative justice can adjust to the very local circumstances of injustices and their causation, and thereby cater to the particular needs and challenges of an injustice context, political adaptability can be taken as evidence that restorative justice lacks an adequate vision of social justice. It could be argued restorative justice can fit into any dominant political framework because it is little more than a palliative technique that softens the immediate harms of injustice and provides a less cumbersome means for dealing with minor offences, but offers no lasting vision of justice to which a society can aspire. Without an oppositional vision of justice, restorative justice is unlikely to do more than serve the dominant relations of ruling in our societies. Take, for example, the application of restorative justice principles through Canada's 2003 Youth Criminal Justice Act (YCJA). Serge Charbonneau (2004) argues that although the YCJA recommends the restorative practice of conferencing, it also makes room for punitive responses to violent and repeat young offenders. This dualistic approach to youth justice results in the braiding of restorative and retributive sanctions, with conferencing serving as an initial response for minor offences and the court-based resources of the criminal justice system (CJS) activated only for what are perceived to be more serious cases. The YCJA has helped grow restorative justice in Canada, as illustrated by the fact that only twenty-seven of the 407 operational programs serve adults exclusively. The others work with youth, but many do so for purposes of diverting "less serious" crimes away from the CJS, offering them instead "extrajudicial measures" (Llewelyn 2018). In this way, restorative justice becomes a diluted and co-opted form of justice because it is potentially limited to offences that might otherwise have been ignored by the CJS. Thus, restorative justice supplements and supports the dominant CJS, playing no more than a marginal role within this system by offering a more cost-effective approach for dealing with the small stuff. From this marginal position, restorative justice has little power to call into question the gendered, class-based, or racialized dimensions of the CJS.

For many restorativists, such a future for restorative justice would be anathema to their ambitions. They view restorative justice as part of a broader transformative movement toward making social conflicts more productive and positive. These restorativists might be referred to as communitarians because of their commitment to a restorative justice that fosters transformative community change within and through social relationships (Woolford and Ratner 2003). For communitarians, creative and communicative relationships are the basis for transforming the social world, since we learn through problem solving to confront head-on the obstacles and challenges to societal peace. In contrast, other restorative justice practitioners can be designated as governmentalists because they view restorative justice as merely another tool within the criminal justice toolbox and as a means to assist and support rather than transform the CJS (Woolford and Ratner 2003). In the previous chapter, we mentioned the restorative justice program that affiliated itself with the Great Canadian Superstore to act as its anti-shoplifting arm. This is one example of a governmentalist program. In other cases from our research, we have come across restorative justice agencies that were content to deal only with minor crimes, or which used community accountability panels to moralize to young offenders. All of these groups can be understood to be governmentalist, since they appear intent on advancing an uncritical governmentality among offenders, directing them on how to regulate their own behaviour in a more conciliatory and non-disruptive manner, but these agencies show little interest in exploring the broader context of power in which the offences took place, or in empowering victims and offenders in a way that would enable them to question social injustices.

John Braithwaite (2002) has similarly distinguished between social justice and administrative practitioners, also capturing this contrast between the desired ends forwarded in different segments of the restorative justice movement (see also the "continuum of restorative possibilities" suggested by Mika and Zehr 2003: 138–139, as well as Van Ness and Strong 2002 and Sharpe 2004). This division in the world of restorative justice between community/justice and governance/administration-oriented programs is thus one that is played out in many different jurisdictions.

How can one advance a vision of social justice within the restorative movement without foreclosing the conversation about what exactly justice is? Pavlich (2007) has rightfully critiqued the tendency toward developing universal principles of restorative justice that are intended to apply in all restorative contexts. Such fixed notions of the "correct values" guiding restorative justice only serve to straightjacket and limit our approach to specific instances of injustice, and, it is the flexibility and attention to situational specificity that are two of the most attractive features of restorative justice. Even worse, the establishment of unchanging principles of restorative justice encourages sedimentation of restorative justice thinking, which could lead the movement to fail to adequately reflect upon and critique its own principles and practice. A restorative justice that is a work in progress, which is always in the process of forming and reforming itself, is most likely to be resist such rigidity. Zernova and Wright (2007: 104), who embrace a restorative justice in flux and support a "politics of difference" with respect to the existing divisions in restorative justice contend:

> Maybe it could be beneficial for restorative justice advocates to focus not on developing unified visions and eliminating diversity but on learning to live and struggle with differences. Some may feel that their task is to develop restorative justice as an improvement on criminal justice; others may believe that restorative justice should pursue the larger aim of building a fairer society.

The question remains, however: how can restorative justice be transformative if it is defined by differences, and if it is in a constant state of identity formation? The lessons of transformation handed down from earlier periods of revolution suggest such change is brought by a vanguard steeped in revolutionary ideology. How, some might ask, can restorative justice bring about transformative change unless it follows a similar script? But in these "post-Socialist times" (Fraser 1997), we do not have at our disposal a unifying ideology to direct change. What we have instead are a diverse array of actors who are similarly troubled by the intersectional strife and callous meanness of the neoliberal era. The task for these individuals and groups is to find a means to negotiate their differences while working with a general common purpose, and this is not likely to occur through ideological closure, which risks excluding some concerns while privileging others (for example, highlighting class oppression while overlooking gendered inequalities). With increasing global turmoil, such as market recession and environmental destruction, resulting from a lengthy period of neoliberal deregulation, the time has perhaps never been riper for restorativists to join the multitude of dissatisfied voices in pressing for social change.

Restorativists, however, cannot simply pursue a radical vision of transformation and ignore immediate needs within the CJS that must be addressed. Even a restorative justice program that aspires toward transformation must engage in the present world and provide services that are of clear benefit to existing clients. Therefore, the project of transformation need not be divorced from everyday attempts to reform criminal justice. The goal may be one of broader transformation, but ex-offenders still require assistance in reintegrating into their communities (such as help with job and apartment seeking), victims still need support in overcoming the harmful effects of crime (such as via therapeutic services), and communities still function better when they are less fearful. Criminal justice improvements are also part of a broader conversation about our vision for a future world, although they cannot be permitted to narrow or rigidly define our thinking about what is possible.

TRANSFORMATIVE JUSTICE

To maintain the balance between immediate needs and the goal of transformation, as well as to navigate the seeming contradiction of expressing transformation as a goal and yet wanting to keep the future of restorative justice open and indeterminate, the terms "social justice" and "transformation" must be refined. Our emphasis will be upon what we refer to as transformative justice rather than social justice or transformation, since it better captures the active nature of justice as an ongoing project rather than as a fully imaginable or realizable end. That is to say, one cannot fully prescribe what the future justice will look like, and a crucial lesson of world history is that attempts to socially engineer a totalized vision of a just world too often end in corruption, authoritarianism, and disaster (Scott 1998). Nazism and Stalinism are but two examples of visions of justice taken as prescribed ends for which any means were justified. Thus, like Pavlich, our notion of transformative justice does not come with a fully articulated definition of what the future world should look like. However, we know enough about the nature of injustice that some basic guidelines can be devised to help us in our pursuit of transformative justice. These guidelines, or signposts, are not envisioned here as a full and final end goal for the restorative justice movement, but, rather, as categories of injustice and remedy to guide thought and action without severely restricting our creativity.

A provisional understanding of transformation was offered in Chapter 1, where it was suggested that restorative justice offers opportunities for personal and social change. Restorative justice offers the potential for collective discussion of problems in our society, and through this discussion, we can learn about ourselves, and concentrate our efforts on changing ourselves, but also obtain a deeper understanding of our societies and what might require changing therein for a better world to arise. In this sense, the transformative potential of restorative justice rests within its process, which allows people to reflect deeply upon the many causes of injustice. However, it would be naïve to expect restorative justice meetings will necessarily gravitate toward anti-oppressive criticisms of self and world. What is to prevent a meeting from simply rationalizing existing relations of domination? For example, a community that finds patriarchal domination to be beneficial to community life may not use a restorative justice meeting dealing with spousal abuse to address the more widespread domination of women within the community. Instead, they may place pressure on the female complainant in the case to simply accept her role and to stop stirring up trouble (Acorn 2004). In this regard, restorative justice possesses no necessary critical political content, making some transformative guidelines necessary.

RECOGNITION, REDISTRIBUTION, AND REPRESENTATION

Nancy Fraser's (1997, 2000) three-dimension theory of justice provides at least a starting point for some transformative guidelines. For Fraser, injustices typically demand one or more of the following responses: recognition, redistribution, and representation. *Recognition* is needed in response to injustice of a cultural-symbolic nature. When someone misrecognizes you, they may impute upon you a wrong identity (for example, calling a Nehiyaw person an "Indian") and/or devalue your social status based upon this imputed identity (as in racist discourse). Cultural-symbolic injustices can result in social exclusion, forced assimilation, or even attempts at extermination. With respect to injustices of a criminal nature, in many instances, there is a form of misrecognition at play, since crime disempowers an individual and deprives him or her of a sense of personal "dominion," to borrow the language of Braithwaite and Petit (1990).

When misrecognition occurs, recognition is due. If a person is assaulted (sexual or non-sexual), for example, a just response must involve recognition of their bodily integrity and rights to physical safety. Or, if a person is the victim of a racist hate crime, they, at minimum, require recognition of their equal human worth.

However, Fraser notes recognition can be either affirmative or transformative in its response to cultural-symbolic injustices. Affirmative recognition tends to be superficial; it does not address the patterned cultural-symbolic injustices that are at the root of misrecognition. Affirmative repair in response to racism, for example, may provide public recognition of the equality of a targeted person or group, but does little to challenge our misguided patterns of racial thinking through which we imagine something as contentious as race to actually exist. In such a case, a member of an ethnic minority who comes to school to find a racist epithet scrawled upon their locker would receive affirmative repair when the perpetrator of this deed is caught, required to clean the locker, apologize, and write a research essay on the harms of racism. Here, the emphasis has been placed upon modifying individual behaviour without attempting to address broader processes of racism at the school or in society. In contrast, a transformative approach would seek to challenge structures of symbolic domination by interrogating the roots of cultural injustice. Therefore, if it were to be transformative, a restorative justice session dealing with the same case would want to do more than procure an apology and an essay from the person who vandalized school property with racist graffiti. It would need to examine more broadly the racial tensions at the school and in the community to understand their source and to inspire students to think critically toward the category of race. Such a project would seek to educate students and community members about the structural dimensions of racism, its roots, and its human consequences. Say, for example, the graffiti had targeted an Indigenous student. This would present the opportunity for discussion of colonialism and the ways in which it disadvantaged and devalued Indigenous communities, but also for education on the continued resistance and strength of Indigenous peoples in the face of these demoralizing and racist assaults on their communities. The goal of these efforts, in short, would be to destabilize operative systems of racialized valuation.

It should be noted with the above examples, though, that conflicts are rarely solely cultural. Modes of symbolic domination introduce and prop up systems of material deprivation. In the case of racism against Indigenous peoples, for example, the devaluation of Indigenous cultures is not simply an insult to their status as valuable and equal human groupings. It is also part and parcel of the ongoing settler colonial dispossession of Indigenous territories. From the beginning of the settler colonial project in Canada and the US, Indigenous nations were devalued to deny their stewardship over their territories and to justify their erasure so that they could be replaced by settlers (Tuck and Yang 2012; Wolfe 2006). Symbolic struggles have material consequences. These are consequences not just for the material well-being of members of a dominated group, but also for their relationship to their territories and ecology. For this reason, recognition, even when promoted as transformative recognition, is seldom by itself sufficient to redress an injustice.

Redistribution is needed for violations of a socio-economic nature. Socio-economic injustices include the harms of economic exploitation (such as low wages that do not reflect one's contribution to economic production), marginalization from economic rewards (such as the exclusion of ethnic, gender, or racial groups from certain occupations, or the way in which men are more likely to be promoted than their female co-workers), and material deprivation in relation to other groups (such as the fact women tend to be paid less than men for similar work) (Fraser 1997). Criminal injustices also tend to involve wrongs of a socio-economic nature, both in motivating circumstances for a crime (for example, an offender may feel marginalized from the system of economic rewards because they are unable to find a job with adequate pay) and in its results (for example, a victim may feel materially deprived as a result of the offence). As with responses to cultural-symbolic injustices, the forms of redistributive remedy offered in the aftermath of socio-economic injustice can be affirmative or transformative. Affirmative forms of redistribution offer only a minor surface redistribution of resources, such as in the form of small compensatory payments or community work in lieu of such a payment. A transformative form of redistribution would aspire toward a deeper restructuring of our economy and system of work. Such an approach would need to redress the broader system of inequality in our society, which is itself the criminogenic seedbed of a great deal of social injustice. For a restorative approach to be transformative, more must occur than the simple redistribution of money or services from offender to victim. Instead, consideration needs to be given to the social conditions that made the injustice possible. At the root of crime are issues like poverty, social disorganization, and economic marginalization, and unless these are addressed, a community is unlikely to create for itself conditions amenable to peaceful co-existence. Thus, a transformative restorative justice program would, for example, have a clear interest in working alongside anti-poverty groups to tackle issues of community poverty and to advocate for living wages for all community members. A transformative restorative approach cannot simply stop at an agreement on compensation; it must move toward challenging the structured patterns of exclusion from fair economic participation.

The final remedy, *representation,* is offered in response to political injustices that deny individuals and groups a sense of social belonging and of inclusion in processes of decision making and political framing. When groups or individuals are denied a voice in political matters, or denied political membership, they are deprived of fundamental rights within a democratic society. The response to this injustice can once again be affirmative or transformative. Affirmative representation provides only a token voice so the participation of the formerly excluded individual or group does not prove too disruptive to the system. This is the remedy offered through tools like victim impact statements, which are intended to correct the exclusion of victims from court proceedings, but do so by only providing the merely consultative inclusion of the victim's point of view and thereby also serve to bolster the legitimacy of national criminal justice frameworks. In contrast, a transformative approach would seek to critique systems of representation that deny participation to certain groups and individuals in our societies. In this sense, restorative justice has already built into it a more transformative approach to participatory injustices, since it allows for the active participation of victims, offenders, and community members in justice decision making. This is not to suggest, however, that restorative justice could not be more transformative in this regard, and its efforts could be directed toward fostering even broader forms of public participation in justice decision making. For instance, transformative restorative justice programs in Indigenous communities could press for broader powers of representation in the form of self-determination for Indigenous peoples. While contemporary practices of circle sentencing offer affirmative representation of Indigenous voices in local justice processes, transformative representation in these circumstances would involve greater community control over political and legal matters within community life. Such powers would enable communities, if they so choose, to pursue remedy for the many injustices in their midst, such as housing, addiction, violence, and the continuing legacy of residential schools.

These analytical guideposts offer direction for a transformative restorative justice. In each case — in terms of recognition, redistribution, and representation — the distinction between affirmative and transformative remedies allows us a model through which we can gauge the adequacy of a given response to injustice and can serve as guidelines for restorative justice programs. Moreover, it offers us a transformative ideal that demands a thorough interrogation of existing conditions of domination rather than just a facile response to immediate harms. Anything less than a transformative approach to injustice tends to only scratch the surface of the problem, ignoring its deeper cultural, structural, and political roots.

It is also the case that injustices of misrecognition, maldistribution, or misrepresentation intersect. Therefore, the respective remedial strategies selected will have an impact on one another. Fraser (1997) argues that transformative strategies of recognition, redistribution, and representation tend to align most favourably, as a combination of affirmative and transformative strategies can lead to contradictions and the canceling out of the transformative effort by the logic of the corresponding affirmative approach. In other words, if a restorative justice program were to support a more transformative redistributive strategy that sought to address more broadly the problem of Indigenous poverty but took an affirmative strategy toward recognizing Indigenous identities as subsumed under a racialized category, the net effect could be to essentialize Indigenous peoples in a manner that makes the transformative redistributive strategy appear a special dispensation to a particular ethnic group rather than the just dues of original peoples wrongly dispossessed of their lands.

A note of caution. What Fraser offers us is an analytical framework for assessing our justice intentions. Like any analytical framework, it requires a simplification. As well, like any theoretical perspective, it must be approached as a fallible framework open to deconstruction. As we try to separate and carve out categories of justice, for example, we might not fully capture the entanglements between our categories. Is territorial dispossession simply matter of maldistribution or also an assault upon the culture of an Indigenous group whose identity is bound by their relationship to territory? And what about the representational needs of the territory itself? Does it receive a voice in the political decision making that impacts its deep ecology? As well, Fraser's framework draws on a European liberal philosophical tradition that takes for granted the overarching liberal-democratic framework of the nation-state without fully contending with conflicts over the state's claim to sovereignty and the competing sovereignties within the borders of a specific state. Here, too, Indigenous justice assertions challenge the framing we have set forth. These guidelines provide some initial starting points for discussing transformative justice, but they can only reach true transformative potential through being subject to ongoing critique and revision in conversation with groups and individuals whose experiences of injustice are the key stakes of our transformative efforts.

With these guidelines in hand, as well as the caution we note above, one might still rightfully ask: but what is transformative justice? This is a fair question and our answer may not satisfy all readers. This is because we will not give our definition of transformative justice any content other than the guidelines proposed above, which we note are a rough framework, themselves open to critical reflection and reappraisal. This is because transformative justice is an ongoing practice through which we must continually strive toward a better world. Given the many contexts of injustice, as well as their temporal and regional variations, it is not possible to prescribe one notion of transformative justice that will fit all circumstances. What we are left with instead is a need to seek to live justly in relation to an ever-increasing diversity of wronged human and other-than-human parties. Our responsibility is to try to meet their justice needs, even if fully meeting these needs is impossible. This is one of the paradoxes of justice Jacques Derrida signals in his discussion of justice as an "experience of the impossible." We must try to do justice through our limited tools of communication, even though perfect communication, where one fully understands the intersecting experiences of injustice lived by a single individual, remains impossible since we can never fully place ourselves in the life experiences of another. Not to act is unacceptable, but not to recognize the limits of our action is hubris. Therefore, we still strive to create practical communicative circumstances in which justice can be approached, but also oscillate back to our critical stance in order to challenge our own approximations of justice. This is not dissimilar to our approach in writing this book. You are currently reading the second volume of *The Politics of Restorative Justice*, which reflects an effort to challenge the initial framing of these problems, which contained many gendered, class-based, settler-colonial, and other assumptions despite the best intention of the original author. This second volume will also be a fallible text. It would not suffice to not engage students in the topic of restorative justice and instead to wait for our own perfect cognition of the topic. But it also would be an act of bad faith to pretend that we have presented the final word. Just as one seeks to intervene and foster social change through a book, but also recognize that later amendment or substantive revision will be required, so too does transformative justice require everyday engagement alongside the

Figure 8.1
Responses to Injustice

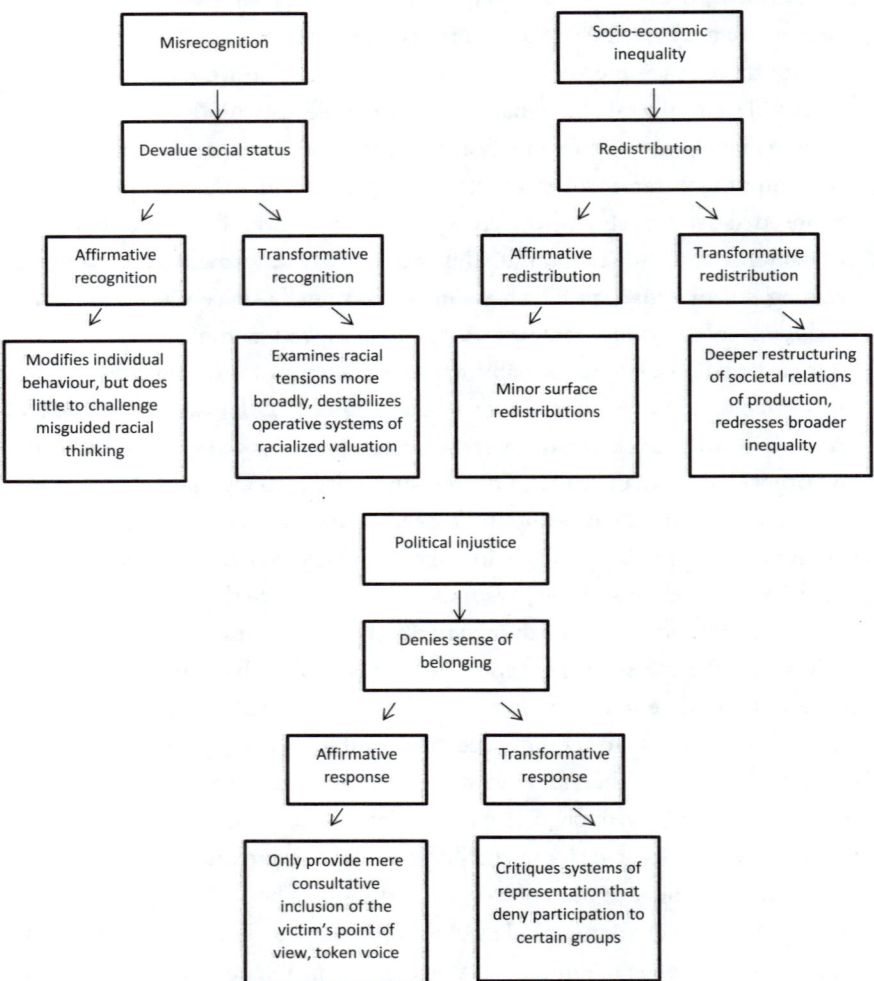

relentless pursuit of critique. Transformative justice is the process of multiplying voices and struggles. It is the project of acting for social change while refusing calcification of one's ideas. It demands justice for those who suffer injustice, and yet does not appropriate the voices of those who suffer, pretending to fully enunciate their demands. It displays empathy for their suffering, but humility allows this empathy to unsettle taken-for-granted assumptions about the world, as well as the way we act within it (LaCapra 1999).

An example of how we may try to practice this type of transformative impulse can be found amongst part of the feminist anti-violence movement. Mainstream feminist groups have come under increasing criticism for focusing too narrowly on gender at the expense of other forms of inequality. As a result, they may rely too heavily on the CJS as a response to gendered forms of violence such as sexual assault and intimate partner violence (Bernstein 2010; Bumiller 2008). Racialized women in particular are vocal about the ways that the alliance with the CJS comes at the expense of racialized and poor men and communities (Richie 2015). Feminists critical of criminalization have looked for alternative ways of responding to harm. Yet for many, restorative justice is not an adequate alternative (Kim 2018). They point to the same limitations we discuss here, particularly the ways in which restorative justice operates within and supports the CJS and thus remains, at best, as an affirmative form of justice. Instead, various groups and communities are using transformative justice practices to address gendered violence. Philly Stand Up (PSU) in Philadelphia is one example. They are a small collective that assists people who have been harmed by sexual violence and those who have used sexual violence to harm others. Though their work looks similar to restorative justice — they facilitate face-to-face encounters and focus on meeting victim needs and holding individuals accountable — they explicitly reject restorative justice:

> TJ [transformative justice] offered a conceptual apparatus that directly linked our sexual assault work with the various political projects and leanings in our lives, from economic justice to radical mental health, and, most substantially, prison abolition. Working from a transformative justice framework means that PSU acknowledges the broader systems of oppression (e.g., racism, male supremacy, capitalism, and the prison-industrial complex) that instigate sexual assault. (Kelly 2011: 49)

The group engages with social movement building with others dedicated to these same injustices, offer public education sessions, and engage in regular self-education practices. While this example is, again, not meant to ossify any ideas about what transformative justice may look like going forward it does allow us to see that it is not an impossible dream. There are people and groups, including INCITE! who we profile in Box 8.1, that are trying to realize transformative justice now.

Box 8.1 INCITE!: How Do We Address Violence within Our Communities?

We are told to call the police and rely on the criminal justice system to address violence within our communities. However, if police and prisons facilitate or perpetrate violence against us rather than increase our safety, how do we create strategies to address violence within our communities, including domestic violence, sexual violence, and child abuse, that don't rely on police or prisons?

Developing community-based responses to violence is one critical option. Community accountability is a community-based strategy, rather than a police/prison-based strategy, to address violence within our communities. Community accountability is a process in which a community — a group of friends, a family, a church, a workplace, an apartment complex, a neighborhood, etc. — work together to do the following things:

• Create and affirm values & practices that resist abuse and oppression and encourage safety, support, and accountability

• Develop sustainable strategies to address community members' abusive behavior, creating a process for them to account for their actions and transform their behavior

• Commit to ongoing development of all members of the community, and the community itself, to transform the political conditions that reinforce oppression and violence

• Provide safety & support to community members who are violently targeted that respects their self-determination

We at INCITE!:

• Maintain a space by and for women, transpeople, and gender non-conforming people of color

• Center our political analysis and community action in the struggle for liberation

• Support sovereignty for indigenous people as central to the struggle for liberation

- Oppose all forms of violence which oppress women, transpeople, and gender non-conforming people of color and our communities

- Recognize the state as the central organizer of violence which oppresses women, transpeople and gender nonconforming people of color and our communities

- Recognize these expressions of violence against women, transpeople, and gender non-conforming people of color as including colonialism, police brutality, immigration policies, reproductive control, etc

- Link liberation struggles which oppose racism, sexism, classism, heterosexism, ableism, ageism, transphobia, and all other forms of oppression

- Support coalition building between women, transpeople, and gender non-conforming people of color

- Recognize and honor differences across cultures

- Encourage creative models of community organizing and action

- Promote shared leadership and decision-making

- Recognize and resist the power of co-optation of our movement

- Support these principles not only in our actions, but in the practices within our own organizations

- Support the creation of organizational processes which encourage these principles and which effectively address oppressive individual and institutional practices within our own organizations

- Discourage any solicitation of federal or state funding for INCITE! activities

Source: <https://incite-national.org/community-accountability/>.

THE POLITICS OF TRANSFORMATION

With this (albeit fluid) definition in mind, the challenge for restorative justice is that, as it gains greater political appeal, stronger efforts are made to use restorative justice as a tool of political domination and governance, and therefore to accentuate its affirmative potential while the project of transformative justice slips by the wayside. To strategize how we might combat this tendency, it is useful to return to the three senses of politics: the political context of restorative justice; the politics of governance inherent in restorative justice; and restorative justice as a form of strategic political action. Through consideration of these three elements of restorative justice, some guidance can be offered to those who wish to maintain a restorative course toward a relentlessly transformative justice.

The Political Context of Restorative Justice

As has been stressed throughout, restorative justice operates in a political context. Understanding this context is therefore essential to implementing a transformative restorative justice, since this context shapes the structural and cultural conditions that a transformative approach would need to address. For example, in the current neoliberal context of criminal justice, one can observe the flexibility of neoliberal governments in their willingness to consider affirmative forms of recognition, redistribution, and representation. Indeed, it is within the neoliberal era that one can witness a greater recognition of victims, the development of restitution and compensation programs to redistribute funds to victims, and the more widespread use of victim impact statements as a form of victim representation (Woolford and Ratner 2008a). None of these efforts threaten the neoliberal social order. In fact, they achieve quite the opposite result. All of these remedies for victims of crime help construct a notion of victimhood that complements a neoliberal view of the world. The victim is represented as an isolated individual who was wronged for no other reason than the depravity of the offender. This harm is perceived to require remedy in the form of individual compensation and some limited venting through the victim impact statement, but the victim is largely restricted from any other performance of victimhood (that is, there is little room for a forgiving and non-vindictive victim under this model). The contemporary approach to victims, then, although an improvement over previous times when the victim was simply ignored, is still largely affirmative since it serves to reproduce a worldview in which the victim is an isolated sufferer and their experience is in no way held to be symptomatic of broader social structural problems.

Restorative justice is suited for co-optation by neoliberal regimes because it can be used for these sorts of affirmative purposes. Restorative justice can siphon off criticisms of and anxieties toward the courts. It can provide a less costly venue for dealing with minor crimes so the retributive system can direct its energies and punitive resources toward what neoliberals consider more serious criminal violations. Thus, restorative justice does not replace the punitive violence of the state; instead, it serves to supplement and help focus this violence on those cases deemed most deserving. In this sense, restorative justice can be useful in helping neoliberal governments contend with a potential contradiction in their strategies of governance. Neoliberal governments need to maintain a sense of being tough on crime, but criminal justice systems are incredibly costly and cumbersome to administer. Restorative justice, therefore, allows these governments to divert less controversial crimes away from the system, while focusing their resources on those that represent, in their view, the greatest public dangers. In this sense, it allows the neoliberal state to rule some offenders with its "left hand," using more cooperative restorative justice processes, while reserving the punitive might of its "right hand" for "dangerous" others (Wacquant 2001; Bourdieu 1998).

An affirmative restorative justice also fails to disrupt dominant patterns for designating risk in our society. The punishing "right hand" of the state is directed predominantly toward working-class, racialized, and marginalized youth who are perceived to be "dangerous" because of their actual or potential involvement in street crimes. Meanwhile, the unacceptable loss of life and large public and personal expense caused by corporate crime is given less criminal justice attention. Turning again to the example of Maple Leaf Foods, Michael McCain has been afforded public acceptance because of his act of condolence and settlement payments to the victims of the listeriosis outbreak. However, he is not subject to the punitive arm of the state, despite what some would perceive as "dangerous" behaviour, especially since his company is one of the many that lobbied the Conservative government to place responsibility for food inspection more directly in the hands of the food industry. Consistent with their neoliberal ideological leanings, the Conservatives considered allowing the food industry to police itself, saving government and private dollars, but placing the public at greater risk of future food-related disease outbreaks (Canadian Press 2008). For these reasons and others, restorativists must be critically aware of the neoliberal discourses that shape the logic of governance in their jurisdictions and must seek to devise strategies to avoid their restorative justice programs being swept away in the sea of neoliberalism and contributing to this growing imbalance.

One problem with the portrayal of neoliberalism thus far, however, is that, as mentioned in Chapter 6, neoliberalism is not a unitary philosophy of governance. Neoliberalism is an adaptable logic that forms itself to its specific context. For this reason, scholars and students can play a role in educating restorativists by conducting detailed studies of the local contours of neoliberalism within specific regions and jurisdictions.

Affirmative restorative justice can also be used to extending intersecting modes of domination because it might be used to provide only lip service recognition to the injustice experiences of poor, gendered, racialized, and/or LGBTQ individuals. In so doing, restorative justice might work to pacify or make less disruptive such individuals, offering them surface inclusion and consideration in terms of their specific justice needs without combating the underlying context of domination in which they exist. For example, a restorative justice that is not outwardly transphobic will not address the housing and employment challenges faced by trans people. And a restorative justice program that seeks to introduce "colourblind" practices will do nothing to challenge the system of white advantage within North America. These are important aspects of the context in which restorative justice operates, and a restorative justice that fails to unite with other groups seeking the elimination of intersecting forms of domination will always find itself in the position of serving as a minor salve for major injustices of our social world.

Restorative Justice as Governance

A related concern is that restorative justice is, in its own right, a modality of governance. Restorative justice provides insights and tools that allow individuals to better govern themselves. This is not, in and of itself, a bad thing. What Foucault (1994) refers to as the "care of the self" can be a reflexive sense of who we are that allows us to disrupt the ways in which power operates upon our minds and bodies. However, the internalized self-governance promoted by restorative justice can also be an imposition of onerous social control if it asks people to become passive and non-confrontational. The fact that conflict resolution techniques can be used to appease and pacify rather than to transform has been noted by several critical scholars (Dyck 2006; Pavlich 1996a, 1996b; Woolford 2005). For example, a university ombudsperson schooled in restorative justice techniques might function as a sort of mediator for student-professor conflicts. If a professor has been accused of sexual harassment of female students, the ombudsperson can convene a confidential mediation session that allows the parties to resolve the problem. The professor may come to understand his actions make the female students uncomfortable, and students may regain a modicum of trust that he will no longer act in this inappropriate manner. However, what has occurred here is remarkably convenient for preserving that status quo state of affairs on the university campus. The issues of professorial power, of chilly climates, and of sexual harassment have all been buried with the resolution of this case as simply an interpersonal conflict. Likewise, an Indigenous nation dealing with widespread sexual violence and addiction within their community may be well aware that the histories of Canadian settler colonialism and residential schooling have played a significant role in provoking these conditions. Nonetheless they may be required or encouraged by state gatekeepers to the circle sentencing process to concentrate their efforts on dealing with the immediate concerns of healing individuals and family from violence and substance abuse, and to leave aside their broader and more time-consuming critique of Canadian settler colonialism. It seems, therefore, that at every step, the transformative power of restorative justice is reduced and exchanged for the (albeit very understandable) pragmatics of resolving the immediate problem.

Put in everyday terms, there is nothing inherently wrong with restorative justice promoting that people learn how to communicate effectively and resolve conflicts on their own, unless this is encouraged in a manner where the person does not reflect on the nature of the conflict and seeks instead to automatically resolve conflict, regardless of whether the conflict might serve a productive purpose.

For these reasons, restorative justice must acknowledge it does offer governance, and it must seek to govern well. Gil (2006: 509) discusses this issue:

> Expanding critical consciousness in everyday social encounters, as well as in professional service settings, involves political discourse. When people interact socially and professionally, their actions and communications can either conform to, or challenge, the social status quo and prevailing patterns of human relations. When people speak and act in accordance with "normal" expectations, they reinforce, by implication, the existing social order and its "common sense" consciousness.

According to Gil, restorative justice needs to create opportunities for the "emergence of critical consciousness." Such a consciousness would not simply reproduce the normative relations of our social and political worlds; it would instead be inspired to question these worlds and to look toward alternative possibilities. If restorative justice is to govern well, it can only do so by encouraging its participants to be critical agents capable of challenging unfair norms and practices within their everyday lives. It can only do so by moving conflict resolution beyond the limits of affirmative repair. It can only do so by helping people become more than just automatic repressors of conflict — they must become agents capable of assessing their internalized habits and assumptions about the world, allowing them to disrupt patterns of domination that are embedded in their day-to-day worlds.

Restorative Justice and Strategic Political Action

Restorative justice theorists often place a great deal of emphasis on ideational change — that is, on the need for a new lens or paradigm (Zehr 1990; Redekop 2007). As noted above, ideational change, such as a newfound "critical consciousness," is important, since we need to open space for new views of the world to take hold if we want to sponsor transformative justice. However, a political strategy for promoting social change is also necessary. It is on this level that it is most crucial that restorative justice act as a social movement, with elements within that movement dedicated to networked disruptions of structural violence. The following are a series of strategic slogans that might be useful to those pursuing transformative restorative justice:

1. *Play to Restorative Strengths*: The practice that most clearly distinguishes restorative justice from other justice processes is its emphasis on open-ended, multi-party communication. In its attempt to create forums in which citizens can communicate their thoughts and feelings on specific matters of injustice, as well as on broader issues of criminal and social justice, restorative justice also overlaps with theories of deliberative democracy that seek to increase citizen input into governance (see Parkinson and Roche 2004; Dzur and Olson 2004; and Braithwaite and Petit 1990 for related ideas; see also Chapters 3 and 6). Parkinson and Roche (2004: 506) view restorative justice as "a vibrant, grassroots example of deliberation in practice." However, they do not feel restorative justice has yet fully met the deliberative standards of inclusiveness, equality between participants, transformative power, scope and decisiveness, and accountability. Thus, an engagement with theories of deliberative democracy provides restorative justice with evaluative tools through which it can assess the democratic adequacy of its practices: has restorative justice done enough to

include all potential participants? Does it institute sufficient measures to ensure equality between participants? Does it provide participants with meaningful transformative power in the sense that they can bring change to their lives and worlds? Does it extend the democratic scope of decision making across all populations? Does it create channels for ensuring democratic accountability so that we are collectively responsible for our democratic decisions? Restorative justice, in many of its forms, strives toward positive answers to all of these questions, but these deliberative ideals could still be realized to a greater degree. It should, however, also be noted this strategic slogan is about more than just the internal evaluation of restorative justice; it also has significant bearing on how restorative justice represents itself publicly. If restorative justice is part of a larger movement to extend and invigorate democratic principles beyond their contemporary neoliberal form, it will find itself partnered with other groups seeking to transform our democratic institutions. Restorative justice should, therefore, attach itself to this broader public discussion on what it means to be a participatory and deliberative democracy. Thus, a restorative justice agency in a poor neighbourhood cannot just commit itself to handling the crime component of community life, while matters of racism and ethnic tension, gendered poverty, community economic development, and other such issues are left to likewise isolated agencies. If what restorative justice does well is to foster discussion and deliberation, and if the issues dealt with by these agencies are directly connected to the criminal problems addressed through restorative justice, then broader deliberative processes must be established to together tackle the interlinking problems of poverty, race and gender inequality, and crime.

2. *Ideas Are Not Enough*: There is occasionally the sense in the restorative justice literature that if our ideas are sufficiently appealing and firmly rooted to our moral systems of thought (spiritual and otherwise), we will inevitably convert the non-believers and bring them to see the light of restorative justice. Unfortunately, ideas alone are rarely enough to shift hegemonic patterns of thought and behaviour. Even when verbal agreement is achieved and someone concedes restorative justice seems like a good idea, there still exists a bulwark of deeply

habituated and institutionalized practice that must be addressed. Restorative justice must, therefore, strive to change not only thoughts, but also deeply embedded habits. Efforts should be made to encourage participatory and deliberative practices in day-to-day life. This means restorative justice must be about more than simply holding victim-offender mediations when specific instances of crime occur. It also entails support for town hall meetings, public forums, local consultations, and other exercises in local decision making and problem solving. Democratic participation, however, does not only mean engagement in public discussion. At times, more radical intervention is required to expand the terrain of public debate. In instances where specific concerns cannot gain any traction on the public agenda, civil disobedience, protest, and legal challenges are often necessary. This sort of confrontational behaviour may seem contrary to the restorative worldview, but we sometimes come up against social and historical circumstances that prevent full discussion of our concerns. Rosa Parks' decision to take a seat reserved for white bus riders was an act of civil disobedience that sparked larger protests. These protests, although certainly not restorative in any direct sense, helped to pry open a political order that was reluctant to discuss matters of racial equality. In this sense, there are times when confrontational action is necessary to create the conditions for cooperation and to help re-pattern human behaviour. Could victims and ex-offenders together march upon city hall to demand that the brutal poverty of their neighbourhoods be addressed? Could restorative practitioners band with like-minded agencies to lobby for better social services in their communities? Efforts such as these must be made to achieve tangible benefits to everyday people and to attack the roots of crime and injustice.

3. *There Are Opponents*: Following from the previous slogan, it would be nice to think restorative justice is in everyone's interests. The unfortunate truth is some people are deeply invested in the existing CJS. The current system provides them with status, authority, legitimacy, and wealth. This is even true of governmentalist restorative justice programs that offer their compromised and diluted versions of restorative justice. Others are emotionally attached to the idea of retribution and will not be easily swayed to let it go. Indeed, in multicultural socie-

ties, we must admit there are cultural sectors of these societies for whom retribution is deeply ingrained. A more restorative system is likely to be experienced by many as a form of rupture in that it breaks down, for some, material benefits, as well as sensibilities they have long used to understand their world. There are towns for which the main driver for employment is the local prison. There are professionals whose practices have long been based within a retributive culture. There are people who have long seen the salve for their social fears to lie in concrete walls and bars. There is no painless transformation toward restorative justice, and restorativists must work to make all of these invested groups part of the conversation. Weaning individuals from emotional and cultural attachments to punitive justice may well be a long-term project that requires intergenerational efforts to open people to non-punitive justice ideals. In contrast, those with deeply vested economic and political interests in the current CJS — those whose jobs and incomes depend on our extensive prison system, for example, or those neoliberal politicians who gain political capital by grandstanding on "law and order" issues — will be unlikely to allow anything but an affirmative form of restorative justice to take hold. The reality is, then, that there may come a time when more protest and direct action is needed to lead these gatekeepers from their entrenched positions.

4. *Seek Participatory Rather than Professional Legitimacy:* Professionalization is increasingly becoming the norm in conflict resolution circles. The long debate over whether it is better to have local laypersons facilitating restorative justice, or whether specific training is required to ensure appropriate restorative practice, appears to have been won by the latter group. And no one can deny training and professional standards are useful in many circumstances. Conflicts are complex phenomena, and people should be as well-prepared as they can be to facilitate them rather than blindly feeling their way through. However, this does not mean the assessed quality of a facilitator should be based upon their professional status. A certificate in hand should not be enough to establish facilitator credentials; instead, more should depend on the perspectives of the participants in restorative justice. Did this person empower the participants? Were participants satisfied with the process? Did the facilitator open the discussion to considera-

tion of broader structural injustices? Such questions should be central when determining the legitimacy of facilitators. Moreover, facilitator training should be directed toward standards other than those typical of lawyers and other conflict resolution professionals. For example, Dyck (2006: 530) notes, "One of the key reasons why the structural dimension is often ignored is that many restorative justice programs focus their training almost exclusively on the development of interpersonal communications skills." Facilitators simply are not trained to identify and address structural imbalances. They are also not trained in linking specific individual troubles to broader social injustices. Nor do they receive advice on assessing the nature of government and how to navigate governing ideological presuppositions. In sum, it is not inevitable that professional involvement in restorative justice result in the co-optation or dilution of transformative justice. For Olson and Dzur (2004: 151), "Democratic professionals seek to open up their domains of authority to lay participants, to share tasks, and to share in the construction of norms that constrain and direct professional action" (see Shapland et al. 2006 for evidence of professional acceptance of restorative justice principles). In this sense, the professional status of a restorative justice practitioner is not a badge of authority to be worn to better regulate restorative sessions, but a means for facilitating more productive discussion.

5. *Link Up and Network*: To quote Dyck (2006: 542) once again, "A transformative practice would see restorative justice agencies investing time and energy in developing accountable relationships with advocacy and social action groups in our communities." By recognizing the ways in which our work is related to these groups, we would become less inclined to work in isolation or, as is sometimes the case, against them. This encapsulates well the slogan "Link Up and Network." There are a multitude of social actors and groups working toward a similar set of goals. The affirmative practice of restorative justice isolates injustices from their broader social conditions. In contrast, a transformative practice understands these injustices as part of a bigger picture, which is difficult to address from an isolated spot in the vast arrangement of society. Therefore, restorative justice groups must network beyond the realm of criminal justice, taking into consideration their common goals with community economic

development, anti-poverty, anti-racism, feminist, LGBTQ, and other such groups. By linking their activities, these groups can exert pressure upon the state and civil society from multiple positions, creating a more broad-based effort to shift dominant patterns of thought and action.

6. *Keep Going*: Restorative justice should not allow itself the luxury of completion. It is an ideal that can always be improved upon, that can always be further advanced. To think otherwise is to allow stasis to set in and allow us to get too comfortable. For this reason, transformative justice does not end with the full realization of economic redistribution, cultural recognition, and social representation. Each of these projects will have its unintended consequences, and new injustices will arise in the pursuit of a better world. A transformative justice that is not sensitized to these possibilities risks falling into the traps of dogmatism, through which an idealized vision is held desperately no matter what contradictory evidence has arisen to suggest that problems within the vision exist. No matter what successes we achieve in terms of gaining new resources for our communities, we must continue to critically evaluate these achievements and press them further. For example, a new community program that offers micro-loans and other funding incentives to marginalized community members may be a success achieved by a restorative justice agency in concert with other local groups. But that agency must still examine closely how these loans are distributed: are they equally available to all community members? Are there any groups who are excluded from the program?

7. *Commit to Reflexivity*: There is no restorative core that must be protected from all criticism. A reflexive engagement means we must be willing to challenge all elements of our thought, including the guiding presuppositions of the restorative justice ethos. The goal is to uncover the subterranean politics lurking within these assumptions and to devise new understandings of restorativeness when the old ones fail. Even the restorative ethos should remain open to critique, since a blind faith in the power of communication to heal social rifts can sometimes mask structural inequalities that are at the base of those rifts — as if to say, "Talk it out, but don't probe too deeply into structurally embedded forms of social injustice."

FINAL THOUGHTS

We have sought to navigate two conceptions of the world: a world of process that is open and indeterminate, and a world of regularity in which structured patterns of domination maintain an overarching system of power. Although these may seem, upon first glance, contradictory, the truth is things remain in movement, even though general patterns can be discerned. Restorative justice must embrace this unsettled state, allow for a degree of uncertainty, and yet commit to a notion that patterns can change for the better.

In the end, restorative justice is a movement with many competing parts. Those that affirm the present social order appear, for the moment, to be winning out and this, in our view, is unfortunate. The potential of restorative justice is to be part of something bigger. Through an enabling politics networked with other social justice movements, restorative justice can aspire toward transformative justice.

QUESTIONS FOR DISCUSSION

1. Choose one of the structural injustices from Chapter 6 (age, gender, race, sexual identity). How might restorative justice respond in an affirmative justice way and a transformative justice way to an offender positioned unequally?
2. What are some of the practical barriers to restorative justice as social movement? What are some of the opportunities for it to mobilize?
3. We argue that restorative justice must help people become agents capable of assessing their internalized habits and assumptions about the world, allowing them to disrupt patterns of domination. Are there habits or assumptions about crime, conflict, harm, injustice, or justice that restorative justice has troubled for you? How might you bring your knowledge about restorative justice into the various aspects of your life to disrupt patterns of domination?

REFERENCES

Abel, Richard L. 1982. "The Contradictions of Informal Justice." In R. Abel (ed.) *The Politics of Informal Justice: The American Experience* Volume 1. New York: Academic Press.
Achilles, Mary, and Lorraine Stutzman-Amstutz. 2006. "Responding to the Needs of Victims: What Was Promised, What Has Been Delivered." In D. Sullivan and L. Tifft (eds.), *Handbook of Restorative Justice: A Global Perspective*. London and New York: Routledge.
Acker, James R. 2006. "Hearing the Victim's Voice Amidst the Cry for Capital Punishment." In D. Sullivan and L. Tifft (eds.), *Handbook of Restorative Justice: A Global Perspective*. London and New York: Routledge.
Acorn, Annalise E. 2004. *Compulsory Compassion: A Critique of Restorative Justice*. Vancouver: UBC Press.
Adam, Heribert. 2001. "Divided Memories: Confronting the Crimes of Previous Regimes." *Telos* 118: 87–109.
Adelberg, Ellen, and Claudia Currie (eds.). 1987. *Too Few to Count: Canadian Women in Conflict with the Law*. Vancouver: Press Gang Publishers.
Agamban, Giorgio. 1993. *The Coming Community*. Minneapolis: University of Minnesota Press.
Aggestam, K. 1995. "Reframing International Conflicts: 'Ripeness' in International Mediation." *Paradigms*, 9, 2: 86–106.
Agozino, Biko. 2004. "Imperialism, Crime, and Criminology: Towards the Decolonization of Criminology." *Crime, Law, and Social Change*, 41, 4: 343–358.
Ahladas, Yiota, and Ben Sachs-Hamilton. 2008. "Community Is No Cliché: It Works... the Burlington Way." *Yes Magazine*. <http://yesmagazine.org/article.asp?ID=2538>.
Ahmed, Sara. 2004. *The Cultural Politics of Emotion*. New York: Routledge.
Alcoff, Linda, and Laura Gray. 1993. "Survivor Discourse: Transgression or Recuperation?" *Signs: Journal of Women in Culture and Society*, 18: 260–90.
Alexander, Jeffrey C. 2004. "On the Social Construction of Moral Universals: The 'Holocaust' from War Crime to Trauma Drama." In J. Alexander, R. Eyerman, B. Giesen, N.J. Smelser and P. Sztompka (eds.), *Cultural Trauma and Collective Identity*. Berkeley: University of California Press.
Anderson, Elijah. 1999. *The Code of the Street: Decency, Violence and the Moral Life of the Inner City*. New York and London: W.W. Norton.

Arvin, Maile, Eve Tuck, and Angie Morrill. 2013. "Decolonizing Feminism: Challenging Connections Between Settler Colonialism and Heteropatriarchy." *Feminist Formations*, 25, 1: 8–34.

Ashworth, Andrew. 2003. "Responsibilities, Rights and Restorative Justice." In G. Johnstone (ed.), *A Restorative Justice Reader: Texts, Sources, Context*. Cullompton, UK: Willan Publishing.

Backhouse, Constance, Donald McRae, and Nitya Iyer. 2015. *Report of the Task Force on Misogyny, Sexism and Homophobia in Dalhousie University Faculty of Dentistry*. <https://cdn.dal.ca/content/dam/dalhousie/pdf/cultureofrespect/DalhousieDentistry-TaskForceReport-June2015.pdf>. Accessed September 26, 2018.

Balfour, Gillian, and Elizabeth Comack. 2014. "Introduction." In Gillian Balfour and Elizabeth Comack (eds.), *Criminalizing Women: Gender and (In)Justice in Neo-Liberal Times*, 2nd edition. Halifax: Fernwood Publishing.

Barnett, Randy. 1977. "Restitution: A New Paradigm of Criminal Justice." *Ethics*, 87, 4: 279–301.

Bartky, Sandra Lee. 1990. *Femininity and Domination: Studies in the Phenomenology of Oppression*. New York: Routledge.

Bartlett, W., and J. Le Grand. 1993. *Quasi-Markets and Social Policy*. Basingstoke: Palgrave Macmillan.

Bauman, Zygmunt. 2001. *Community: Seeking Safety in an Insecure World*. Cambridge: Polity Press.

Benhabib, Seyla. 1992. *Situating the Self: Gender, Community and Postmodernism in Contemporary Ethics*. New York: Routledge.

____. 1996. "Toward a Deliberative Model of Democratic Legitimacy." In S. Benhabib (ed.), *Democracy and Difference: Contesting the Boundaries of the Political*. Princeton, NJ: Princeton University Press.

Bernstein, Elizabeth. 2010. "Militarized Humanitarianism Meets Carceral Feminism: The Politics of Sex, Rights, and Freedom in Contemporary Antitrafficking Campaigns." *Signs: Journal of Women in Culture and Society*, 36, 1: 45–71.

Blackstone, William. 1765. *Commentaries on the Laws of England*. Vol. 1. Oxford: Clarendon Press.

Bonta, James, Jennifer Rooney, and Suzanne Wallace-Capretta. 1998. *Restorative Justice: An Evaluation of the Restorative Resolutions Project*. Ottawa: Solicitor General of Canada.

Borrows, J. 2016) "Heroes, Tricksters, Monsters, and Caretakers: Indigenous Law and legal Education." *McGill Law Journal*, 61, 4: 795–846.

Bottoms, A.E. 1995. "The Philosophy and Politics of Punishment and Sentencing." In C. Clarkson and R. Morgan (eds.), *The Politics of Sentencing Reform*. Oxford: Clarendon Press.

____. 2003. "Some Sociological Reflections on Restorative Justice." In A. von Hirsch, J. Roberts, A.E. Bottoms, K. Roach, and M. Schiff (eds.), *Restorative Justice and Criminal Justice: Competing or Reconcilable Paradigms?* Oxford, UK: Hart Publishing.

Bouffard, Jeff, Maisha Cooper, and Kathleen Bergseth. 2017. "The Effectiveness of Various Restorative Justice Interventions on Recidivism Outcomes Among Juvenile Offenders." *Youth Violence and Juvenile Justice*, 15, 4: 465–480.

Bourdieu, Pierre. 1987. "The Force of Law: Toward a Sociology of the Judicial Field."

Hastings Law Journal, 38: 805–853.

———. 1990. *The Logic of Practice*. Cambridge: Polity Press.

———. 1998. *Acts of Resistance: Against the Tyranny of the Market*. New York: New Press.

Braithwaite, John. 1989. *Crime, Shame and Reintegration*. Cambridge, UK: Cambridge University Press.

———. 1994. "Thinking Harder About Democratizing Social Control." In J. Alder and J. Wundersitz (eds.), *Family Conferencing and Juvenile Justice: The Way Forward of Misplaced Optimism?* Canberra: Australian Institute of Criminology.

———. 1999. "Restorative Justice: Assessing Optimistic and Pessimistic Accounts." *Crime and Justice: A Review of Research*, 25: 1–127.

———. 2002. *Restorative Justice and Responsive Regulation*. New York: Oxford University Press.

———. 2003. "Restorative Justice and a Better Future." In G. Johnstone (ed.), *A Restorative Justice Reader: Texts, Sources, Context*. Cullompton, UK: Willan Publishing.

Braithwaite, John, and Kathleen Daly. 1994. "Masculinities, Violence and Communitarian Control." In T. Newburn and E. Stanko (eds.), *Just Boys Doing Business? Men, Masculinities and Crime*. London: Routledge.

Braithwaite, John, and Stephen Mugford. 1994. "Conditions of Successful Reintegration Ceremonies: Dealing with Juvenile Offenders." *British Journal of Criminology*, 34, 2: 139–171.

Braithwaite, John, and Philip Petit. 1990. *Not Just Desserts: A Republican Theory of Criminal Justice*. Oxford: Clarendon Press.

Brockes, Erin. 2018. "As Sylvia Plath Knew, If You're Going to Be a Victim, You'd Better Be a Good One." *The Guardian*, November 1. <https://www.theguardian.com/commentisfree/2018/nov/01/woman-victim-credible-christine-blasey-ford>.

Brooks, Roy L. 2003, "Reflections on Reparations." In J. Torpey (ed.), *Politics and the Past: On Repairing Historical Injustices*. Lanham, NJ: Rowman and Littlefield.

Browning, Christopher R. 2004. *The Origins of the Final Solution: The Evolution of Nazi Jewish Policy, September 1939–March 1942*. With contributions by Jürgen Matthäus. Lincoln, NE: University of Nebraska Press and Yad Vashem, Jerusalem.

Bruce, Jasmine. 2013. "Understanding 'Back Stage' and 'Front Stage' Work in Restorative Justice Conferences: The Benefits of Using Ethnographic Techniques." *Current Issues in Criminal Justice*, 25, 1: 517–526.

Bumiller, Kristin. 2008. *In an Abusive State: How Neoliberalism Appropriated the Feminist Movement Against Sexual Violence*. Durham: Duke University Press.

Burchell, Graham. 1993. "Liberal Government and Techniques of the Self." *Economy and Society*, 22, 3 (August): 267–282.

Burger, Chief Justice Warren. 1979. "Address Before the National Conference on the Causes of Popular Dissatisfaction with the Administration of Justice, April 7–9, 1976." Reprinted in A.L. Levin and R.R. Wheeler (eds.), *The Pound Conference: Perspectives on Justice in the Future*. St Paul, MN: West Publishing.

Burgess-Proctor, Amanda. 2006. "Intersections of Race, Class, Gender, and Crime: Future Directions for Feminist Criminology." *Feminist Criminology*, 1, 1: 24–47.

Butler, Judith. 1990. *Gender Trouble: Feminism and the Subversion of Identity*. New York: Routledge.

Cameron, Angela. 2006. "Stopping the Violence: Canadian Feminist Debates on Restorative Justice and Intimate Violence." *Theoretical Criminology*, 10, 1: 49–66.

Canadian Press. 2008. "Deregulating Food Inspection Too Risky: Union." CTV News, November 8. <AW: https://www.ctvnews.ca/deregulating-food-inspection-too-risky-union-1.339451>.

Card, Claudia. 2010. *Confronting Evils: Terrorism, Torture, Genocide*. Cambridge: Cambridge University Press.

CBC News. 2009. "Manitoba Métis Win Hunting Rights Case." CBC News, January 8. <https://www.cbc.ca/news/canada/manitoba/manitoba-m%C3%A9tis-win-hunting-rights-case-1.784627>.

Center for American Progress. 2016. *Unjust: How the Broken Criminal Justice System Fails LGBT People*. Boulder, CO: Center for American Progress.

Charbonneau, Serge. 2004. "The Canadian Youth Criminal Justice Act 2003: A Step Forward for Advocates of Restorative Justice?" In E. Elliott and R.M. Gordon (eds.), *New Directions in Restorative Justice: Issues, Practice, Evaluation*. Cullompton, UK: Willan.

Christie, Nils. 1977. "Conflicts as Property." *British Journal of Criminology*, 17, 1: 1–15.

____. 1986. "The Ideal Victim." In E.A. Fattah (ed.), *From Crime Policy to Victim Policy*. London: MacMillan.

Christodoulidis, Emilios A. 2000. "'Truth and Reconciliation' as Risks." *Social & Legal Studies*, 9, 2: 179–204.

Chunn, Dorothy, and Dany Lacombe (eds.). 2000. *Law as a Gendering Practice*. Oxford: Oxford University Press.

Clifford, James. 1988. *The Predicament of Culture: Twentieth-Century Ethnography, Literature, and Art*. Cambridge, MA: Harvard University Press.

Cohen, Albert K. 1965. "The Sociology of the Deviant Act." *American Sociological Review*, 30: 5–14.

Cohen, Stanley. 1985. *Visions of Social Control: Crime, Punishment, and Classification*. Oxford: Polity Press.

Cole, Tim. 1999. *Selling the Holocaust: From Auschwitz to Schindler, How History Is Bought, Packaged, and Sold*. New York: Routledge.

Columbia Law School. 2017. "Kimberlé Crenshaw on Intersectionality, More than Two Decades Later." <law.columbia.edu/pt-br/news/2017/06/kimberle-crenshaw-intersectionality>.

Comack, Elizabeth. 2014. "Part II Introduction." In Gillian Balfour and Elizabeth Comack (eds.), *Criminalizing Women: Gender and (In)Justice in Neo-Liberal Times*, 2nd edition. Halifax, NS: Fernwood Publishing.

Comack, Elizabeth, and Gillian Balfour. 2004. *The Power to Criminalize: Violence, Inequality, and Law*. Halifax, NS: Fernwood Publishing.

Consedine, Jim. 1995. *Restorative Justice: Healing the Effects of Crime*. Lyttleton, NZ: Ploughshares.

____. 2003. "The Maori Restorative Tradition." In Gerry Johnstone (ed.), *A Restorative Justice Reader: Texts, Sources, Context*. Cullompton, UK: Willan Publishing.

Cote, Jim, and Anton Allahar. 1995. *Generation on Hold: Coming of Age in the Late Twentieth Century*. New York: NYU Press.

Coy, Patrick G., and Timothy Hedeen. 2005. "A Stage Model of Social Movement Co-optation: Community Mediation in the United States." *The Sociological Quarterly*, 26: 405–435.

Crawford, Adam. 2003. "The Prospects for Restorative Youth Justice in England and Wales: A Tale of Two Acts." In K. McEvoy and T. Newburn (eds.), *Criminology, Conflict Resolution and Restorative Justice*. Houndsmills, Basingstoke, Hampshire: Palgrave Macmillan.

Crawford, Adam, and Tim Newburn. 2002. "Recent Developments in Restorative Justice for Young People in England and Wales: Community Participation and Representation." *British Journal of Criminology*, 42: 476–485.

Crenshaw, Kimberle. 1991. "Mapping the Margins: Intersectionality, Identity Politics, and Violence against Women of Color." *Stanford Law Review*, 43, 6: 1241–1299.

Cunneen, Chris. 1997. "Community Conferencing and the Fiction of Indigenous Control." *Australian and New Zealand Journal of Criminology*, 30: 292–311.

———. 2002. "Restorative Justice and the Politics of Decolonisation." In E. Weitkamp and H. Kerner (eds.), *Restorative Justice: Theoretical Foundations*. Cullompton, UK: Willan Publishing.

———. 2006. "Exploring the Relationship Between Reparations, the Gross Violation of Human Rights, and Restorative Justice." In D. Sullivan and L. Tifft (eds.), *Handbook of Restorative Justice: A Global Perspective*. London and New York: Routledge.

———. 2007. "Reviving Restorative Justice Traditions." In G. Johnstone and D.W. Van Ness (eds.), *Handbook of Restorative Justice*. Cullompton, UK: Willan Publishing.

Curtis-Fawley, Sarah, and Kathleen Daly. 2005. "Gendered Violence and Restorative Justice: The Views of Victim Advocates." *Violence Against Women*, 11, 5: 603–638

Daly, Kathleen. 2003. "Restorative Justice: The Real Story." In Gerry Johnstone (ed.), *A Restorative Justice Reader: Texts, Sources, Context*. Cullompton, UK: Willan Publishing.

———. 2006. "The Limits of Restorative Justice." In D. Sullivan and L. Tifft (eds.), *Handbook of Restorative Justice A Global Perspective*. London and New York: Routledge.

Daly, Kathleen, and Russ Immarigeon. 1998. "The Past, Present, and Future of Restorative Justice: Some Critical Reflections." *Contemporary Justice Review*, 1: 21–45.

Daly, Kathleen, and Julie Stubbs. 2006. "Feminist Engagement with Restorative Justice." *Theoretical Criminology*, 10, 1: 9–28.

Dean, Mitchell. 1999. *Governmentality: Power and Rule in Modern Society*. London: Sage.

Delbo, Charlotte. 1995. *Auschwitz and Ater*. New Haven, CT: Yale University Press.

Delgado, Richard, and Jean Stefancik. 2017. *Critical Race Theory*, 3rd edition. New York: New York University Press.

Derrida, Jacques. 1992. "Force of Law: The 'Mystical Foundation of Authority.'" In D. Cornell, M. Rosenfeld, and D.G. Carlson (eds.), *Deconstruction and the Possibility of Justice*. London: Routledge.

Deutsch, M. 1973. *The Resolution of Conflict: Constructive and Destructive Processes*. New Haven, CT: Yale University Press.

Diani, Mario. 1992. "The Concept of Social Movement." *The Sociological Review*, 40,

1: 1–25.
Dickie, Bonnie. 2000. *Hollow Water* (film). National Film Board of Canada.
Dietrich, Noelle. 2018. "The Closure Factor: An Autoethnographical Analysis of the Justness of Restorative Justice after Murder." Unpublished MA thesis, University of Manitoba.
Dignan, James, Anne Atkinson, Helen Atkinson, Marie Howes, Jennifer Johnstone, Gwen Robinson, Joanna Shapland, and Angela Sorsby. 2007. "Staging Restorative Justice Encounters Against a Criminal Justice Backdrop: A Dramaturgical Analysis." *Criminology & Criminal Justice*, 7, 1: 5–32.
Dryzek, J.S. 2000. *Deliberative Democracy and Beyond*. Oxford: Oxford University Press.
Duff, R.A. 2003. "Restorative Punishment and Punitive Restoration." In Gerry Johnstone (ed.), *A Restorative Justice Reader: Texts, Sources, Context*. Cullompton, UK: Willan Publishing.
Duguid, S. 2000. *Can Prisons Work? The Prisoner as Object and Subject in Modern Corrections*. Toronto, ON: University of Toronto Press.
Durkheim, Emile. 1984 [1933]. *The Division of Labour in Society*. New York: Free Press.
Dyck, David. 2006. "Reaching Toward a Structurally Responsive Training and Practice of Restorative Justice." In D. Sullivan and L. Tifft (eds.), *Handbook of Restorative Justice: A Global Perspective*. London and New York: Routledge.
Dzur, Albert W., and Susan M. Olson. 2004. "The Value of Community Participation in Restorative Justice." *Journal of Social Philosophy*, XXXV, 1 (Spring): 91–107.
Elias, Robert. 1986. *The Politics of Victimization: Victims, Victimology and Human Rights*. Oxford: Oxford University Press.
Elliott, Elizabeth, and Robert M. Gordon (eds.). 2005. *New Directions in Restorative Justice: Issues, Practice, Evaluation*. Cullompton, UK: Willan Publishing.
Ewick, P., and S.S. Silbey. 1998. *The Common Place of Law: Stories of Popular Legal Consciousness*. Chicago: University of Chicago Press.
Fattah, Ezzat A. (ed.). 1992. *Towards a Critical Victimology*. New York: St. Martin's Press.
Federal-Provincial-Territorial Working Group on Restorative Justice. 2016. *Restorative Justice in the Canadian Criminal Justice Sector*. Ottawa: Correctional Services Canada.
Fein, Helen. 1993. *Genocide: A Sociological Perspective*. London: Sage Publications.
Fisher, R., and W. Ury. 1991. *Getting to Yes: Negotiating Agreement Without Giving In*, 2nd edition. New York: Penguin Books.
Fishkin, J.S. 1991. *Democracy and Deliberation: New Directions for Democratic Reform*. New Haven, CT: Yale University Press.
Fisk, Milton. 1993. "Introduction: The Problem of Justice." In M. Fisk (ed.), *Key Concepts in Critical Theory: Justice*. New Jersey: Humanities Press.
Fitzpatrick, Peter. 1995. "The Impossibility of Popular Justice." In S. Engle Merry and N. Milner (eds.), *The Possibility of Popular Justice: A Case Study of Community Mediation in the United States*. Ann Arbor: University of Michigan Press.
Foucault, Michel. 1977. *Discipline and Punish: The Birth of the Prison*. New York: Pantheon Books.
____. 1991. "Governmentality." In G. Burchell, C. Gordon and P. Miller (eds.), *The Foucault Effect: Studies in Governmentality with Two Lectures by and an Interview with Michel Foucault*. Chicago: University of Chicago Press.

_____. 1994. *Ethics, Subjectivity and Truth*. New York: New Press.
Frank, Anne. 1995 [1947]. *The Diary of a Young Girl*. New York: Doubleday.
Fraser, Nancy. 1992. "Rethinking the Public Sphere: A Contribution to the Critique of Actually Existing Democracy." In Craig Calhoun (ed.), *Habermas and the Public Sphere*. Cambridge, MA: MIT Press.
_____. 1997. *Justice Interruptus: Critical Reflections on the "Postsocialist Condition."* New York: Routledge.
_____. 2000. "Rethinking Recognition." *New Left Review*, 3 (May–June): 107–120.
_____. 2003. "From Discipline to Flexibilization? Rereading Foucault in the Shadow of Globalization." *Constellations*, 10, 2: 160–171.
Gaarder, Emily. 2015. "Lessons from a Restorative Circles Initiative for Intimate Partner Violence." *Restorative Justice*, 3, 3: 342–367,
Galaway, B., and J. Hudson (eds.). 1996. *Restorative Justice: International Perspectives*. Monsey, NY: Criminal Justice Press.
Garfinkel, Harold. 1956. "Conditions of Successful Degradation Ceremonies." *American Journal of Sociology*, 61: 420–424.
Garland, David. 2001. *The Culture of Control: Crime and Social Order in Contemporary Society*. Chicago: University of Chicago Press.
Gavrielides, Theo. 2007. *Restorative Justice Theory and Practice: Addressing the Discrepancy*. Helsinki: European Institute for Crime Prevention and Control.
_____. 2014. "Bringing Race Relations into the Restorative Justice Debate: An Alternative and Personalized Vision of 'the Other.'" *Journal of Black Studies*, 45, 3: 216–246.
Giddens, Anthony. 1991. *Modernity and Self-Identity: Self and Society in the Late Modern Age*. Stanford, CA: Stanford University Press.
Gil, David G. 2006. "Toward a 'Radical' Paradigm of Restorative Justice." In D. Sullivan and L. Tifft (eds.), *Handbook of Restorative Justice: A Global Perspective*. London and New York: Routledge.
Gilligan, Carol. 1982. *In a Different Voice: Psychological Theory and Women's Development*. Cambridge: Harvard University Press.
Goffman, Erving. 1993/1959. *The Presentation of Self in Everyday Life*. New York: Anchor Books.
_____. 1967. *Interaction Ritual: Essays on Face-to-Face Behavior*. New York: Pantheon Books.
Goldschmidt, Siegfried. 1945. *Legal Claims Against Germany*. New York: Dryden Press.
Goodhand, Margo. 2017. *Runaway Wives and Rogue Feminists: The Origins of the Women's Shelter Movement in Canada*. Halifax and Winnipeg: Fernwood Publishing.
Goschler, Constantin. 1991. "The United States and *Wiedergutmachung* for Victims of Nazi Persecution: From Leadership to Disengagement." In A. Frohn (ed.), *Holocaust and Shilumim: The Policy of Wiedergutmachung in the Early 1950s*. Washington, DC: German Historical Institute.
_____. 2004. "German Compensation to Jewish Nazi Victims." In J.M. Diefendorf (ed.), *Lessons and Legacies IV: New Currents in Holocaust Research*. Evanston, IL: Northwestern University Press.
Gramsci, Antonio. 1971. *Selections from the Prison Notebooks (Selections)*. New York: International Publishers.

Gustafson, David L. 2016. "Victim Offender Mediation Program Fraser Region." *Community Justice Initiatives Association Annual Report*, Fraser Region, British Columbia, pp. 6–7.

Habermas, Jürgen. 1984. *The Theory of Communicative Action: Reason and the Rationalization of Society*, volume 1. Boston: Beacon Press.

———. 1989. *The Structural Transformation of the Public Sphere*. Cambridge, MA: Polity Press.

———. 1990. *Moral Consciousness and Communicative Action*. Cambridge, MA: MIT Press.

———. 1999. *Between Facts and Norms: Contributions to a Discourse Theory of Law and Democracy*. Cambridge, MA: MIT Press.

Haig-Brown, Celia. 1988. *Resistance and Renewal: Surviving the Indian Residential School*, Vancouver: Tillacum Library.

Hampton, Jean. 1998. "Punishment, Feminism, and Political Identity: A Case Study in the Expressive Meaning of Law." *Canadian Journal of Law and Jurisprudence*, 11, 1: 23–45.

Hannah-Moffat, Kelly, and Margaret Shaw. 2001. *Taking Risks: Incorporating Gender and Culture into the Classification and Assessment of Federally Sentenced Women in Canada*. Ottawa: Status of Women.

Hardt, Michael, and Antonio Negri. 2000. *Empire*. Cambridge, MA: Harvard University Press.

———. 2004. *Multitude: War and Democracy in the Age of Empire*. New York: Penguin.

Harrington, Christina B. 1985. *Shadow Justice: The Ideology and Institutionalization of Alternatives to Court*. Westport, CT: Greenwood Press.

Harris, Nathan, Lode Walgrave and John Braithwaite. 2004. "Emotional Dynamics in Restorative Conferences." *Theoretical Criminology*, 8, 2: 191–210.

Hart-Landsberg, Martin. 2006. "Neoliberalism: Myths and reality." *Monthly Review*, 57, 11. <http://www.monthlyreview.org/0406hart-landsberg.htm>.

Hartman, Yvonne. 2005. "In Bed with the Enemy: Some Ideas on the Connections between Neoliberalism and the Welfare State." *Current Sociology*, 53, 1: 57–73.

Hay, Colin. 2006. "Political Ontology." In R.E. Goodin and C. Tilly (eds.), *The Oxford Handbook of Contextual Political Analysis*. Oxford: Oxford University Press.

Hayner, Priscilla B. 2002. *Unspeakable Truths: Facing the Challenge of Truth Commissions*. New York and London: Routledge.

Herf, Jeffrey. 1997. *Divided Memory: The Nazi Past in the Two Germanys*. Cambridge, MA: Harvard University Press.

Herman, Susan. 2004. "Is Restorative Justice Possible Without a Parallel System for Victims?" In H. Zehr and B. Toews (eds.), *Critical Issues in Restorative Justice*. Monsey, NY and Cullompton, UK: Criminal Justice Press and Willan Publishing.

Hofrichter, Richard. 1982. "Neighborhood Justice and the Social Control Problems of American Capitalism: A Perspective." In Richard Abel (ed.), *The Politics of Informal Justice: The American Experience*, volume 1. New York: Academic Press.

———. 1987. *Neighborhood Justice in Capitalist Society: The Expansion of the Informal State*. New York: Greenwood.

Hogarth, John. 1971. *Sentencing as a Human Process*. Toronto: University of Toronto Press.

Hogeveen, Bryan. 2006. "Unsettling Youth Justice and Cultural Norms: The Youth Restorative Action Project." *Journal of Youth Studies,* 9, 1: 47–66.

Hogeveen, Bryan, and Joanne Minaker. 2008. *Youth, Crime and Justice: Issues of Power and Justice.* Toronto: Pearson.

Hogeveen, Bryan, and Andrew Woolford. 2006. "Critical Criminology and Possibility in the Neoliberal Ethos." *Canadian Journal of Criminology and Criminal Justice,* 48, 5: 681–702.

Hubbard, Tasha. 2014. "Buffalo Genocide in Nineteenth-Century North America: 'Kill, Skin, and Sell.'" In Andrew Woolford, Jeff Benvenuto, and Alexander Hinton (eds.), *Colonial Genocide in Indigenous North America.* Durham: Duke University Press.

Hudson, Barbara. 2003. *Justice in the Risk Society.* London: Sage.

___. 2006. "Beyond White Man's Justice: Race, Gender and Justice in Late Modernity." *Theoretical Criminology,* 10, 1: 29–47.

Hunt, Ronald. 2000. "Conferencing a Serious Arson Case." <https://www.iirp.edu/news/conferencing-a-serious-arson-case>.

Illich, Ivan. 1977. *Towards a History of Needs.* New York: Pantheon Books.

Illich, Ivan, Irving Zola, John McKnight, and Harley Shaiken. 1977. *Disabling Professions.* London: Marion Boyars.

INCITE! <https://incite-national.org/>. Accessed May 7, 2019.

Jameson, Frederic. 1991. *Postmodernism, or, the Cultural Logic of Late Capitalism.* Durham, NC: Duke University Press.

Jelinek, Yeshayahu A. 1990. "Political Acumen, Altruism, Foreign Pressure or Moral Debt: Konrad Adenauer and the 'Shilumim.'" *Tel Aviver Jahrbuch für Deutsche Geschichte* 19: 77–102.

Jessop, Bob. 2002. "Liberalism, Neoliberalism, and Urban Governance: A State-Theoretical Perspective." *Antipode,* 34, 3: 452–472.

Johnson, Holly, and Karen Rodgers. 1993. "A Statistical Overview of Women and Crime in Canada." In Ellen Adelberg and Claudia Currie (eds.), *In Conflict with the Law: Women and the Canadian Justice System.* Vancouver: Press Gang Publishers.

Johnstone, Gerry. 2002. *Restorative Justice: Ideas, Values, Debates.* Devon, UK: Willan Publishing.

___. 2004. "How, and in What Terms, Should Restorative Justice Be Conceived?" In H. Zehr and B. Toews (eds.), *Critical Issues in Restorative Justice.* Cullompton, UK: Willan Publishing.

Johnstone, Gerry, and Daniel Van Ness. 2007. "The Meaning of Restorative Justice." In G. Johnstone and D.W. Van Ness (eds.), *Handbook of Restorative Justice.* Cullompton, UK: Willan Publishing.

Kant, Immanuel 1873. *Fundamental Principles of the Metaphysics of Morals.* London: Longmans, Green, & Co.

Kay, Jonathan. 2009. "The Folly of Native Sentencing Circles." *National Post,* January 20.

Kay, Judith W. 2006. "Murder Victims' Families for Reconciliation: Story-Telling for Healing, as Witness, and in Public Policy." In D. Sullivan and L. Tifft (eds.), *Handbook of Restorative Justice: A Global Perspective.* London and New York: Routledge.

Kelly, Esteban L. 2011. "Philly Stands Up: Inside the Politics and Poetics of

Transformative Justice and Community Accountability in Sexual Assault Situations." *Social Justice*, 37, 4: 44–57.

Kilty, Jennifer. 2014. "Examining the 'Psy-Carceral Complex' in the Death of Ashley Smith." In Gillian Balfour and Elizabeth Comack (eds.), *Criminalizing Women: Gender and (In)Justice in Neo-Liberal Times*, 2nd edition. Halifax: Fernwood Publishing.

Kim, Hubert. 1999. "German Reparations: Institutionalized Insufficiency." In Roy L. Brooks (ed.), *When Sorry Isn't Enough: The Controversy over Apologies and Reparations for Human Injustice*. New York: New York University Press.

Kim, Mimi. 2018. "From Carceral Feminism to Transformative Justice: Women-of-Color Feminism and Alternatives to Incarceration." *Journal of Ethnic & Cultural Diversity in Social Work*, 27, 3: 219–233.

Konowal, Charles. 1997. *Glimmer of Hope* (film). National Film Board of Canada.

Koontz, Claudia. 2003. *The Nazi Conscience*. Cambridge, MA: Belknap Press.

Kriesberg, Louis. 2008. "Waging Conflicts Constructively." In S. Byrne, J. Senehi, D. Sandole, and I. Staroste-Sandole (eds.), *Conflict Resolution: Core Concepts, Theories, Approaches and Practices*. London: Routledge.

Kritz, Neil J. 1995. *Transitional Justice: How Emerging Democracies Reckon with Former Regimes*. Washington, DC: United States Institute of Peace Press.

Krog, Antjie. 1998. *Country of My Skull: Guilt, Sorrow, and the Limits of Forgiveness in the New South Africa*. New York: Three Rivers Press.

Kueneman, Rodney. 2008. "The Origins and Role of Law in Society." In Rick Linden (ed.), *Criminology: A Canadian Perspective*, volume 5. Toronto: Thomson-Nelson.

Kurki, L. 2000. "Restorative Justice and Community Justice in the United States." *Crime and Justice*, 27: 235–303.

LaCapra, Dominick. 1999. "Trauma, Absence, Loss." *Critical Inquiry*, 25, 4: 696–727.

Lajeunesse, Therese. 1996. *Evaluation of Community Holistic Circle Healing, Hollow Water First Nation, Volume 1: Final Report*. Manitoba: Thérèse Lajeunesse & Associates.

Laroque, Emma. 1997. "Re-Examining Culturally Appropriate Models in Criminal Justice Applications." In Michael Asch (ed.), *Aboriginal and Treaty Rights in Canada: Essays on Laws, Equality, and Respect for Difference*. Vancouver: UBC Press.

Latimer, J., C. Dowden, and D. Muise. 2001. *The Effectiveness of Restorative Justice Practices: A Meta-Analysis*. Ottawa: Department of Justice, Canada.

Latour, Bruno. 1991. *We Have Never Been Modern*. Cambridge: Harvard University Press.

Levi, Primo. 1989. *The Drowned and the Saved*. New York: Vintage International.

Levrant, S., F.T. Cullen, B. Fulton, and J.F. Wzniak. 1999. "Reconsidering Restorative Justice: The Corruption of Benevolence Revisited?" *Crime and Delinquency*, 45: 3–27.

Lewis, Ruth, Rebecca Emerson Dobash, Russell Dobash, and Kate Cavanagh. 2001. "Law's Progressive Potential: The Value of Engagement with the Law for Domestic Violence." *Social & Legal Studies*, 10, 1: 105–130.

Llewellyn, Jennifer. 2007. "Truth Commissions and Restorative Justice." In G. Johnstone and D.W. Van Ness (eds.), *Handbook of Restorative Justice*. Cullompton, UK: Willan

Publishing.

———. 2018. "Realizing the Full Potential of Restorative Justice." *Policy Options*, May. <http://policyoptions.irpp.org/magazines/may-2018/realizing-the-full-potential-of-restorative-justice/>.

Llewellyn, Jennifer, Bruce Archibald, Donald Clairmont, and Diane Crocker. 2013. "Imagining Success for a Restorative Approach to Justice: Implications for Measurement and Evaluation." *Dalhousie Law Journal*, 36, 2: 281–316.

Llewellyn, Jennifer, and Robert Howse. 1998. *Restorative Justice: A Conceptual Framework*. Ottawa: Law Commission of Canada.

Llewellyn, Jennifer, Jacob MacIssac, and Melissa MacKay. 2015. *Report from the Restorative Justice Process at the Dalhousie University Faculty of Dentistry*. <https://cdn.dal.ca/content/dam/dalhousie/pdf/cultureofrespect/RJ2015-Report.pdf>. Accessed September 26, 2018.

Maglione, Giuseppe. 2017. "Embodied Victims: An Archaeology of the 'Ideal Victim' of Restorative Justice." *Criminology & Criminal Justice*, 17, 4: 401–417.

Maier, Charles S. 1988. *The Unmasterable Past: History, Holocaust, and German National Identity*. Cambridge, MA: Harvard University Press.

Mamdani, Mahmood. 2000. "The Truth According to the TRC." In I. Amadiume and A. An-Na'im (eds.), *The Politics of Memory: Truth, Healing & Social Justice*. London: Zed Books.

———. 2001. *When Victims Become Killers: Colonialism, Nativism, and the Genocide in Rwanda*. Princeton, NJ: Princeton University Press.

Marchak, Patricia. 2008. *No Easy Fix: Global Responses to Internal Wars and Crimes against Humanity*. Montreal and Kingston: McGill-Queen's University Press.

Marshall, Tony F. 1999. *Restorative Justice: An Overview*. London: Home Office, Research Development and Statistics Directorate.

Martinson, R. 1974. "What Works? Questions and Answers about Prison Reform." *The Public Interest*, Spring: 22–54.

Matthews, Roger (ed.). 1988. *Informal Justice?* London: Sage.

Matza, David. 1990. *Delinquency and Drift*. New Brunswick, NJ: Transaction.

Maxwell, Gabrielle, and Allison Morris. 1993. *Family, Victims and Culture: Youth Justice in New Zealand*. Wellington: Special Policy Agency and Institute of Criminology, Victoria University of Wellington.

Maxwell, Gabrielle, Allison Morris, and Hennesey Hayes. 2006. "Conferencing and Restorative Justice." In D. Sullivan and L. Tifft (eds.), *Handbook of Restorative Justice: A Global Perspective*. London and New York: Routledge.

Maynard, Robyn. 2017. *Policing Black Lives: State Violence in Canada from Slavery to the Present*. Halifax & Winnipeg: Fernwood Publishing.

McCold, Paul. 2006. "The Recent History of Restorative Justice, Mediation, Circles, and Conferencing." In D. Sullivan and L. Tifft (eds.), *Handbook of Restorative Justice: A Global Perspective*. London: Routledge.

McCold, Paul, and Benjamin Wachtel. 1998. "Restorative Policing Experiment: The Bethlehem Pennsylvania Police Family Group Conferencing Project." Pipersville, PA: Community Service Foundation.

McCold, Paul, and Ted Wachtel. 1998. "Community Is Not a Place: A New Look at

Community Justice Initiatives." *Contemporary Justice Review*, 1, 1: 71–85.
____. 2002. "Restorative Justice Theory Validation." In E. Weitkamp and H. Kerner (eds.), *Restorative Justice: Theoretical Foundations*. Cullompton, UK: Willan Publishing.
McEvoy, Kieran, and Anna Ecksson. 2006. "Restorative Justice in Transition: Ownership, Leadership, and 'Bottom-Up' Human Rights." In D. Sullivan and L. Tifft (eds.), *Handbook of Restorative Justice: A Global Perspective*. London and New York: Routledge.
McEvoy, Kieran, and Tim Newburn. 2003. "Criminology, Conflict Resolution and Restorative Justice." In K. McEvoy and T. Newburn (eds.), *Criminology, Conflict Resolution and Restorative Justice*. Houndsmills, Basingstoke, Hampshire: Palgrave Macmillan.
McGlynn, Clare, Julia Downes, and Nicole Westmarland. 2017. "Seeking Justice for Survivors of Sexual Violence: Recognition, Voice and Consequences." In E. Zinsstag and M. Keenan (eds.), *Restorative Responses to Sexual Violence: Legal, Social and Therapeutic Dimensions*. London: Routledge.
McGlynn, Clare, Nicole Westmarland, and Nikki Godden. 2012. "'I Just Wanted Him to Hear Me': Sexual Violence and the Possibilities of Restorative Justice." *Journal of Law and Society*, 39: 213–240.
McLachlin, Beverly. 2004. "Judging in a Democratic Society." Sixth Templeton Lecture on Democracy, University of Manitoba, June 3.
Meierhenrich, Jens. 2008. *The Legacies of Law: Long-Run Consequences of Legal Development in South Africa, 1652–2000*. Cambridge, MA: Cambridge University Press.
Merton, Robert. 1938. "Social Structure and Anomie." *American Sociological Review*, 3, 5: 672–682.
Miers, David. 1989. "Positivist Criminology: A Critique." *International Review of Victimology*, 1: 3–22.
Mika, Harry, and Howard Zehr. 2003. "A Restorative Framework for Community Justice Practice." In K. McEvoy and T. Newburn (eds.), *Criminology, Conflict Resolution and Restorative Justice*. Houndsmills, Basingstoke, Hampshire: Palgrave Macmillan.
Mill, John Stuart. 1993 [1861]. "On the Connection Between Justice and Utility." In M. Fisk (ed.), *Key Concepts in Critical Theory: Justice*. New Jersey: Humanities Press.
Miller, Susan, and LeeAnn Iovanni. 2013. "Using Restorative Justice for Gendered Violence: Success with a Postconviction Model." *Feminist Criminology*, 8, 4: 247–268.
Milloy, John S. 1999. *A National Crime: The Canadian Government and the Residential School System, 1879 to 1986*. Winnipeg, MB: University of Manitoba Press.
Mills, C. Wright. 1959. *The Sociological Imagination*. New York: Oxford University Press.
Minow, Martha. 1999. *Between Vengeance and Forgiveness: Facing Genocide and Mass Violence*. Boston: Beacon Press.
Monture-Angus, Patricia. 1999. *Journeying Forward: Dreaming First Nations' Independence*. Halifax, NS: Fernwood Publishing.
Moore, D.B., and T.A. O'Connell. 2003. "Family Conferencing in Wagga Wagga: A Communitarian Model." In G. Johnstone (ed.), *A Restorative Justice Reader: Texts,*

Sources, Context. Cullompton, UK: Willan Publishing.
Morris, Ruth. 1994. *A Practical Path Toward Transformative Justice.* Toronto: Rittenhouse.
Morrison, Brenda. 2006. "School Bullying and Restorative Justice: Toward a Theoretical Understanding of the Role of Respect, Pride, and Shame." *Journal of Social Issues,* 62, 2: 371–392.
____. 2007. "Schools and Restorative Justice." In G. Johnstone and D.W. Van Ness (eds.), *Handbook of Restorative Justice.* Cullompton, UK: Willan Publishing.
Moses, Siegfried. 1944. *Jewish Post-War Claims.* Tel Aviv: Irgun Olej Merkaz Europa.
Murphy, Jeffrie G., and Jean Hampton. 1988. *Forgiveness and Mercy.* Cambridge, UK: Cambridge University Press.
Nader, Laura. 1990. *Harmony Ideology: Justice and Control in a Mountain Zapotec Village.* Stanford, CA: Stanford University Press.
Naffine, Ngaire. 1987. *Female Crime: The Construction of Women in Criminology.* Winchester: Allen & Unwin.
Nancy, Jean-Luc. 1991. *The Inoperative Community.* Minneapolis: University of Minnesota Press.
Napoleon, Val. 2004. "By Whom, and by What Processes, Is Restorative Justice Defined?" In H. Zehr and B. Toews (eds.), *Critical Issues in Restorative Justice.* Cullompton, UK: Willan Publishing.
Nelund, Amanda. 2016. "Engendering Alternative Justice: Criminalized Women, Alternative Justice, and Neoliberalism." PhD diss. University of Manitoba.
____. 2017. "The Marginalised Woman: Thinking Beyond Victim/Offender in Restorative Justice." *Restorative Justice,* 5, 3: 408–419
Niven, Bill. 2002. *Facing the Nazi Past: United Germany and the Legacy of the Third Reich.* London and New York: Routledge.
Novick, Peter. 1999. *The Holocaust in American Life.* Boston: Mariner Books.
Offe, Claus. 1997. *Varieties of Transition: The East European and East German Experience.* Cambridge, MA: MIT Press.
Olson, Susan M., and Albert W. Dzur. 2004. "Revisiting Informal Justice: Restorative Justice and Democratic Professionalism." *Law & Society Review,* 38, 1: 139–176.
Osiel, Mark. 1999. *Mass Atrocity, Collective Memory and the Law.* New Brunswick, NJ: Transaction.
Parkinson, John, and Declan Roche. 2004. "Restorative Justice: Deliberative Democracy in Action?' *Australian Journal of Political Science,* 39, 3: 505–18.
Pavlich, George. 1996a. *Justice Fragmented: Mediating Community Disputes Under Postmodern Conditions.* London: Routledge.
____. 1996b. "The Power of Community Mediation: Government and Formation of Self." *Law and Society Review,* 30: 101–27.
____. 2001. "The Force of Community." In H. Strang and J. Braithwaite (eds.), *Restorative Justice and Civil Society.* Cambridge: Cambridge University Press.
____. 2005. *Governing Paradoxes of Restorative Justice.* London: GlassHouse Press.
____. 2007. Ethics, Universal Principles, and Restorative Justice." In G. Johnstone and D.W. Van Ness (eds.), *Handbook of Restorative Justice.* Cullompton, UK: Willan Publishing.

Peachey, Dean E. 2003. "The Kitchener Experiment." In G. Johnstone (ed.), *A Restorative Justice Reader: Texts, Sources, Context*. Cullompton, UK: Willan Publishing.

Pennell, Joan, and Gale Burford. 2002. "Feminist Praxis: Making Family Group Conferencing Work." In H. Strang and J. Braithwaite (eds.), *Restorative Justice and Family Violence*. Cambridge, UK: Cambridge University Press.

Pepinsky, Harold E., and Richard Quinney (eds.). 1990. *Criminology as Peacemaking*. Bloomington, IN: Indiana University Press.

Phlean, Bryan. 1998. "Hollow Water Healing: Straightforward, Honest." *Windspeaker*, January 1.

Picard, Cheryl A. 1998. *Mediating Interpersonal and Small Group Conflict*. Ottawa: Golden Dog Press.

Pitts, Gordon. 2008/2018. "The Testing of Michael McCain." *Globe and Mail*. November 28/updated April 30, 2018. <theglobeandmail.com/report-on-business/the-testing-of-michael-mccain/article598005/>.

Pollard, Sir Charles. 2001. "'If Your Only Tool Is a Hammer, All Your Problems Will Look Like Nails.'" In H. Strang and J. Braithwaite (eds.), *Restorative Justice and Civil Society*. Cambridge: Cambridge University Press.

Power, Samantha. 2002. *"A Problem from Hell": America and the Age of Genocide*. New York: Basic Books.

Pranis, Kay. 2005. *The Little Book of Circle Processes: A New/Old Approach to Peacemaking*. Intercourse, PA: Good Books.

Pross, Christian. 1998. *Paying for the Past: The Struggle over Reparations for Surviving Victims of the Nazi Terror*. Baltimore: Johns Hopkins University Press.

Ptacek, James (ed.). 2010. *Restorative Justice and Violence Against Women*. Oxford: Oxford University Press.

Putnam, Robert. 2000. *Bowling Alone: The Collapse and Revival of American Community*. New York: Touchstone.

Puxon, Grattan. 1981. "Gypsies Seek Reparations." *Patterns of Prejudice*, 15: 21–25.

Rawls, John. 1971. *A Theory of Justice*. Cambridge, MA: Belknap Press of Harvard University.

_____. 1993. "Justice as Fairness: Political not Metaphysical." In M. Fisk (ed.), *Key Concepts in Critical Theory: Justice*. New Jersey: Humanities Press.

Raye, Barbara E., and Ann Warner Roberts. 2007. "Restorative Processes." In G. Johnstone and D.W. Van Ness (eds.), *Handbook of Restorative Justice*. Cullompton, UK: Willan Publishing.

Redekop, Paul. 2007. *Changing Paradigms: Punishment and Restorative Discipline*. Scottdale, PA: Herald Press.

Richards, Kelly. 2011. "Restorative Justice and 'Empowerment': Producing and Governing Active Subjects through 'Empowering' Practices." *Critical Criminology*, 19: 91–105.

Richie, Beth. 2015. "Reimagining the Movement to End Gender Violence: Anti-Racism, Prison Abolition, Women of Color Feminisms, and Other Radical Visions of Justice." *University of Miami Race & Social Justice Law Review*, 5, 2: 257–273.

Robinson, Nehemiah. 1944. *Indemnification and Reparations — Jewish Aspects*. New York: Institute of Jewish Affairs.

Roche, Declan. 2007. "Restitution and Restorative Justice." In G. Johnstone and D.W. Van Ness (eds.), *Handbook of Restorative Justice*. Cullompton, UK: Willan Publishing.

Rose, Nikolas. 1993. "Government, Authority and Expertise in Advanced Liberalism." *Economy and Society*, 22, 3 (August): 283–99.

———. 1996. "Governing 'Advanced' Liberal Democracies." In A. Barry, T. Osborne, and N. Rose (eds.), *Foucault and Political Reason: Liberalism, Neo-liberalism and Rationalities of Government*. UCL Press.

———. 1999. *Powers of Freedom: Reframing Political Thought*. Cambridge, UK: Cambridge University Press.

Ross, Rupert. 1996. *Returning to the Teachings: Exploring Aboriginal Justice*. Toronto: Penguin Books.

Rossner, Meredith. 2011. "Emotions and Interaction Ritual: A Micro-Analysis of Restorative Justice." *British Journal of Criminology*, 51: 95–119.

———. 2013. *Just Emotions: Rituals of Restorative Justice*. Oxford: Oxford University Press.

Rousseau, Pierre. 2009. *NP Editor*, February 2.

Roy, Eleano Ainge. 2017. "New Zealand River Granted Same Legal Rights as Human Being." *The Guardian*, March 16. <theguardian.com/world/2017/mar/16/new-zealand-river-granted-same-legal-rights-as-human-being>.

Rypi, Anna. 2017. "'You Don't Have to Say Straight Out…': Directed Impression Management at Victim-Offender Mediation Pre-meetings." *Sociological Focus*, 50, 3: 261–276.

Sagi, Nana. 1980. *German Reparations: A History of the Negotiations*. Jerusalem, Israel: Magnes Press, Hebrew University.

Schrastetter, Susanna. 2003. "The Diplomacy of *Wiedergutmachung*: Memory, the Cold War, and the Western European Victims of Nazism, 1956–1964." *Holocaust and Genocide Studies*, 17 (Winter): 459–479.

Scott, James C. 1998. *Seeing Like a State: How Certain Schemes to Improve the Human Condition Have Failed*. New Haven: Yale University Press.

Sebba, Leslie. 1980. "The Reparations Agreements: A New Perspective." *Annals of the American Academy of Political and Social Science*, 450: 202–212.

Selva, L.H., and R.M. Böhm. 1987. "A Critical Examination of the Informalism Experiment in the Administration of Justice." *Crime and Social Justice*, 29: 43–57.

The Sentencing Project. 2018. *Capitalizing on Mass Incarceration: US Growth in Private Prisons*. Washington: The Sentencing Project.

Seven Generations Education Institute. 2015. "Seven Grandfather Teachings." <http://www.7generations.org/?page_id=2396>.

Shapland, J., A. Atkinson, H. Atkinson, E. Colledge, J. Dignan, M. Howes, J. Johnstone, G. Robinson, and A. Sorsby. 2006. "Situating Restorative Justice Within Criminal Justice." *Theoretical Criminology*, 10, 4: 505–532.

Shapland, Joanna, Gwen Robinson, and Angela Sorsby. 2011. *Restorative Justice in Practice: Evaluating What Works for Victims and Offenders*. London and New York: Routledge.

Sharpe, Susan. 2004. "How Large Should the Restorative Justice 'Tent' Be?" In H. Zehr and B. Toews (eds.), *Critical Issues in Restorative Justice*. Cullompton, UK:

Willan Publishing.

———. 2007. "The Idea of Reparation." In G. Johnstone and D.W. Van Ness (eds.), *Handbook of Restorative Justice*. Cullompton, UK: Willan Publishing.

Sherman, Lawrence, and Heather Strang. 2007. *Restorative Justice: The Evidence*. London: The Smith Institute.

Sherman, Lawrence, Heather Strang, Evan Mayo-Wilson, Daniel J. Woods, and Barak Ariel. 2015. "Are Restorative Justice Conferences Effective in Reducing Repeat Offending? Findings from a Campbell Systematic Review." *Journal of Quantitative Criminology*, 31, 1: 1–24.

Shonholtz, Raymond. 1984. "Neighborhood Justice Systems: Work, Structure and Guiding Principles." *Mediation Quarterly*, 5: 3–30.

Simmel, Georg. 1908. *The Sociology of Georg Simmel*. (K. Wolff, ed.). New York: Free Press.

Skelton, Ann, and Cheryl Frank. 2004. "How Does Restorative Justice Address Human Rights and Due Process Issues?" In H. Zehr and B. Toews (eds.), *Critical Issues in Restorative Justice*. Cullompton. UK: Willan Publishing.

Stern, Vivian. 2006. *Creating Criminals: Prisons and People in a Market Society*. London: Zed Books.

Strang, Heather. 2001. *Victim Participation in a Restorative Justice Process*. Oxford: Oxford University Press.

Stuart, Barry. 1996. "Circle Sentencing: Turning Swords into Ploughshares." In B. Galaway and J. Hudson (eds.), *Restorative Justice: International Perspectives*. Monsey, NY: Criminal Justice Press.

Stuart, Barry, and Kay Pranis. 2006. "Peacemaking Circles: Reflections on Principal Features and Primary Outcomes." In D. Sullivan and L. Tifft (eds.), *Handbook of Restorative Justice: A Global Perspective*. London and New York: Routledge.

Stubbs, Julie. 2002. "Domestic Violence and Women's Safety: Feminist Challenges to Restorative Justice." In Heather Strang and John Braithwaite (eds.), *Restorative Justice and Family Violence*. Cambridge: Cambridge University Press.

Sullivan, Dennis, and Larry Tifft. 2001. *Restorative Justice: Healing the Foundations of Our Everyday Lives*. Monsey, NY: Willow Tree.

———. 2006. "Introduction: The Healing Dimension of Restorative Justice: A One-World Body." In D. Sullivan and L. Tifft (eds.), *Handbook of Restorative Justice: A Global Perspective*. London and New York: Routledge.

Supreme Court of Canada. 1975. Murdoch v. Murdoch, 1 S.C.R. 423 Date: 1973-10-02. <https://scc-csc.lexum.com/scc-csc/scc-csc/en/item/5346/index.do>.

Sykes, Gresham M., and David Matza. 1957. "Techniques of Neutralization: A Theory of Delinquency." *American Sociological Review*, 22, 6: 664–670.

Tauri, Juan M. 2009. "An Indigenous Perspective on the Standardisation of Restorative Justice in New Zealand and Canada." *Indigenous Policy Journal*, xx, 3 (Fall): 1–24.

———. 2014. Criminal Justice in Contemporary Settler Colonialism. *African Journal of Criminology and Justice Studies*, 8, 1: 20–38.

Tavuchis, Nicholas. 1991. *Mea Culpa: A Sociology of Apology and Reconciliation*. Stanford, CA: Stanford University Press.

Taylor, Jillian. 2018. "Restorative Justice at the Centre of Manitoba's New Plan to

Keep People out of Jail." CBC **News, 9** March. <http://www.cbc.ca/news/canada/manitoba/manitoba-justice-system-modernization-strategy-1.4568641>.

Teitel, Ruti. 2000. *Transitional Justice*. New York: Oxford University Press.

Thom, Brian. 2006. "The Paradox of Boundaries in Coast Salish Territories." Paper presented at Indigenous Cartographies and Representational Politics; an International Conference. Ithaca, NY: Cornell University, March 3–5.

Tickell, A., and J.A. Peck. 1995. "Social Regulation after Fordism: Regulation Theory, Neoliberalism and the Global–Local Nexus." *Economy and Society*, 24, 3 (August): 357–386.

Toews, Barb, and Howard Zehr. 2004. "Preface." In H. Zehr and B. Toews (eds.), *Critical Issues in Restorative Justice*. Cullompton, UK: Willan Publishing.

Torpey, John. 2001. "'Making Whole What Has Been Smashed': Reflections on Reparations." *The Journal of Modern History*, 73 (June): 333–358.

____. 2003. "Introduction." In J. Torpey (ed.), *Politics and the Past*. Oxford: Rowman and Littlefield Publishers.

____. 2006. *Making Whole What Has Been Smashed: On Reparations Politics*. Cambridge, MA: Harvard University Press.

Truth and Reconciliation Commission. 1996. *Amnesty Hearing Transcripts: Killing of Griffiths Mxenge, Part 1*. Durban, South Africa: Truth and Reconciliation Commission.

Tuck, E., and K.W. Yang. 2012. "Decolonization Is Not a Metaphor." *Decolonization: Indigeneity, Education & Society*, 1, 1: 1–40.

Turk, Austin. 1969. *Criminality and Legal Order*. Chicago: Rand McNally.

Tutu, Desmond. 1999. *No Future Without Forgiveness*. New York: Image, Doubleday.

Umbreit, Mark, Robert B. Coates, and Betty Vos. 2006. "Victim Offender Mediation: An Evolving Evidence-Based Practice." In D. Sullivan and L. Tifft (eds.), *Handbook of Restorative Justice: A Global Perspective*. London and New York: Routledge.

Umbreit, Mark, and Howard Zehr. 1996. "Restorative Family Group Conferences: Differing Models and Guidelines for Practice." *Federal Probation*, 60, 3: 24–29.

United Nations. 2007. *Handbook of Restorative Justice Programs*. New York: United Nations.

United Nations Economic and Social Council. 2000. *Basic Principles on the Use of Restorative Justice Programmes in Criminal Matters*. Adopted by the Social Council and its Substantive Session of 2002/12. <https://www.un.org/ruleoflaw/blog/document/basic-principles-on-the-use-of-restorative-justice-programmes-in-criminal-matters/>.

Van Ness, Daniel. 1993. "New Wine and Old Wineskins: Four Challenges of Restorative Justice." *Criminal Law Forum*, 4, 2: 251–276.

Van Ness, Daniel, and Karen Heetderks Strong. 2002. *Restoring Justice*. Cincinnati: Anderson.

Van Wormer, Katherine. 2009. "Restorative Justice as Social Justice for Victims of Gendered Violence: A Standpoint Feminist Perspective." *Social Work*, 54, 2: 107–116.

Villa-Vicencio, Charles. 2006. "Transitional Justice, Restoration, and Prosecution." In D. Sullivan and L. Tifft (eds.), *Handbook of Restorative Justice: A Global Perspective*.

London and New York: Routledge.

Wacquant, Loïc. 2001. "The Penalization of Poverty and the Rise of Neoliberalism." *European Journal on Criminal Policy and Research*, 9, 4 (Winter): 401–412.

———. 2004. "Critical Thought as Solvent of Doxa." *Constellations*, 11, 1 (Spring): 97–101.

———. 2009 *Punishing the Poor: The Neoliberal Government of Social Security*. Durham: Duke University Press.

Walgrave, Lode. 2002. "From Community to Domination: In Search of Social Values for Restorative Justice." In E. Weitekamp and H.J. Kerner (eds.), *Restorative Justice: Theoretical Foundations*. Cullompton, UK: Willan Publishing.

———. 2004. "Has Restorative Justice Theory Appropriately Responded to Retribution Theory and Impulses?" In H. Zehr and B. Toews (eds.), *Critical Issues in Restorative Justice*. Cullompton, UK: Willan Publishing.

Walkate, Sandra. 1989. *Victimology: The Victim and the Criminal Justice Process*. London: Unwin Hyman.

———. 2006. "Changing Boundaries of the 'Victim' in Restorative Justice: So Who Is the Victim Now?" In D. Sullivan and L. Tifft (eds.), *Handbook of Restorative Justice: A Global Perspective*. London and New York: Routledge.

Weber, Max. 1946. *From Max Weber: Essays in Sociology*. (H.H. Gerth and C. Wright Mills eds.) New York: Oxford University Press.

Weisel, Elie. 2006 [1972]. *Night*. New York: Hill and Wang.

Weitekamp, Elmar. 2003. "The History of Restorative Justice." In G. Johnstone (ed.), *A Restorative Justice Reader*. Cullompton, UK: Willan.

White, Rob. 2008. "Restorative Justice, Inequality, and Social Change." In C. Brooks and B. Schissel (eds.), *Marginality & Condemnation: An Introduction to Criminology*, 2nd edition. Black Point, NS and Winnipeg, MB: Fernwood Publishing.

Wiebe, Rudy, and Yvonne Johnson. 1999. *Stolen Life: The Journey of a Cree Woman*. Toronto: A.A. Knopf Canada.

Williams, Michelle Y. 2013. "African Nova Scotian Restorative Justice: A Change Has Gotta Come." *Dalhousie Law Journal*, 36, 2: 419–459.

Wilson, Richard. 2001. *The Politics of Truth and Reconciliation in South Africa: Legitimizing the Post-Apartheid State*. Cambridge, UK: Cambridge University Press.

Wolfe, P. 2006. "Settler Colonialism and the Elimination of the Native." *Journal of Genocide Research*, 8, 4: 387–409.

Woolford, Andrew. 2005. *Between Justice and Certainty: Treaty-Making in British Columbia*. Vancouver: University of British Columbia Press.

———. 2019. "Decriminalizing Settler Colonialism: Entryways to Genocide Accusation and Canadian Absolution." In George Pavlich and Matthew Unger (eds.), *Entryways and Criminalization*. University of Alberta Press.

Woolford, Andrew, and James Gacek. 2016. "Genocidal Carcerality and Indian Residential Schools in Canada." *Punishment & Society*, 18, 4: 400–419.

Woolford, Andrew, and R.S. Ratner. 2003. "Nomadic Justice: Restorative Justice on the Margins of Law." *Social Justice*, 30: 177–194.

———. 2005. "Selling Mediation: The Marketing of Alternative Dispute Resolution." *Peace and Conflict Studies Journal*, 12, 1: 1–21.

———. 2008a. *Informal Reckonings: Conflict Resolution in Mediation, Restorative Justice and Reparation*. London: Routledge-Cavendish.

———. 2008b. "Mediation Games: Justice Frames." In S. Byrne, J. Senehi, D. Sandole, and I. Staroste-Sandole (eds.), *Conflict Resolution: Core Concepts, Theories, Approaches and Practices*. London: Routledge.

———. 2015. *This Benevolent Experiment: Indigenous Boarding Schools, Genocide and Redress in Canada and the United States*. Lincoln and Winnipeg: University of Nebraska Press and University of Manitoba Press.

———. 2018. "Decriminalizing Settler Colonialism: Entryways to Genocide Accusation and Canadian Absolution." In George Pavlich and Matthew Unger (eds.), *Entryways and Criminalization*. Edmonton: University of Alberta Press.

Woolford, Andrew, and Stefan Wolejszo. 2006. "Collecting on Moral Debts: Reparations, the Holocaust, and the Porrajmos." *Law & Society Review*, 40, 4: 871–902.

Wright, Martin. 1991. *Justice for Victims and Offenders: A Restorative Response to Crime*. Milton Keynes: Open University Press.

Wright, Martin, and Guy Masters. 2002. "Justified Criticism, Misunderstanding, or Important Steps on the Road to Acceptance." In E. Weitkamp and H. Kerner (eds.), *Restorative Justice: Theoretical Foundations*. Cullompton, UK: Willan Publishing.

Yazzie, R., and J.W. Zion. 2003. "Navajo Restorative Justice: The Law of Equality and Justice." In G. Johnstone (ed.), *A Restorative Justice Reader: Texts, Sources, Context*. Cullompton, UK: Willan Publishing.

Youngblood Henderson, James Sa'ke'j, and Wanda D. McCaslin. 2005. "Exploring Justice as Healing." In W.D. McCaslin (ed.), *Justice as Healing: Indigenous Ways*. St. Paul: Living Justice Press.

Zehr, Howard. 1985. "Retributive Justice, Restorative Justice." *New Perspectives on Crime and Justice: Occasional Papers of the MCC Canada Victim Offender Ministries Program and the MCC U.S. Office of Criminal Justice*, September (4).

———. 1990. *Changing Lenses: A New Focus for Crime and Justice*. Scottdale, PA: Herald.

———. 1995. "Justice Paradigm Shift? Vales and Visions in the Reform Process." *Mediation Quarterly*, 12, 3 (Spring): 207–216.

Zernova, Margarita, and Martin Wright. 2007. "Alternative Visions of Restorative Justice." In G. Johnstone and D.W. Van Ness (eds.), *Handbook of Restorative Justice*. Cullompton, UK: Willan Publishing.

Zinsstag, Estelle, and Marie Keenan (eds.). 2017. *Restorative Responses to Sexual Violence: Legal, Social, and Therapeutic Dimensions*. London and New York: Routledge.

Zweig, Ronald W. 1987. *German Reparations and the Jewish World: A History of the Claims Conference*. Boulder, CO: Westview Press.

INDEX

adversarialism, 9, 58, 74, 115, 116
Alcoholics Anonymous, 117
amnesties, 89–95, 99
Anishinaabe, 64–66, 183–184
Anthropocene, 177
apartheid, 14–15, 33, 89–94, 103
apologies
    individual, 8, 60, 109, 110, 122, 136, 184, 201
    state, 32–33, 71, 98
Australia, 55, 79, 101, 109

Badgley Commission, The, 45
Benhabib, Seyla, 42, 45, 62
Blasey Ford, Christine, 129–130
Borrows, John, 64
Braithwaite, John, 52, 59–62, 79, 102, 108, 110, 141, 187, 196, 197–198, 201, 214
Butler, Judith, 157

Canadian Charter of Rights and Freedoms, 26
capitalism, 44, 75–76, 141–142, 152, 167–173, 207
Children, Young Persons and Their Families Act, New Zealand, 79
Christie, Nils, 31–32, 52, 57, 99, 125
Circle of Support and Accountability (COSA), 26–27, 87–88
class, 16, 21, 22, 55, 56, 67, 75–76, 109, 118, 127, 143, 160–162, 165, 167, 199, 211
Coetzee, Dirk Johannes, 91–94

colonialism, 43, 44, 54–55, 63–64, 79, 121, 145, 150, 201
comfort women, 32–33
commemoration, 95, 97–98
communicative ethics, 40–42, 47, 63
communitarians, 197
community
    becoming, 145
    definition, 143–147
    exclusionary notions, 143–147, 192
    of care, 144, 192
community accountability panels, 99–100, 164, 197
Community Holistic Circles of Healing (CHCH), 104–106, 183–184
community justice centres, 74
Conference on Jewish Claims Against Germany, 96–97
Crenshaw, Kimberlé, 42–43, 67, 165–166,
criminal justice
    Republican Theory 62–63
criminal justice system (CJS), 28–30, 182–185, 190–191
criminalization, 135, 141, 207
critical race theory, 42–43, 64, 158–159
culture
    defined, 173–174

Dalhousie Dentistry Scandal, 34–36
Daly, Kathleen, 8, 17, 18, 62, 79, 156, 182–185, 195–196
David Suzuki Foundation, 17
deconstruction, 43–47, 122, 131, 158,

192, 204
degradation ceremonies, 59–61
deinstitutionalization, 56, 75
deliberative democracy, 62–63, 214–216
deprofessionalization, 56
Derrida, Jacques, 43–47, 69, 131, 192, 205
Diné, 82, 87
diversion, 100, 185–186
drift, 59, 163, 186
due process, 51, 185, 187
Duff, R.A., 184–185
Durocher, Rene, 5–6, 175

Earth First, 17
ecological rights, 176–177
epistemology, 55, 69, 71
Ethelbert of Kent, Laws of, 51
essentialism, 42, 163, 173, 204
ethic of care, 42

facilitators
    professionalization, 148–149, 217–218
    techniques, 111–115
    training, 148–150, 217–218
family violence, 19, 21, 80, 121, 123, 130, 148, 156–157, 183, 213
feminism, 1, 39, 42–43, 45, 64, 68, 80, 109, 123, 127, 155–157, 195, 207
Foucault, Michel, 51–52, 116–117, 188–189, 212
Frank, Anne, 126
Fraser, Nancy, 198, 200–205

gatekeepers/gatekeeping, 25, 27, 30, 161–162, 183, 190, 213, 217
gender/gendering, 16, 21–22, 28, 56, 67, 80, 115, 129–130, 154–157, 159–160, 165–166, 191, 197, 199, 205, 207, 208–209, 212, 215
genocide, 12, 29, 50
Gilligan, Carol, 42
Goffman, Erving, 111–112

Goodon, Will, 43
governmentality, 167–168, 170, 188–190, 197
Gramsci, Antonio, 22, 134

Habermas, Jürgen, 23, 37, 40–45, 62–63
harmony ideology, 117
hegemony, 22
heteronormativity, 21
heteropatriarchy, 21
Hollow Water, Manitoba, 103–106, 183–184
Holocaust, 50–51, 95–97, 126
hospitality, 145, 192
Hudson, Barbara, 64, 66, 68, 156
human rights, 15, 16, 62, 88–89, 90–91, 99, 103, 158–159, 174

identity, 42, 56, 59, 61–62, 66, 67, 121–123, 125–128, 130–131, 134, 145–146, 154, 158, 181, 200–201
INCITE!, 207–209
Indian Act, Canada, 54–55, 89
Indian residential schools, 70–71, 89, 183, 203, 213
Indigenous Peoples
    Australia, 55, 109
    Canada, 21, 40, 43–44, 53–55, 63–64, 70–72, 81–89, 109, 150, 154–155, 158–159, 166, 176, 191, 201–205, 213
intersectionality, 1, 42–43, 46–47, 64, 67, 155, 156, 158, 165–166

John Howard Society, 6, 102, 196
Johnson, Yvonne, 29
Johnstone, Gerry, 51, 52, 122, 144
justice
    affirmative, 201–212, 214, 217, 218
    definition, 23
    recognition, 200–206, 210, 212, 219
    redistribution, 200–206, 210, 219
    representation, 200–206, 210, 219

transformative, 1, 14–16, 20–22, 195–220

Kant, Immanual, 23, 37, 40, 41
Kavanaugh, Brett, 129
Kennedy, Richard, 184
King, Martin Luther Jr., 36, 148

labelling, 59, 61, 133
LGBTQ, 159–160, 212, 219

Māori, 63, 79, 176, 178
Maple Leaf Foods, 135–139, 211
marijuana, 28, 135
Marshall, Tony, 8, 23
McCain, Michael, 135–139, 211
McLachlin, Justice Beverley, 38
Mi'kmaq Legal Support Network, 88
Mills, C. Wright, 46, 150
Montgomery Bus Boycott, 36
Murdoch v. Murdoch, 39
Mxenge, Griffiths, 91–94

Nanaboozhoo, 64
National Centre for Victims of Crime, 19
Nazis/Nazism, 50, 95–97, 126–127, 143, 199
neoliberalism, 20–21, 56–57, 131, 159, 166–173, 188, 191, 195, 198–199, 210–212, 217
net widening, 36, 100, 185–186, 187, 188
nothing works, 56
Nova Scotia Restorative Justice Program (NSRJP), 27, 88

offenders
  reintegration, 7, 9, 26–27, 61, 79–80, 87–88, 100–101, 109, 141, 161, 182, 189, 199
  risk, 100, 133, 162, 171, 186, 189, 211
  stigma, 58, 59, 61, 100, 102, 134, 141, 186

Onashowewin, 166
ontological insecurity, 170
ontology, 55, 69, 71
other-than-humans, 31, 175–179, 205

Parks, Rosa, 34, 36, 41, 216
patriarchy, 16, 39, 121, 127–128, 129, 156–157, 165, 200
Pauchay, Christopher, 82–87
Pavlich, George, 2, 23, 28, 59, 74, 117, 120, 122, 141–143, 171, 189–192, 198, 199, 212
peacemaking criminology, 31
performativity, 129, 157
plea bargain, 9, 10–11, 182
popular punitiveness, 174

race/racism/racialization, 16, 21, 22, 30, 36, 42, 64, 67, 109, 127, 145, 154–155, 158–159, 164, 165, 201–202, 207
Rawls, John, 37–41
recidivism, 20, 27, 86, 88, 102–103, 106–107, 161
reintegrative shaming, 69, 79, 141
relational/relationality, 11, 31, 64, 66, 90, 159, 160, 177
reparations, 32, 76, 91, 94–99, 127
responsibilization, 142, 169, 171
restorative justice
  definition, 6–15
  ethos, 49–72, 74, 101, 116, 181, 187, 219
  ideal traits of, 10–12
  morphological properties, 12–14
  social movement, 13, 17–20, 22, 120, 173, 183, 194, 195, 198, 200, 207, 214, 220
  transformative, 1, 14–15, 16, 20, 22, 28, 111, 154, 173, 195–220
restorative justice practices
  family group conferencing (FGC), 79–80
  family group decision making (FGDM), 80

healing circles, 82–88, 104–106, 183
peacemaking circles, 82–83
pre-charge/post-charge, 25–27
sentencing circles, 55, 82–87, 99, 104–105, 203, 213
sentencing/ post-sentencing, 25–27, 76, 79, 120–121
victim offender mediation (VOM), 76–79, 81, 110
victim offender reconciliation (VOR), 76–79, 81, 110
Restorative Resolutions, 102, 196
retributive justice/retribution, 6, 53, 58–59, 129, 171–172, 181–187, 196, 211, 216–217
Roma, 96–97, 143
Rossner, Merideth, 110–11

San Francisco Community Boards (SFCB), 74–75
selection bias, 109
sentencing
    disproportionate sentencing, 186–187
settler colonialism, 16, 21–22, 54, 71, 109, 159, 202, 213
sexual violence, 45, 68, 95, 103, 154, 156, 160, 183, 207, 213,
social capital, 103, 144
social death, 68
South African Truth and Reconciliation Commission (SATRC), 14–15, 89–95, 99, 103
Struefert, Don, Mary and Carin, 11–12, 14, 25
Sullivan, Guy, 11–12, 14, 25
Swanson, Jim, 11

Task Force on Misogyny, Sexism and Homophobia in Dalhousie University, Faculty of Dentistry, 34–36
Tauri, Juan, 63–64, 158–159
techniques of discipline, 117–118, 142
techniques of neutralization, 140

technologies of the self, 117–118, 171
teleology, 69
Truth and Reconciliation Commission of Canada, 69–72, 89
Turk, Austin, 32
Tutu, Bishop Desmond, 89–90

Ubuntu, 90
Umbreit, Mark, 76, 185
United Nations, 7, 29, 171
United Nations Convention on the Prevention and Punishment of the Crime of Genocide (1948), 29
United Way, The, 18

Van Ness, Daniel, 17, 57, 118, 123, 185, 195, 198
victims
    definition, 122–132
    ideal versus deserving, 125, 130–131
    narratives, 125–130
    needs, 122
    rights, 7, 9, 19, 128
welfare state/welfarism, 56, 57, 142, 167, 169, 173, 188
Whanganui River, 176, 178–179
white collar crime, 135, 162
World War II, 50, 95, 126–127, 167

Yantzi, Mark, 76
youth
    "at risk", 118, 162–163, 211
    definition, 162–163
    labelling, 99–100
Youth Criminal Justice Act, Canada, 7, 196–197
Youth Justice and Criminal Evidence Act, England and Wales, 7
Youth Restorative Action Project (YRAP), 164–165

Zehr, Howard, 28, 31, 57–59, 99, 181, 182, 185, 188, 198, 214